PARTITIONED REPRESENTATIONS

STUDIES IN COGNITIVE SYSTEMS

VOLUME 8

The titles published in this series are listed at the end of this volume.

PARTITIONED REPRESENTATIONS

A Study in Mental Representation, Language Understanding and Linguistic Structure

by

JOHN DINSMORE
Department of Computer Science,
Southern Illinois University at Carbondale, U.S.A.

SPRINGER SCIENCE+BUSINESS MEDIA, B.V.

Library of Congress Cataloging-in-Publication Data

Dinsmore, John, 1949-
Partitioned representations : a study in mental representation, language understanding, and linguistic structure / John Dinsmore.
p. cm. -- (Studies in cognitive systems ; v. 8)
Includes bibliographical references and indexes.
ISBN 978-94-010-5584-0 ISBN 978-94-011-3574-0 (eBook)
DOI 10.1007/978-94-011-3574-0
1. Psycholinguistics. 2. Comprehension. I. Title. II. Series.
P37.5.C66D56 1991
401'.9--dc20 91-23610
CIP

ISBN 978-94-010-5584-0

Printed on acid-free paper

**To Kymrie, Warren
and Alma**

TABLE OF CONTENTS

Preface

Cognitive science is a field that began with the realization that researchers in varied disciplines—psychology, artificial intelligence, linguistics, philosophy, formal semantics, neuroscience, and others—had taken on a common set of problems in representation and meaning, in reasoning and language. Nevertheless, cognitive science as a whole enjoys no common methodology or theoretical framework, and is in danger of becoming even more fragmented with time. There are two reasons for this. First, cognitive science is built on existing methodologies that have different historical origins. As a result, the psychologist's truth is different from the linguist's truth. The artificial intelligence researcher's truth is different from the philosopher's truth. The neuroscientist's truth is different from the formal semanticist's truth. All too often there is little or no recognition of the relevance of work in other disciplines to one's own concerns. Second, cognitive scientists tend to develop theories around isolated problems. For instance, there are theories about how humans categorize concepts, about how humans analyze linguistic expressions syntactically, about how the English tense system works semantically, about how humans reason about space or reason about time, about how goal-directed problem solving occurs, about how the brain computes, and so on. Too little attention has been given to recognizing commonalities or unifying principles that might underlie all of these tasks, or to whether different compartmentalized theories are even mutually consistent. What are called for are unifying theories which explain many cognitive abilities at the same time and which can simultaneously be justified from multiple methodological perspectives.

Language and Mental Representation

My work on partitioned representations began over a decade ago in La Jolla, when I was a graduate student in linguistics at the University of California at San Diego. There, I began looking at the so-called *projection problem for presupposition*, a very intriguing and subtle problem that attracted much interest among linguists throughout much of the seventies and that was to become the topic of a chapter of my dissertation. This was a time in which linguistics was dominated by the generative school, which, as a matter of methodological conviction, viewed language in isolation from virtually all other cognitive factors in the name of the "autonomous language faculty," a time when the *cognitive linguistics* of Langacker, Lakoff and Fauconnier was just beginning to challenge this practice. It seemed to me that the proposed generative accounts of the projection problem for presupposition completely missed the point in offering a formalism powerful enough to *describe* the problem, but failing to ask the most critical question: *Why* do presuppositions behave the way they do?

My feeling was that underlying the projection problem was something to do with how we humans conceptualize and reason about the world. I proposed what seemed to me to be an intuitively natural model for structuring information, based on what I at that time called *worlds*, but now call *spaces*, local conceptual domains representing coherent possible realities such as possibilities or belief systems. I found that if one simply looks at presuppositions in terms of processing strategies at work *within* these local domains, an immediate, explanatory and far more general account of the projection problem emerged.

I was surprised and delighted to discover that Gilles Fauconnier, in an independent line of linguistic research, was coming to some remarkably similar conclusions about the nature of representation. He proposed that the many long standing problems of reference—opacity and transparency, attributiveness and referentiality, *de dicto* and *de re*, and so forth—had to do with the ability of different *mental spaces* to represent the existence of distinct objects, along with the role of *connectors* to establish counterpart relations between such objects.

In the ensuing years an impressive array of linguistic problems have been catalogued for which partitioned representations are accountable. Some of these have to do with the semantics and pragmatics of discourse. Some with accessibility of anaphoric reference. A problem that I have given a lot of attention to is that of tense and aspect. Almost all previous work in this area had referred to Reichenbach's very vague and totally unexplicated concept of *reference time*. I discovered that reference time could be clearly *defined* in terms of the three-level model of language understanding, and that once it was so defined an almost complete and unified account of *both* the semantics (and thereby adverbial co-occurrence) *and* the pragmatics of tenses and aspects emerged as particular instances of more general principles elucidated in the theory.

Mental Representation and Function

One of my very early and now dominant concerns in developing the theory of partitioned representations is whether the theory could be justified and constrained *as a theory of mental representation*, that is independently of its ability to explain particular linguistic facts. For instance, how do we know what spaces exist or what particular structures spaces enter into? What does it mean to attribute a proposition or the existence of some object to a space? How do spaces support reasoning and information retrieval? There were two reasons for such concerns. First, the study of these problems is a legitimate task in its own right; these considerations naturally accompanied the beginning of my career in *artificial intelligence* in the early eighties. Second, I was concerned that without general answers to these questions the use of the theory to explain linguistic facts would lack rigor. In particular, the linguist working within this framework would be free to posit any elaborations of the basic model of mental representation he wanted to, in order to account for any particular problem at hand with no real commitment to the testability of the elaborations. Linguists had already showed a great propensity for this kind of thing.

I began developing logical and computational models of partitioned representations in order to better understand their functionality. The logic, PR, approximates certain features of mental representation, but is simple enough to study formally. In particular, it specifies the conditions under which spaces can be set up to guarantee *soundness*, i.e., correct inference. In the computational model,

Spaceprobe, the use of spaces in reasoning, and in language processing, can be observed. The *three-level theory* of language processing specifies the interaction of the partitioning framework with language processing. In brief, I discovered a tight correspondence between the constraints necessary in the computational and logical models to guarantee their functionality, and the partitioning structures suggested by linguistic evidence.

The functionality of partitioned representations in reasoning lies in their ability to decompose complex information, modal, hypothetical, temporal or the like, by distributing that information over very concrete and fairly autonomous domains of representation and reasoning. Reasoning processes within spaces is what I call *parochial reasoning*. The functionality of partitioned representations in language processing lies in their ability to background large amounts of information made implicit in the way spaces are configured or embedded one in another. Most linguistic processing is also made parochial.

Partitioned Representations as an Interdisciplinary Topic

I have given a lot of attention in my research to looking for precedents and parallel lines of thinking in research in various disciplines. This search has been surprisingly fruitful. The framework of partitioned representations is related to a number of models or theories of representation and language processing from a variety of disciplines.

In Linguistics

Gilles Fauconnier's theory of *mental spaces*, as mentioned, accounts for problems in reference—opacity, transparency, attributiveness, specificity and the like—that had been the focus of much research especially in the philosophy of language for decades. George Lakoff has attempted to integrate the concept of mental spaces into his work on *image schemata.*

In Logic

Conditional proofs and similar logical techniques of constructing subproofs in *natural deduction* are exactly parallel to reasoning in partitioned representations. Another correspondence exists with Hans Kamp's *discourse representation theory.* Kamp demonstrated that with the assumption of the existence of such intermediate representations onto which natural language discourse could be mapped and which could then be attributed a semantics directly, many paradoxes in the analysis of the logic of conditionals, quantifiers and tenses were overcome.

In Artificial Intelligence

Many existing computational systems employed what are easily identified as what I am calling partitioned representations, each one developed, however, with some particular narrow application in mind. Among these are various implementations of *belief spaces* as well as the *context-layered data bases* used in planning systems.

In Psychology

Some work specifically concerned with counterfactual reasoning can be seen to exhibit space-like structures as in partitioned representations. Phillip Johnson-Laird motivates the theory of *mental models* as largely analogical representations that could better explain human performance in applying logical syllogisms better than logic- or rule-based models and describes the use of multiple mental models in representing and reasoning about propositional attitudes and conditionals, similar to the way spaces are used in partitioned representations.

The theory of partitioned representations, though highly constrained, is at the same time general enough to preserve the insights expressed in these various other theories and models very well.

Partitioned Representations: the Book

This book charts a course from mental representations—the hidden structures of human knowledge—through the processes involved in understanding human language, to the actual observed structures of language—the syntactic, semantic and pragmatic patterns visible at the surface level. It takes the position that the nature of the language understanding process emerges from the *structure of mental representation* and that the surface structure of language is best explained in terms of the manner in which language understanding proceeds.

This book is organized into three parts. The first part, *Nuts and Bolts* discusses methodology and presents the principles of partitioned representations as well as the three-level model of language processing based on those representations. The second part, *Studies in Language*, looks at specific ways in which the three-level model of language understanding and the theory of partitioned representations it presupposes are reflected in the structure of English. It explores many of the consequences of the model for linguistic theory and the philosophy of language. The third part, *Formal Models*, is treated as an appendix in the realization that many general readers in cognitive science are not entirely comfortable with the kinds of formalism it makes use of. It consolidates the formal results of the investigation of the computational and logical properties of partitioned representations.

This book has its biases. The perspectives most represented here are those of linguistics and artificial intelligence, my particular areas of training. In particular this book is seen as making a contribution to what has become known as *cognitive linguistics*, a theoretical perspective—found, for instance, in the works of Langacker, Lakoff and Fauconnier—that sees language very much as an integral part of general cognitive processing. It is also seen as making a contribution to *knowledge representation*, the field that, using computational means, seeks to develop models of aspects of human-like reasoning. It is also seen as making a contribution to *natural language processing*, the area that, also often using computational means, develops models with human-like abilities in the comprehension and production of discourse. This book will also have something to say about *formal logic* and will discuss a host of *philosophical* issues, especially in the philosophies of language and mind. Finally, this book takes care to address issues in connectionism vs. symbolism, issues that are on many researchers minds at this time.

This book gives some, but certainly inadequate, attention to the discussion of *psychological* issues, issues that should to my mind be central to this project. This relative neglect is a consequence of weaknesses in my own background. Nevertheless I do see the theory of partitioned representations as making some important claims, and will take pains to identify points at which more psychologically oriented research would be relevant for their verification.

ACKNOWLEDGEMENTS

I would like to express my gratitude to those who awakened my early interest in language and cognition: Gilles Fauconnier, Yuki Kuroda, Ron Langacker, Ed Klima and Shirley Silver. These are people that I admire enormously, and whom I have been extremely fortunate to have had as teachers. I would like to thank all of those who have been associated with, or have at one time or another given useful feedback on, the research reported here. These include Gilles Fauconnier, Tony Maida, Mylen Epik, Ng Kee Hian, Pong Likhitaworn, Chris Moehle, Madhukar Thakur, Mark Johnson, Margaret Winters, Geoff Nathan, Elizabeth Kidwell, Sally and Walter Sedelow, Al Bethke, Martha Evens, John Barnden and Luis Calero. I would also like to thank anonymous reviewers of *Cognitive Science, Journal of Philosophical Logic, Language and Cognitive Processes, New Generation Computing* and Kluwer's *Cognitive Systems* series, who presumably know who they are. Thanks also to Jackie Muehler for some of the artwork; to Margaret, Gilles, Luis and the above mentioned Kluwer reviewers for reading an earlier draft of the book; and to James Fetzer and Simon Ross for their interest in this project and for being so easy to work with.

PART ONE

NUTS AND BOLTS

CHAPTER ONE

Mental Representation

Before we look at the theory of partitioned representations, a broader view of the investigation of mental representations is called for. For instance, what is a theory of mental representation supposed to do? How we know whether a particular theory does it? What role do computer models play in the study of representations? We want to become clear about what issues are being addressed in order to fix the position of the research reported here within the broader world of cognitive science. This first chapter starts with a wide-angle view of the world of issues in representation, understanding and language structure with which cognitive scientists try to cope. The next chapter will then zoom in on the territory in which our story begins.

Cognitive science is at a crossroads. In these beginning years of its history it has been guided primarily by the methodological assumptions of *symbolism*, assumptions that are, by the way, with some qualifications more or less consistent with the research reported here. Yet many of the most fundamental assumptions of this paradigm are under increasing attack. In this chapter I will begin by looking at symbolic theories of representation and their underlying assumptions. Then I will show where the critical weaknesses in the traditional paradigm lie, and review the *connectionist paradigm*, often presented as a alternative to the symbolic paradigm.

I will then discuss the role of computational and logical *models* of mental representation. I will finally summarize the criteria needed to justify theories and models of representation, criteria that reflect the multidisciplinary perspective of this book and that will be imposed in the development of the theory of partitioned representations.

SYMBOLISM: THE CLASSICAL PARADIGM

The central principles that characterize traditional work in the symbolic paradigm are:

- that there are such things as *symbols*, which can be combined into larger *symbolic structures* (or *expressions*),
- that these symbolic structures have a *combinatorial semantics* whereby what a symbolic structure represents is a function of what the parts represent, and
- that at the same time all cognitive *processes* (reasoning) are manipulations of these symbolic structures.

The best known statement of the assumptions underlying the symbolic paradigm is *physical symbol system hypothesis* of Newell and Simon (1976) and Newell (1982). I say that these principles are *central* in the sense that symbolic theories tend to conform to these principles, but that, as we will see, often deviate from them in restricted ways. Figure 1.1 represents these principles graphically.

Examples of Symbolic Theories of Representation

By way of illustration, let's look at some typical theories of representation that have been researched in psychology and artificial intelligence.

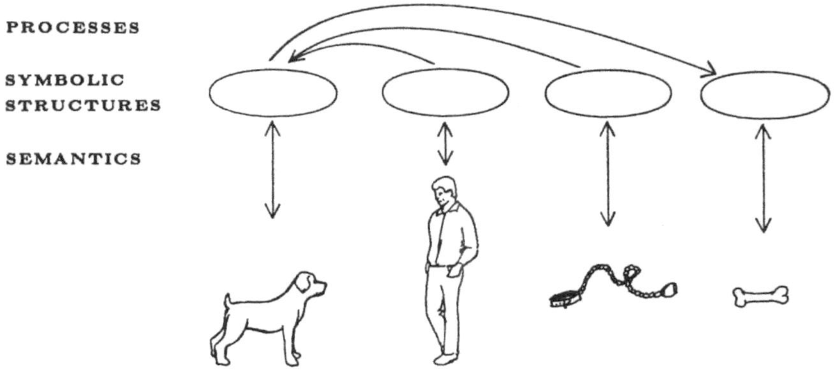

Fig. 1.1. The dual role of symbolic structures.

Logic-based representations. The artifacts that have most inspired the development of cognitive science are probably the computer and symbolic logic. A *logic-based system* (e.g., Walker, et al. 1987, Genesereth and Nilsson 1987), in particular, the *predicate calculus*, generally consists of:

- a set of primitive *symbols.*
- a set of *syntactic rules* that specify how symbols can be combined into *formulas.*
- a parallel set of *semantic rules* that specify how the denotations of expressions are derived from the denotations of their parts.
- a set of *rules of inference* that specify the derivation of formulas from other formulas (the rules of inference often work in combination with a set of *axioms*, formulas or formula schemas that extend the range of the rules of inference).

For example, the following are some logical formulas.

```
owns(Fred, Fido)
owns(Fred, object_89)
dog(Fido)
bone(object_89)
(dog(X) & bone(Y)) --> yearns_for(X,Y)
(owns(X, Y) & owns(X,Z) & yearns_for(Y,Z))
   --> gives(X,Y,Z)
```

These might be interpreted to say that Fred owns Fido, that Fido is a dog, that Fred owns a bone, that (all) dogs yearn for (all) bones, and that when one owned thing yearns for another owned thing then the common owner gives the yearnee to the yearner. Observe that the meanings of the formulas are built from the meanings of the parts. Simple facts are expressed using a *predicate*, representing some type of relation, along with a set of *arguments*, representing objects that enter into the relation. More complex meanings are expressed by introducing *connectives* or higher-level predicates. A rule of inference generally works by matching some set of *conditions* and specifying a *consequent* that can be derived. For instance, from the formulas above we should easily be able to derive

```
gives(Fred, Fido, object_89)
```

As a cognitive model or as an *artificial intelligence* (*AI*) system, a logic-based system maintains a *knowledge base*, a set of formulas representing what the system knows. It also requires a *procedure* for applying rules of inference to determine what actually *is* inferred. These rules may be triggered in response to new knowledge, either coming from outside the system or by inference from inside the system, or in response to goals of the system.

Among the advantages of logic-based representations are that they are highly expressive (you can find a way to represent almost anything) and have a well-understood semantics (the representations themselves and what they stand for in the real world are related systematically). They succeed in modeling the idea of inference, which in simple cases seem to correspond to the kinds of common-sense reasoning that people are able to perform. They are also very adaptable; AI researchers have been exploring extensions of these systems that are able to reason inductively as well as deductively, jump to conclusions, reason probabilistically and so on.

Associative networks. Associative networks (Quillian 1968, Findler 1979) represent knowledge in graph-like structures involving *nodes* representing concepts, interconnected with links labeled for the relations holding between concepts. Whereas a given symbol is characterized by a unique *name* in a logic-based system, it is generally characterized by a *location* in an associative network from which related concepts can be accessed. Figure 1.2 represents a small associative network. Node labels are not actually part of the representation, but are glosses added to suggest the semantic interpretations. In the early work (Quillian 1968) on these networks it was proposed that the meaning of a node depends on its location in the network, and therefore could change with changes in the network. Hence, these networks are often called *semantic networks.* It has never been clear to me how this would work, or how this would differ from the claim that the symbol **Fred** in a logic-based system changes meaning with changes in the set of premises or derived formulas that mention **Fred**. In any case, associative networks are often treated, at least within artificial intelligence, as reflecting the predicate-argument structure of logic-based systems. The key difference between associative networks and logic-bases systems, however, is in the fact that there is effectively one large representational structure with many paths among symbols rather than a set of discrete formulas.

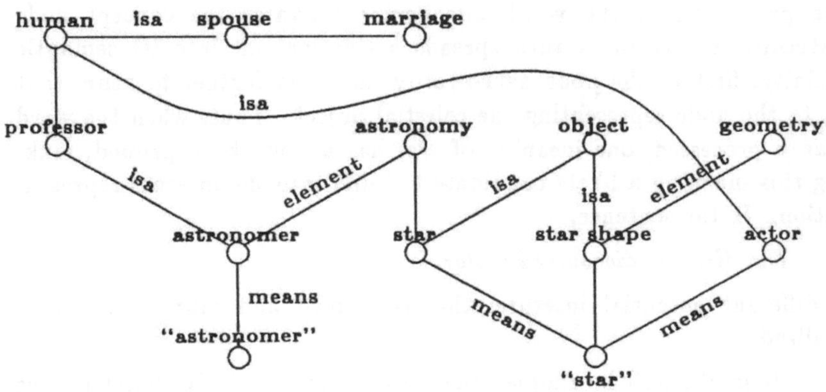

Fig. 1.2. A associative network.

This organizational difference in associative networks manifests itself in the nature of the reasoning processes that occur in these networks. In the early models, access to a concept was controlled by the *activation* of the node representing that concept. Should a concept become activated, that activation will generally *spread* out along links to nodes in the original node's *semantic vicinity* thus increasing *their* levels of activation.*

One implication of spreading activation in associative networks is found in natural language understanding, for instance. Those concepts corresponding to nodes at which the most activation has accumulated tend to become relevant interpretations for otherwise ambiguous or underspecified linguistic expressions. For instance, in the sentence**

---

* Connectionist systems, discussed a little later, involve somewhat similar mechanisms.

** Since I will be discussing language processing throughout most of this book, but will use English-like sentences to represent parts of internal representations, it will be important to distinguish sentences of natural language discourse from the (generally partitioned) internal representations of the meanings of these sentences. Internal representations will be written in **boldface** while English sentences themselves will be displayed in *italics*. Internal representations of linguistic expressions will be quoted in boldface. Fully capitalized words will be used as metavariables for saying things about *sets* of representations.

The astronomer discovered a star.

the processing of the word *astronomer* activates the concept node **astronomer** which in turn spreads activation out into its semantic vicinity, first to the node **astronomy** and then further to **star**, that is, to the node representing the celestial object. Thus, when the word *star* is processed, one meaning of *star* has already been primed, making this meaning a likely candidate to build into the internal representation. In the sentence,

The director discovered a star.

a different potential interpretation is primed and more than likely realized.

It might well be claimed that already in associative networks we find some stretching of some of the central premises of the symbolic paradigm: Although spreading activation is assumed to operate over symbolic structures, we have factors that affect the manner of symbolic processes but are not themselves parts of symbolic structures, namely activation levels. Presumably the level of activation associated with a node at a given time does not change the semantic interpretation of the node, so that association is *non-symbolic.*

In many associative network models the passing of discrete symbolic *markers* in a much more controlled manner replaces spreading activation (Fahlman 1979). Marker passing, however, is capable of achieving many specific inferences through graph-traversal instead of by rule application. Extensions of the semantic network framework often incorporate logic-like structures and processes (e.g., Shapiro 1979, Sowa 1984, Hendrix 1978). The links serve as an indexing mechanism to facilitate matching one structure against another and finding intersections of sets or concepts.

It is important to observe with regard to associative networks that the organization of symbolic structures can have a profound influence on the relative ease of cognitive processing. This point will be made repeatedly in this book.

Frames, schemas and scripts. Some of the most pervasive kinds of cognitive processes which we would like to capture are those of categorizing objects, events, situations, sequences of events and situations, and so on, into *recurrent* types about which we can make generalizations, in order to better understand the instances at hand. For instance, suppose you get a glimpse of a small animate object and observe only that it has feathers. You are likely to immediately conclude that it is a bird and therefore that it flies, walks on two legs, lays eggs (if it is a female), sings (if it is a male) and so on. Many such inductive inferences turn out to be difficult to capture in a natural way in logic-based systems. *Schemas* (Rumelhart 1980), of which *frames* (Minsky 1975) and *scripts* (Schank and Abelson 1977, Schank 1982) can be seen as subtypes, are representational structures that are designed to capture exactly these kinds of generalizations in one place.

For instance, a *script* might represent the typical sequence of events involved in going to eat in a restaurant (entering, being seated, getting a menu, selecting an order, receiving food, eating, and so on), or the typical components of a hot summer day (shorts, bikinis, sunglasses, cold drinks, water sports, and so on). In reasoning about a specific sequence of events, appropriate scripts can be located, correspondences between elements of the script and the specific specific instance established, and the instance elaborated appropriately. Figure 1.3 illustrates the application of such a script. After acquiring some perhaps limited information about some events, represented by the solid links in the lower oval, the system might recognize that the events instantiate the script, represented by the upper oval. Correspondences between certain objects in the instance and objects in the script, represented by the dashed arrows, are established making the information of the script accessible when reasoning about the instance. This information in the script, said to be *inherited* by the instance, is taken to implicitly say something about the instance, and thus to supplement what is already known about the instance.

More specifically, understanding the following discourse fragment would involve application of the **restaurant** script, and probably also a **breakfast** script.

> *Fred and Mabel went into the diner. The waitress jotted down their order of pancakes.*

A lot of information, not explicit in the story, becomes available by inheritance from the restaurant script. For instance, we can assume that Fred and Mabel sat down, that they *ate* pancakes, that they paid for the pancakes, that it is probably morning, and so on.

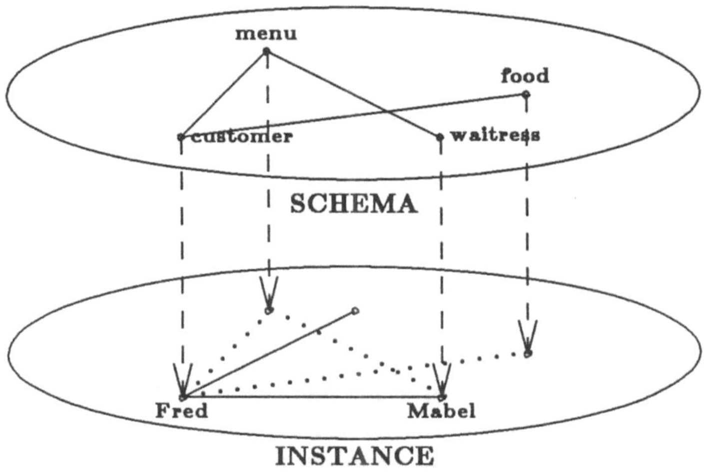

Fig. 1.3. The application of the restaurant script to the understanding of the description of a particular restaurant situation.

A primary motivation for these structures is in their efficiency in producing many of the common-sense inferences that humans find natural. Scripts have been particularly effective in computational natural language understanding systems in providing the background necessary for successful interpretation (Schank and Riesbeck 1981). For instance, definite noun phrases like *the dog* normally require that a unique object that satisfies the description be somehow identifiable by the hearer or reader in the speech setting. Often a schema allows the existence of such an object to be inferred immediately in the absence of explicit mention. Thus, the restaurant script in the example above contains a representation of a wait-person which becomes the waitress referenced by *the waitress.*

Frames, schemas and scripts are not complete theories of mental representation in themselves, only organizational structures that capture certain aspects of cognition. Generally they make use, at least in computational models, of an underlying associative network. In fact, inheritance is often implemented in these models by passing markers along these links.

Analogical representations. Kosslyn (1980), Funt (1980), Johnson-Laird (1983) and others advocate representations which are image-like, in the sense that the representations utilize a *medium* which corresponds, or is analogous, to a part of the reality being represented. A roadmap is a good example for illustrating the idea of an analogical representation. The medium consists of markings on a two-dimensional sheet of paper. What is represented is some area of the surface of the earth. Directionality, distance and area are intrinsic properties of both the paper and the earth's surface. Accordingly, putting a labeled dot on the map implicitly represents the relations of distance and direction of some city to all other cities and other objects on the map.

Generally, analogical models of mental representation are in fact used in representing spatial information. Johnson-Laird proposes the theory of *mental models*, which will be mentioned often in the course of this book, as a psychologically more realistic account of human reasoning processes than those that use logical rules of inference. (Mental models actually mix analogical representations with some propositional features.) For instance, in interpreting a sentence of the form

A is to the right of B.

object B is located and object A is placed in a location relative to B falling within a suitable range of coordinates, but also consistent with the spatial arrangement of other objects positioned in the mental model.

What an analogical medium of *mental* representation might be, is an open question. Presumably it is not paper, but it may be neural tissue or some means of forming a grid of representations. In computer models, typically two- or three-dimensional arrays are declared to give a convenient medium.

In general. Mental representations are abstract. They are not something that we can see or hear. We only know about them indirectly, in observations of human behavior, through introspection, by drawing analogies to other systems or artificially constructed models, and so on. Defining and justifying a particular theory of representation is a slippery business. In fact, it is often unclear whether a particular theory really says something that might be demonstrably true of human cognition, or whether it simply provides a conceptual perspective or vocabulary in terms of which the facts about human cognition can be interpreted. As Brachman (1979) has convincingly argued, failure to establish a methodological perspective has resulted in much misunderstanding about the differences among models of representation. For instance, Hayes (1979b) shows how from one perspective frames can be regarded as nothing more than a notational variant of predicate calculus. There are probably no limits the the ability of a proponent of logic-based systems to see predicates and arguments and even quantifiers in associative networks, in schemata or in any other kind of representation. Since I, too, will be arguing, in this book, for a particular theory of mental representation, I will be particularly concerned with identifying what is really at issue in theories of representation.

Levels of Description

The symbolic paradigm traditionally sees cognition in a broad sense as a sandwich. The top slice of bread is variously called the *knowledge level* (Newell 1982), the *intentional* (Dennett 1978) or the *computational* level (Marr 1982). The bottom slice of bread is the level of *hardware implementation* (Marr 1982) or the *physical* level (Dennett 1978). The salami itself is the *symbol* (Newell 1982), *design* (Dennett 1978) or *representations and algorithms* (Marr 1982) level. Let's take a bite.

The intentional level. This represents the functional view of cognition, at which intentionality, belief, obligation and so on are described. An example of an intentional level description would be the following.

> *George wanted to bake a pie, but was sure he was out of apples. Therefore, he stopped by the market on his way to the bowling alley.*

This level also corresponds to the most common way of conceptualizing human behavior in folk psychology (some have argued that this level is *purely* folk psychology).

The symbol level. The central level characterizes the descriptions of theories of representation of the last section. An example of a symbol level description would be the following.

> *George's* **bake-pie** *script activated, with* **myself** *bound to*

> *the* **baker** *role. A search was run on the preconditions of the* **bake-pie** *script, readily finding role bindings for* **oven** *and* **pie-pan,** *but failing to find a binding for* **fruit-filling.** *Immediately a subgoal* **acquire fruit-filling** *was generated.*

At this level we talk about symbolic representations and processes that access those representations, create new symbolic configurations, and so on.

Even within the symbolic level differences of perspective exist. In this book we are interested specifically in identifying *structural primitives*, basic principles used in organizing mental representations, which affect reasoning processes. Brachman (1979) identifies this as the *epistemological level* as opposed, for instance, to the logic level. It is also what Pylyshyn (1984) identifies as the *functional/symbolic level.* This is the level at which one would expect to find a correspondence between the structures manipulated in a cognitive process and the amount of time the process takes.

The implementation level. This has to do with the physical realization of symbolic representations and processes. It is usually identified with the neural brain hardware or, in computational models, with the computer architecture. An example of an implementation level description would be the following.

> *The firing rate of a neuron about an inch above George's left eye surged. Within milliseconds the pulses were felt in synaptically connected neurons and their firing rates began to rise as well.*

In Marr's (1982) view, the implementation level has less to do with the nature of symbolic processes than the intentional level. In fact, it is usually assumed that the same symbolic structures can be realized in multiple hardware implementations. Connectionism, to be discussed momentarily, is often identified with this level.

Social Cognition. Even higher than the intentional level is the *social* level, the level of customs, institutions and economies in which intentional agents operate. This would also include conventional systems like traffic laws and games. I will return briefly to this level of description when I discuss language in Chapter 3.

Levels everywhere. Different levels of description in cognitive science should not be disturbing; the same thing is found in the physical sciences. Quarks and such organize themselves into atoms, atoms into molecules, molecules into solids and fluids. Eventually you get up to the level of big things like tables and oceans, as well as biological organisms like us. Scientific disciplines are largely defined in terms of the level or levels of description they deal with.

The existence of different levels of description in cognition is often justified in terms of the philosophy of *functionalism* (Putnam 1973). Putnam looks at the computer as an specific example: High-level languages, like Lisp and Prolog, for instance, are implemented to run on a lower-level machine architecture, but its properties are relatively independent of the underlying machine. In fact, exactly the same programming language is *multiply realizable* in any number of hardware machines. Understanding a computational system is generally possible only one level at a time. Imagine a student of artificial intelligence, for instance, trying to understand how an expert system works, from a description of the bit-wise contents of a computer's internal memory.

In Putnam's terminology, systems have *macrostructures*, described in a high-level discipline, for which the underlying *microstructures*, described in a lower-level discipline, are for the most part irrelevant, even though the macrostructures are in an important sense based in the microstructures. The objects and processes at the microstructure level organize themselves into objects and processes at the macrostructure level with entirely different properties, such that it is not particularly useful or even possible to reduce the macrolevel descriptions to the microlevel. In particular, the macrostructures cannot be predicted from the microstructures. Thus, the implementational level is the microstructure relative to the symbolic macrostructure. The symbolic level is a microstructure relative to the intentional macrostructure.

Let me end this section with a cautionary note. Levels of description, though necessary, may be independent only to a degree. Schwartz (forthcoming), for instance, looks at Mendelian genetics and molecular biology as two levels of description. He shows that genetics is not reducible to properties of DNA, but that nevertheless the discovery and investigation of DNA has refined our understanding of genetics. The levels thus are not entirely independent. Another example is science as opposed to the scientist. Science is something that develops over a period of decades or centuries, accumulates a body of knowledge, disseminates that knowledge, educates its practitioners, develops theories and paradigms, follows different paradigms at different times in its history, and so forth. The scientist develops his ideas and knowledge over a period of years or decades, accumulates knowledge, develops new theories. In many respects, science is a macrocosm of the scientist, but with some properties peculiar to its own level, but with many properties emerging from the microlevel of the scientist. Another example of properties emerging from the microlevel might be found in the the goal-oriented structures of social and economic systems, which are probably related to the biological drives (satisfying hunger, maintaining body temperature, satisfying the sex drive, etc.) of the component organisms. Even computer architectures can in fact (pace Putnam) often be greatly influence the way in which higher-level computational tasks are subsequently described. For instance, the development of the massively parallel *Connection Machine* has spawned a new area of research in higher-level computer algorithms (Hillis and Steele 1986).

CRACKS IN THE SYMBOLIC PARADIGM

The central idea of the symbolic paradigm is that there are symbolic structures which on the one hand are interpretable semantically (potentially stand for something out there in the world) and on the other hand are exactly those objects that are manipulated by cognitive processes. Figure 1.1 illustrated this. There are two types of objections that can be, and have been, raised about these assumptions. The first is that this account of semantics won't work, that is, the bottom half of Figure 1.1 is wrong. The second is that this account of cognitive processing won't work, that is, the top half of Figure 1.1 is wrong. Otherwise things are fine. Let's look at these two kinds of problems in turn.

Limitations of Symbolic Semantics

Symbolic expressions are supposed to *denote* things out there in the world, at least in some abstract sense.* This is how a cognitive system is able to interact with the world. There are at least two problems with this view of semantics: First, there is evidence that any representation not only *re-presents* reality but also *interprets* reality. It is impossible to talk about semantics as a simple correspondence between representations and an objective reality. This is Putnam's (1988) thesis of *internal realism.* Second, it is unclear how the correspondence between symbols and reality is supposed to arise. This is the *symbol grounding problem.*

Generally the symbolic paradigm presupposes an *objective reality* consisting of objects, including abstract concepts, and relations among objects. A semantics expresses the relationship that exists between representations and the objects and relations existing in the objective reality, that is, between representations and what is represented. This view of semantics has methodological consequences for cognitive science: If cognitive scientists are to accurately describe a semantic system, they need to be able first to describe reality from an objective, *God's eye,* perspective, often assumed to be furnished by science.

Nevertheless, Putnam (1981, 1988), Lakoff (1987) and Winograd and Flores (1986) argue persuasively that there is no such God's eye perspective, that virtually any description is going to rely on one of many alternative ways to *interpret* reality. What objects, properties, relations and so on that are held to exist in reality only make sense from within the theory that motivates the description. This is what Putnam calls *internal realism.* Notice that internal realism doesn't deny a reality out there, it only addresses the limits of our ability to describe that reality.

The simplest kind of example of this principle that I know of are *spatial coordinate systems.* For instance, we can alternatively regard the sun as rising or the earth as turning under the sun with us on it. We can think of a train moving through the forest, or the forest rushing past the window of a train. We can consider Fred to be standing to the right of Mabel facing us, or Fred standing to the left of Mabel

* Traditional semantic accounts depend on *intentional* objects and properties with the *potential* for reference, in order to give *unicorn* and *nibelung,* for instance, different interpretations even though they refer to the same thing in the real world, that is, to nothing.

facing away from us. The point is that to describe spatial information we need first to frame reality in some some coordinate system, that is, adopt some perspective, before we are in a position to describe that reality.

Putnam (1988) himself offers the simple example of describing the number of objects in a room (does a book count as one object, or does each page count as an object?). There is no definitive way to count objects, he argues; it depends on what you decide to count as an object. Of course, objects are basic to the semantics of logics; variables are said to range over objects. Yet the notion of object itself is not fully inherent in reality itself, but is at least partially a matter of an *interpretation* we *impose* on reality. To take some additional examples, are *rivers* to count as distinct objects? A river is nothing more than a rough regularity in the locations and movements of a group of water molecules over an extended period of time. This makes it an abstraction that people find convenient to impose in their understanding of reality. Similar remarks can be made about the ontological status of such things as a *medical practice* as something that belongs to a doctor, can be inherited from a doctor and so on.

Even scientific theories impose their own ontologies and conceptual frameworks on reality, and scientists are able to switch from one theory to another as convenient. Our discussion of levels of description above is a clear illustration of this. Likewise our common-sensical conceptualizations of reality are alternatives quite different from our scientific conceptualizations. In fact, the usually more naive alternative perspectives that people impose are called *folk theories*.*

Additional examples of the human tendency to impose an interpretation on reality are *institutional facts*. Consider a scene in a baseball game. A physical description might look like this: "A person hits a ball with a stick. As a result, the ball reverses direction and, moving at a high speed and with a steep inclination, goes over an opposing fence and lands in the midst of a group of people." What the spectators see is this: "The batter makes a homerun." Thus, the physical description *counts as* something completely different; however, what it counts as is only partially determined by the physical

---

* The existence and usefulness of folk theories is implicitly recognized in AI in what is called *naive physics* (Hayes 1979a).

description and partially determined by the interpretation imposed by certain people in certain specialized contexts.

Or consider a financial interchange. A physical description might look like this: "Fred hands Mabel three small green sheets of paper, and two silver disks of 1 inch and 3/4 inch diameters." Alternatively, a physical description might look like this: "Fred writes $3.35 on a small blue sheet of paper and writes Mable's name at the top and his own signature at the bottom. He then gives the sheet to Mabel." But what either event counts as is this: "Fred pays Mabel $3.25." The accuracy of the description is not inherent in the reality alone, but rather in how we chose to interpret that reality.

A unique but common kind of example of the human ability to impose interpretations on reality is *fiction*. In theater, for instance, the physical actions occurring on stage count as dying, falling in and out of love, going bonkers, being ruined financially, and so on, while in another interpretation they are simply those of actors doing their jobs.

Lakoff and Johnson (Lakoff and Johnson 1980, Lakoff 1987, Johnson 1987) demonstrate the role of metaphor in imposing a complex system of interpretation on reality. For instance, the metaphor *time is money* goes beyond asserting a similarity; it structures our whole conceptualization of time. Suddenly it makes perfect sense to save, lose, spend, budget and waste time.

Even our lowest-level concepts require human interpretation. As Lakoff (1987, pp. 198-9) reports, color concepts cannot be analyzed simply in terms of some range of wavelengths of light measurable with scientific instrumentation. In this case, we can actually see why human representations contribute to the way reality is interpreted. For instance, no object is simultaneously red or green. The reason is not that it is physically impossible to emit red wavelengths and green wavelengths at the same time. The reason is that it is impossible for humans to perceive red and green at the same time because red and green are neurally encoded as opposing responses of the same neurons.

The important question for us is what internal realism means for the methodology of doing semantics in cognitive science. We certainly do not want to give up talking about correspondences between representations and reality; this kind of solipsism would lose sight of one of the essential constraining factors for cognitive theories. One approach, which Lakoff (1987) calls the *world-as-understood*, approach would be to do semantics as before, effectively regarding people's *conception* of reality as the relevant reality. This probably works where there is at least strong intersubjective agreement about the proper folk theory of the relevant aspect of reality. For instance, for the semantic domain of *time* an ontology that accepts *intervals* of time as objects that can ordered linearly, that can overlap, that can be contained one in another, that have a duration and during which events can occur, is unproblematic. This probably also works where fairly abstract issues in semantics are being studied. For instance, for the study of *compositionality* in representations one might proceed without any specific assumptions about reality beyond the mere existence of objects, properties and relations. Everything said about compositionality might be consistent with any number of alternative folk theories. In fact it is probably the emphasis that logical semantics has traditionally placed on compositionality that has allowed researchers to be oblivious to the problems we are looking at in this section.

Nevertheless, there are at least two pitfalls in the *world-as-understood* approach. First, it may miss many important phenomena. In particular, we would like to ask to what extent the form of the representation *helps impose* an interpretation on reality, whereas the world-as-understood effectively accepts the imposed reality as a given. We will see, for instance, in the next chapter some ways in which partitioned representations contribute to the folk theories people construct to understand reality. Second, the world-as-understood approach needs to be able to deal with alternative mutually inconsistent folk theories. I think this is appropriately accommodated if we are careful to preface any semantic description by a statement about the folk theory we are presupposing. It turns out that this second pitfall doesn't arise easily in practice in partitioned representations since the ability to represent multiple perspectives at the same time without mixing up the perspectives is intrinsic in the highly context-dependent form of the representation, as we will see.

Although the shift to internal realism is not fatal to the symbolic paradigm as a whole, internal realism suggests that semantic structure is much richer than traditionally acknowledged, providing a wealth of unanticipated future dissertation topics. Traditional work in semantics can be seen to use a *world-as-understood* model, as an approximation of this much richer semantics. It is fine to build approximate models of aspects of semantics as long as one is careful to recognize where this strategy reaches its limits.

A second problem with symbolic semantics has been *symbol grounding*, the question of what makes symbols represent what they represent. Traditionally, for instance in applications in AI, the solution to this problem is simple, *too* simple: the programmer or designer of the symbolic system decides what object or concept a symbol stands for. As Searle (1980) argues, this won't do. There would have to be some more solid, internal basis for the meaningfulness of symbols. How are concepts acquired? How are symbols allocated to stand for those concepts? How do the denotations of those symbols of those symbols remain fixed? These are outstanding problems for symbolism which have not been thoroughly addressed (see, however, Johnson 1987).

Limitations of Symbolic Processes

Processing in the symbolic paradigm is more seriously problematic than symbolic semantics is. First, there are some processes that seem to manipulate symbolic structures, but cannot be adequately analyzed in symbolic terms. Second, there appear to be many kinds of cognitive processes that involve non-symbolic structures, that is, structures that are semantically empty.

Non-Analyzable processes. There appear to be some processes which *do* involve symbolic manipulations, in the sense of mapping one symbolic structure into another, but nevertheless resist symbolic description, in the sense of a clear specification of the mapping referring only to the symbols involved. As an example, face recognition might be seen abstractly as a mapping that takes a set of symbolic structures representing facial features, and returns a symbol representing some individual. Now, humans can recognize the same face in a variety of contexts, from different angles, under different illuminations, with parts obscured by shadows or other objects, and so on. No boolean combination of features determines the face, as far as any researcher has ever been able to determine, yet a given face is recognized fairly reliably. Dreyfus and Dreyfus (1986) discuss further examples of *holistic representations*, those which do not decompose objects explicitly into component features, in detail and trace the history of the philosophical debate over this issue.

A related problem is that of the ability of a representation scheme to process unusual, faulty or noisy input. Symbolic models, for instance expert systems, are notoriously brittle when presented with partially obscured or distorted objects, anomalous data and so forth. Here, even where the symbolic mapping is analyzable under ideal noise-free conditions, noise introduces a degree of complexity into the mapping which humans, but not symbolic models, are typically capable of overcoming.

Associations between concepts are particularly prominent as resistant to symbolic analysis, even though associations are easily regarded as mappings between symbols. We have looked at semantic priming in our discussion of associative networks above. Recall that in order to predict associations, decidedly non-symbolic features—activations or markers—were incorporated into the representation schemes to overcome the inability of more strictly symbolic models to predict associations. Additional examples important in natural language understanding are the phenomenon of *metonymy*—the reference to one object or concept by means of an expression that stands for an associated object or concept—and the resolution of anaphoric, e.g., pronominal, reference.

In summary, associations and holistic discrimination *can* be seen to map one symbolic representation or set of representations to another, but the symbolic vocabulary often does not seem to allow us to fully *analyze* the mapping, not to the degree that we can predict what representations will get mapped onto what representations, because the conditions under which the rules are applied resist expression as a boolean function of symbolic features. These are what I like to call *mysterious symbolic processes.* Work in connectionism, to which we turn in a moment, indicates that dropping down to a lower subsymbolic level allows such mappings to be analyzed more successfully.

Semantically empty processes. There are many examples of domains of cognitive processing that it would be very difficult to regard as operating on symbols, that is, on semantically meaningful structures in the traditional sense. Easy examples are aesthetic and emotional processes, which interact with more rational decision-making and problem-solving processes in many ways. Understanding the harmonic and melodic structure of music, for instance, must involve a great deal of cognitive processing. An account of such processing should tell us why people perceive music written in D major as bright or in C minor as serene. A theory of such processing may involve the manipulation of high-level structures, but it is difficult to see many points at which a semantics could be meaningful attached.

It is interesting to observe that much of the work on generative grammar in linguistics has exceeded the limits of the symbolic paradigm in this regard by positing *deep structures* that underlie surface linguistic expressions, are structurally dissimilar and are specifically *not* (for instance in the old *interpretive semantics* school) semantically interpreted. These are structures that are manipulated like symbols, and are justified in terms of symbolic consequences, but do not themselves carry a semantics like symbols. A similar example might be frame systems in their common usage as *prototypes* or bearers of default information. Frame systems, as structures that bundle together features commonly associated with some type of object, have been notoriously resistant to semantic analysis as wholes. Yet they are useful as intermediate structures for generating semantically meaningful inferences.

CONNECTIONISM: THE OTHER PARADIGM

In the last decade the importance of a theoretical framework variously known (not entirely synonymously) as *neural networks*, *parallel distributed processing* or *connectionism* has become increasingly prominent in cognitive science. Rumelhart and McClelland (1986), McClelland and Rumelhart (1986) is a very good introduction into this literature. Let's look at the usefulness of connectionism as an alternative or supplement to symbolism. Dinsmore (forthcoming) is, a more thorough discussion of the relationship between the two paradigms.

Connectionist Mechanisms

A connectionist system is a configuration of *units* and weighted *connections* between units. Figure 1.4 illustrates one possible configuration. A unit does nothing but repeatedly update its level of *activation* and produce a level of output, solely on the basis of the outputs and connection weights from immediately associated units, along with its own previous activation.*

Although all processing is achieved in terms of such local interactions, interesting global behavior can be observed as the network of locally interacting units relaxes into a stable state of equilibrium. Units, initially excited by input, spread activation over connections, exciting and inhibiting each other. Over time, the network's energy level settles as coalitions of active units form and the strongest coalition wins out. Information actually resides in the connection weights. For instance, the network of Figure 1.4 might encode some function such that some input appearing as an initial pattern of activation on the input units would result in the appearance of the associated output as a pattern of activation on the output units (this particular configuration is useful as a *pattern associator*).

There is considerable variation among connectionists about how semantics fits into the model or how connectionist semantics is related to symbolic semantics. Most connectionists would advocate

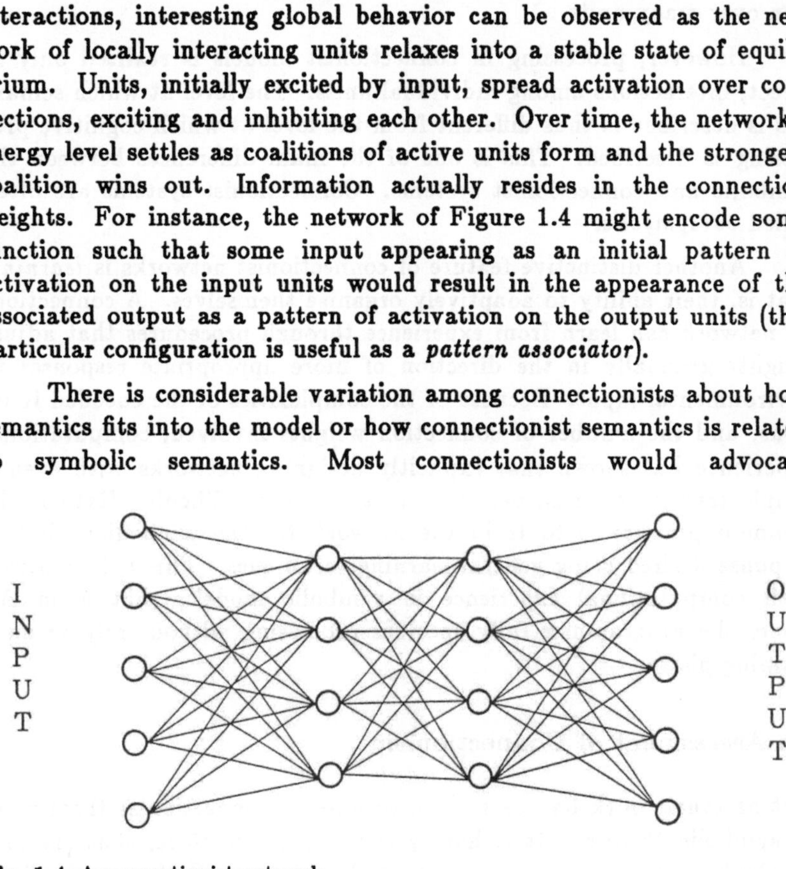

Fig. 1.4. A connectionist network.

---

* Almost always the determination of the activation update involves a *sigma-pi* computation, summing up incoming signals, each of which is the activation value on the other side of a connection scaled down by the weight of the connection. Very typically this sum is then run through a *sigmoid* function that squishes the activation down to fit in the range 0 to 1, or -1 to 1.

distributive models in which objects and concepts are represented as patterns of activity over many units, with each unit participating in many patterns (Hinton 1981). Ultimately representations of things like the San Francisco Giants, motherhood, and generalizations about used car salesmen would therefore be in terms of patterns of activation over many units.

However, processing in connectionist models is realized only in direct, interactions among individual units. The level at which semantics is described is thus different from the level at which cognitive processing is described. This is one of the main differences between the symbolic and connectionist systems. Connectionist systems are often called *subsymbolic*.

Another distinctive feature of connectionist networks is *learning*, that is, their ability to adaptively organize themselves. A connectionist network can learn from experience through procedures that adjust weights gradually in the direction of more appropriate responses to environmental input. Because of the complexities of the encoded functions, and the number of connection weights involved, computational experience has shown that explicitly designing networks with even a simple task in mind is, beyond a certain point, difficult. Rather, the common practice is to train the network for the particular kind of response desired using general learning techniques. This is in contrast with computational experience in symbolic models, that is in AI, where the programmer fully specifies processing without relying on a training phase.

An Assessment of Connectionism

Not as much work has been done to date in connectionist theories as in symbolic theories. It is hardly surprising, therefore, that (1) connectionism has logged fewer substantial achievements than symbolism, (2) fewer clear weaknesses in the connectionist paradigm have been demonstrated, and (3) researchers in connectionism tend to have very high expectations of future success. Looking at the current state of connectionist research, we come to a mixed assessment, but find some impressive results that should raise the eyebrows of any researcher in symbolic cognitive science.

Grounding in neurophysiology. Much of the appeal of connectionism is doubtlessly its basis in brain architecture, which potentially gives it more of a hard science flavor. On the other hand, this basis tends to be quite tenuous. First, many connectionist mechanisms have no known neural counterparts. For instance, the best known learning technique for multi-layered networks, like that in Figure 1.4, requires the propagation of a signal *backward* along connections in a manner that has never been observed physically. Second, many neural mechanisms have no counterparts in connectionist models, for the most part because they are poorly understood. For instance, nothing in connectionist models correspond to hormonal and other chemical mechanisms. It is rare for a connectionist network to exhibit anything like the large-scale anatomical structures observed in the brain. Smolensky (1988) goes so far as making a distinction between connectionist and *neural* networks as different levels of abstraction, connectionist systems being in fact closer to symbolic that to neural systems.

Mysterious processes. Because connectionism typically makes a clear break between processing and semantics, connectionist models are in principle immune to many of the criticisms raised above to symbolic models. First, although certain patterns of activation may denote things out there in the world, there is no requirement that all patterns of activation do this. Thus, processes without semantic counterparts, as found, for instance, in making aesthetic judgements, are entirely consistent with the connectionist paradigm (this is not to say that anyone has any idea of how these would occur in a connectionist network). Likewise, what I have been calling mysterious processes, those which can be described in symbolic terms at both ends but not in the middle, are consistent with the connectionist paradigm.

Not only are mysterious processes consistent with connectionism, many of these processes actually seem to be *predicted* in these models. Connectionist models have been especially successful in low-level information processing tasks that are generally attributed to the peripheral nervous system, and that have fallen in practice outside of the domain of symbolic theories. They tend to be very good at recognizing patterns, such as faces, overcoming noise or faulty input and finding associations between concepts. More generally, they tend to be very good at finding a best match when a number of competing interpretations are available, and completing descriptions by default on the basis of limited information. They seem to aid in making higher-level decisions that have traditionally been very difficult to handle in computational symbolic models. Rumelhart, Smolensky, McClelland and Hinton (1986) demonstrate how connectionist systems handle in a natural way not only the correct application of schemas but also the resolution of conflicts between schemas.

Learning. One of the impressive accomplishments of connectionist research, one that contrasts significantly with the state of symbolic research, is the development of very general learning techniques. By training a connectionist network with input and output patterns a network can do a fairly good job, by simple cumulative connection weight adjustments, at picking up the generalizations that map input reliably onto output. One of the most intriguing results of this research is the ability of these networks to actually create representations as part of the learning process (Rumelhart, Hinton and Williams 1986, Gasser and Lee forthcoming). This promises an initial approach to the symbol grounding problem.

Nevertheless, learning in connectionist systems have some sobering limitations. First, learning is generally achieved by providing highly reliable training instances in a very systematic way, normally iterating over all desirable input-output correspondences a number of times. The quality and systematicity of training by a more realistic, random sampling of the environment would fall far short of that achieved artificially. Second, learning is generally achieved only on the basis of on the order of a *hundred thousand* training instances. The slow speeds of human neural architecture, in contrast to that of the computers on which simulations are run, make so many iterations infeasible. Third, these techniques are unlikely to scale up tractably from the relatively small networks and relatively simple problems for which the have been tested. This is because the time required to train a network could well explode exponentially with an increase in the size of the network (Minsky and Papert 1988, Epilogue).

But aside from the slow rate and lack of reliability of standard connectionist learning techniques, the most pervasive and successful kind of learning in symbolic models is virtually unknown in connectionist models, that is, learning *by being told.* No mechanisms have been proposed for connectionist systems to account for the extremely rapid acquisition by humans of very complex information. This is found, for instance, in natural language understanding, in which sentences are processed in rapid succession, each contributing immediately to an evolving model of the situation a narration is describing, a model that may become part of long term memory. It is found also in the interpretation of conscious rules, like *put the green ones over here and the red ones over there*, that begin to determine behavior immediately after acquisition.

High-level issues. The results in connectionism of interest to cognitive scientists are for the most part achieved under a very limiting assumption, that the environment with which the connectionist system interacts can be adequately represented as a set of binary features. Compositional representations, on the other hand, tend to be unnatural and cumbersome, even for simple relations like John seeing Mary. John might be represented as the activation of some specific unit, or a pattern of activation over a number of units. Likewise for Mary and for the act of seeing. But how does one express that John is the agent of the seeing action and Mary the patient? Quite a lot of research has gone into overcoming this problem (see Blank, Meeden and Marshall, forthcoming, for an overview), none of it quite as adequate as one would like. Additionally, it is hard to get multiple instantiations of a generic representation or schema in a connectionist models (Pinker and Prince 1988) or to set up or forget complex associations between schemas and specific instances quickly as is done through role and variable binding in symbolic models (Barnden and Pollack 1990).

Many of the models that allegedly perform high-level tasks, such as language understanding, are on close inspection not as impressive as the claims made about them. Aizawa (forthcoming) discusses the pervasiveness of what he calls *unreduced mechanisms*, external support in the form of peripheral non-connectionist routines in computational models, or outside interpretations of what the network is supposed to be doing. John McCarthy, in Smolensky (1988), points out the lack of what he calls *elaboration tolerance* in connectionist systems when researchers try to make the systems more inclusive. Lachter and Bever (1988) accuse researchers of sneaking symbolic representations into the design of a connectionist network to give the impression that the higher-level behavior actually emerges from the connectionist architecture.

Are Symbolism and Connectionism a Matter of Different Levels?

The idea that connectionism and symbolism simply deal with different levels sits well with traditional symbolists. The distinction corresponds to the symbolic and implementation levels discussed earlier. How do things look to connectionists? Pinker and Prince (1988) introduce terms for three different positions on this matter: *Implementational connectionism* describes the philosophy that connectionist networks simply provide an alternative means of implementing understood symbolic structures and processes. Implementational connectionism would seem most consistent with the traditional symbolic view. *Eliminative connectionism* describes the opposing, more radical position that the symbolic level is not necessary at all to a complete description of cognition. Finally, *revisionist connectionism* describes a more subtle, intermediate position whereby connectionism will lead to different sets of symbols and operations and to new discoveries about the nature of symbolic processing, even while the levels remain distinct.

I will argue that the eliminativist position cannot be right, since connectionism needs symbolism. Then I will argue that the implementationalist position cannot be right, at least not across the board, because symbolism needs connectionism. Then I want to stake out what I suppose is a version of the revisionist position, *hybridism.*

Connectionism needs Symbolism. Clearly, connectionist networks with significant cognitive abilities will have to be far more complex then the simple computational models that now exist. But as models become more complex, they will become more opaque. For this reason connectionist models cannot dispense with higher-level functional abstractions that summarize large parts of the network structure or behavior. Dyer in his commentary to Smolensky (1988) imagines running a large connectionist network for twenty years and sending it to college and points out that there would be no way to understand what had been produced, even though the network might exhibit intelligent behavior.

The recognition of higher-level structures is in no way inconsistent with the thesis that cognition emerges from connectionist principles. But like many kinds of physical systems, the connectionist architecture can be assumed to organize itself into higher-level structures and processes with their own properties, that call for a higher level of description. We should always look for higher-level organizational principles. In fact, it is difficult to imagine much progress in general cognitive science without recognizing the existence of things like representations for individuals and relations. It is impossible to conceive of an account of deliberate conscious thinking or of scientific theory without such a recognition.

Connectionist theory should develop with an eye to what is observed at the symbolic level, since at the more abstract symbolic level the functionality of cognitive processes is most easily understood. Considerations of functionality serve to constrain connectionist theories and to give connectionist research direction, that is, they give connectionist theories problems to solve. I believe that virtually all connectionist work has in fact proceeded with such considerations in mind.

Symbolism needs connectionism. Dyer, in his commentary to Smolensky (1988), points out that if traditional symbolic operations were simply implemented in connectionist models many of the significant and useful cognitive properties of connectionist models would simply be lost at the symbolic level, where they in fact fulfill a great need. This would include the natural account of mysterious processes which symbolic models don't seem to be capable of fathoming. The fact is that connectionist models seem to provide natural, if somewhat sketchy, solutions to many of the most serious problems that arise in symbolic models.

Hybridism. The successful cognitive scientist of the future may well be one who can shift comfortably from one level to the next according to which provides a better conceptual grasp of the problem at hand, recognizing that two complementary perspectives are more powerful than a single, uniform one.

Cognitive systems are complex, consisting of many component structures and processes. Looking over the range of these components we will often overextend the limits of the descriptive powers of symbolic models in two ways. First, components of the microstructure of cognition may not have organized themselves into higher-level behaviors or structures which are subject to symbolic description. This may be the case, for instance, with emotional responses. Second, symbolic descriptions may simply be incomplete. This would be the case in mysterious processes like face recognition and associations between concepts.

To the extent that connectionist networks have organized themselves into functionally motivated, systematic, high-level behaviors, symbolic descriptions can take over. Often parallel descriptions at the symbolic and connectionist levels may be possible, though the symbolic description in this case is bound to be much simpler. Even when a full account in symbolic terms does not present itself, partial higher-level or functional descriptions of certain aspects of processes may be appropriate supplements to the connectionist description.

As the researcher moves through the various aspects of a cognitive problem moving up or down to the most useful level of description, a model will emerge that will look like a patchwork of symbolic and connectionist components. These are *hybrid models*. In fact, some work with hybrid models has been done. Anderson (1983) describes the subsymbolic, possibly neural, spreading activation mechanism used to measure degree of match for production conditions in ACT* as implementing an associative heuristic. Kwasny and Faisal (forthcoming) describe a natural language parsing system that is based on the symbolic work of Marcus (1978), but make use of a connectionist component to make mysterious high-level decisions about rule application. Lange (forthcoming) provides a general overview of hybrid systems.

METHODS OF MODELS

A *model* is a system, typically embodied in some formalism, computer program or conceptual framework that is taken to be an approximation of some natural system under investigation. From the perspective of cognitive science, systems developed in logic and formal semantics, as well as in artificial intelligence are generally valuable as models in this sense. Much of this study in partitioned representations, especially with regard to the functionality of these representations, is conducted with reference to such models. Let me, therefore, say a few words about models.

Among the purposes for developing cognitive models are the following:

(1) *Conceptual simplicity.* Models are simpler to study. Many properties are shared by a class of systems, the way steamlinedness characterizes almost all flying and swimming things, for instance. If the natural system and some artificial system, the model, belong to the same class of systems, it might be useful to study the model even when many details of the natural system are fairly well understood, in order to make further predictions about the natural system. Mathematical results, for instance, are generally possible only for simple models. Certain theorems have been proven for some connectionist models, for instance, that seem in practice to hold for other connectionist models for which they cannot be proved.

(2) *Explicitness.* Models can exchange accuracy for explicitness. Explicitness has at least the following two advantages. First, explicitness forces the researcher to avoid oversights. Second, an explicit model can serve as a clear reference point from which discrepancies with the facts about the natural system can be recognized. These discrepancies focus the researcher's attention on unsolved problems. Often a model will have a life cycle of progressive refinements, with one version of the model giving way to a better approximation produced in response to observed discrepancies.

(3) *Studying systemic behavior.* A particularly common advantage of models is that a model can help researchers study the behavior of a complex system of components even when the components themselves are poorly understood, by developing approximations of the components. This allows the interaction of the components to be studied independently of the exact properties of the components. This function is particularly important in cognitive science, since cognition involves a lot of processes and structures interacting in complex ways.

Among the pitfalls of models are (1) an unwillingness to replace them with a better approximation when they have outlived their usefulness, and (2) allowing the features peculiar to the formalism used in constructing models, e.g., logic or a computer programming language, to adversely influence theoretical thinking.

Cognitive science has made particular use of, and (probably to some extent adversely) been influenced by, logical and computational models.

Logical models. A system of logic, like the human cognitive system, exhibits compositionality, inference and rationality. One finds some correspondence, though certainly very rough, between what inferences people make easily on the basis of given information, and the length of a logical derivation, at least in noncomplex domains. For instance, given that Fred was born before 1950 and George was born after 1950, we would expect a human to be able to infer that Fred is older than George, just as this is easy to derive in a logic based system, assuming a couple of natural axioms about *before* and *after*.

At worst, the importance of logic in the study of representation might be compared to the importance of the *Turing machine* in the study of computation. The Turing machine is a formally defined theoretical computing device that has the advantage of being very well understood in a mathematical sense but has the disadvantages of being unimplementable (it requires infinite memory capacity) and impractical (if it were implementable, even the simplest computations would take an inordinate amount of time). Nevertheless it provides a formal tool for understanding the properties of real computational devices.

On the other hand logical models have their deficiencies as a theory of human representation, as we have seen, just as Turing machines have practical deficiencies as computers. They fail to account for how meanings adhere to representations, how mysterious processes are achieved, and so on. On the other hand, logical models have proved extremely robust, having gone through progressive refinements over time, primarily in response to their one-time failure to capture certain observed modes of reasoning in a straight-forward way. For instance, in AI the importance of making inferences *by default* in the face of incomplete information has become recognized, not only as something humans do, but also as something intelligent programs must do in many domains in order to produce useful results. Logically minded AI researchers have accordingly developed what they call *nonmonotonic logics* (McDermott and Doyle 1980) in order to better understand the nature of such reasoning.

The objectivist semantics that is normally attached to a logic is also useful in logical models. Observations about meanings and reference are necessary constraints on cognitive theories. Such observations are possible when there is at least an intersubjective understanding among researchers on what meanings are attached to expressions. This might be made possible if researchers share a common *folk theory* about the objects of reference. Unfortunately folk theories are difficult to make explicit, since they presuppose an elaborate context or conceptual framework. Pretending, for purposes of exposition, that the way things are in the folk theory is just the way things are, abstracts away the context, and yields something like a simpler objectivist account. The pitfall is to take the account too seriously to shift the folk theory where appropriate.

Computational models. The contribution of computational models is analogous to the contribution of computer simulations in astronomy, meteorology or economics: The human as a cognizer is a complex system that has many interacting subparts and accepts a wide variety of inputs from various sources, both linguistic and non-linguistic. A theory about the organization of such a complex system is generally very difficult to translate mathematically into predictions about the behavior of the system and therefore difficult to test empirically. A computer simulation of such a theory helps to overcome this difficulty because it *generates* a behavior that can be compared empirically with that of the humans.* Connectionist research has progressed primarily and critically by building and progressively refining computational models.

One of the primary pitfalls peculiar to computational models is that many of the simplifying assumptions are not introduced for their conceptual simplicity, but for their closeness to computer architecture or to the constructs of a particular programming language. For instance, I have developed two computational implementations of partitioned representations. The first of these made use of schema application as the basic underlying reasoning mechanism. The second performed logic-based reasoning. This difference did not reflect a change

* In many people's minds, including my own, there is a big difference between, say, modeling a weather system computationally and modeling cognition. No matter how exact a model of a weather system is, it will never *be* a weather system. On the other hand, if a program succeeds in modeling cognition very exactly, it would seem to be a cognitive system. Searle's (1980) distinguishes *weak AI*, which purports only to model aspects of cognition computationally, and *strong AI*, which claims to be capable, in principle, of creating cognition. He emphatically rejects strong AI, while accepting weak AI.

in my theoretical position, but was based on the choice of programming language. The first implementation was made in *Lisp*, a language that is well suited for representing structures like schemas easily. The second implementation was made in *Prolog*, a logic-based language that is took care of almost all aspects of logic-based reasoning for me.

Artificial Intelligence, the primary source of computational models of representation, is a discipline with one foot in cognitive science and one foot in computer engineering. A system of what AI researchers call *knowledge representation* may or may not be intended as a model of mental representation. Many systems of knowledge representation are oriented toward immediate practical computer applications in expert systems and so on. On the other hand, many are indeed oriented *specifically* toward modeling human intelligence. The viability of a computational system as a model of human cognition depends on how well it simultaneously accords with a number of criteria discussed in the next section.

The use of models in this book. In the appendices, Chapters 10 through 12, I explicitly develop a logical and a related computational model of partitioned representations in order to study the functional properties of the framework in a rigorous way. What I demonstrate clearly is that a logical embodiment of the framework is rational and efficient. I conclude that these properties are preserved in other embodiments. In other parts of the book I borrow some vocabulary and conceptual apparatus from logic and programming to model certain parts of the theory of partitioned representations, though less formally.

ASSESSING THEORIES OF MENTAL REPRESENTATION

Mental representations are not open for direct observation. Cognitive scientists must therefore use indirect evidence to discover the nature of mental representation. Figure 1.5 enumerates some sources of external evidence that cognitive scientists have at their disposal. Particular subfields of cognitive science, for instance artificial intelligence, psychology or linguistics, are in the habit of focusing on one, rarely two, of these sources and ignoring others. I take as a fundamental methodological assumption that all of these sources are relevant and

(1) Experimental Evidence
(2) Neurological Evidence
(3) Functionality
- Expressiveness
- Efficiency
- Rationality

(4) Linguistic Evidence

Fig. 1.5. Assessing theories of representation.

that, moreover, they should *converge* when the implications of an adequate theory of representation are explored.

Experimental Evidence

A theory of mental representation proposes structures or organizational principles which determine the relative rate at which different cognitive processes occur and what the results of those processes will be. Experimental work gives a means for assessing these predictions. Experimental support for a theory of mental representation requires that the system be consistent with quantifiable empirical data, such as human reaction times, in performing different reasoning tasks. For instance, work on priming and associative memory strongly motivates the semantic network model (McKoon and Ratcliff 1980). Work on the effects of context on answering questions about stories strongly motivates the schema model (Bransford and Johnson 1972).

I want to emphasize the ultimate critical importance of experimental evidence in the development of a comprehensive cognitive theory. Unfortunately, experimental support will not, in fact, receive its due concern here—for the most part due to deficiencies in my own background—though it will not be neglected either. I will mention at appropriate points where experimental evidence would be *expected* to bear on the theory of partitioned representations. Occasionally I will cite existing psychological work that does have such a bearing. In this way I hope at least to point out future research areas for the interested experimental psychologist.

Neurological Evidence

Because it is difficult to carry implications from one level of analysis to another, neurological evidence is likely to only weakly constrain cognitive theories. Neurological evidence might come in two forms: *consistency* and *emergent properties*. A cognitive theory may or may not be consistent with the underlying neural architecture. For instance, a theory that proposes that a cognitive process involves a long sequence of serial steps, as in search with backtracking, can probably be dismissed if it is known that humans carry out the process very quickly. The reason has to do with the slowness of neural architecture. An alternative proposal that divides the original process into many parallel subparts is more likely to be consistent with neural evidence, since massive parallelism is supported by a neural architecture. The criterion of consistency is important but weak, weak because a lot of potential higher-level mechanisms are likely to be consistent with what is known about the underlying neural architecture.

Emergent properties have been clearly demonstrated in connectionist research, for instance with regard to associative memory and default reasoning (described traditionally in terms of frames and schemas) as discussed earlier. Nevertheless, also as described above, we cannot expect all higher-level mechanisms to be predicted from, or usefully reduced to, the neural architecture. I suspect that connectionist research will continue to isolate emergent properties. I also suspect that further neurological research, for instance in large-scale anatomical structures, will inspire new ideas of importance for cognitive science. But neurological evidence, because it exists at such a low microlevel, will never provide broad, categorical means of assessing higher-level cognitive theories.

Functionality

Functionality has to do with the ability of the theory to support the computational tasks of which humans are believed to be capable. The mental representation underlies, for instance, such cognitive abilities as visual perception (including recognizing objects), expert-level reasoning, predicting the behavior of interacting physical objects and understanding natural language. The study of functionality is typical of work not only in AI, but also in philosophy and in connectionist research. It involves looking at the global behavior of the theoretical framework and asking if the system is really up to the task it is supposed to accomplish, asking if it exhibits human-like properties like intentional behavior or intelligence. Because of this emphasis on systemic behavior, the study of functionality has traditionally relied extensively on models, logical in philosophy, computational in connectionist research and both logical and computational in AI.

Expressiveness and *efficiency* of reasoning are listed in virtually any textbook on artificial intelligence as the primary factors that motivate specific models of knowledge representation. Usually left implicit in such discussion is *rationality.* Let's look at these three components of functionality in more detail. It is important to realize as we do so that each of these components is only achieved to a degree. One never expects complete expressiveness, perfect efficiency or ideal rationality. Rather there is often a trade off among them.

Expressiveness

Functionality entails that the mental structures should in principle be able to represent any information that humans are able to represent. If humans are able to talk and reason about beliefs, causes, multiple perspectives and nonexistent objects, the model of representation must be able to represent these beliefs, causes, multiple perspectives and nonexistent objects.

Logic-based systems for instance, appeal to many artificial intelligence researchers probably in large part because the systems are of such general expressive power, and have a clearly defined semantics. At one time it troubled researchers that associative networks, in spite of their advantages, did not seem to share this expressive power. The result has been the incorporation of logic-like elements into the associative network formalism to overcome these limitations (Shapiro 1979, Hendrix 1979, Sowa 1984).

On the other hand, there are areas in which logical formalisms seem to be incapable, at least in any natural way, of expressing the knowledge underlying certain cognitive tasks such as face recognition. For this task a logic-based system would seem to need rules of the following form, presupposing some kind of decomposition of the facial image into component features:

color(hair(X), brown) & color(eyes(X), green) &
size(nose(X), 1.33i) → X = Bif

However in practice it seems that no such set of rules ever suffices, as discussed earlier. A human might recognize Bif's face from any variety of angles, from any distance (within certain bounds) and with a number of features distorted or obscured. As we have seen, more success has been achieved in computer face recognition as we have seen by allowing associations to be expressed *subsymbolically* without attempting to decompose higher-level objects into discrete sets of lower-level features. In effect, integrating connectionist features *improves* the expressiveness at the symbolic level, which is good motivation for their incorporation into a theory of representation.

Calling for particular attention are the accurate representation of complex domains, such as those of *belief* and *desire*, *obligation*, and *generalization*. Numerous problems arise here that are well documented especially in the philosophical literature, such as those of opacity of *reference*, and *intentional* vs. *extensional* meanings. Also important is the representation of alternative *perspectives* or *folk theories*, such as seeing the sun as rising and setting as opposed to seeing the earth as rotating under the sun. Perhaps the greatest problem here is to keep these perspectives from interfering and resulting in inconsistent or erroneous representations.

Fundamental to expressiveness is that a complete theory of representation should provide a clear statement of what the relation of the representation to what is represented is, that is, it should provide a *semantics* of some kind. We have already looked at some of the problems in this area, especially with the simplistic assumptions of a direct correspondence between representations and a passive objective reality. Ultimately the study of expressiveness will certainly require an understanding of how representations impose interpretations on reality, e.g., how it is that people recognize certain *fictional* propositions, for instance about Sherlock Holmes' attire, as *true*. We would hope that a theory of mental representation would contribute to this.

Efficiency of Reasoning

Functionality also entails that the system support the kinds of common sense reasoning processes that humans perform well. It is critical to appreciate the importance of the way the *structure* of representations is related to efficiency. An inference that is derived in one representation only through a long multi-step process may simply be implicit in another representation.

A very revealing example of representing a railroad system, attributed to Hubert Dreyfus, illustrates variation between systems of representation in efficiency. The object is to represent all railroad connections in the United States and be able to compute the minimum distance between any two stations in the system. In a logic-based system we might represent the required knowledge as a set of sentences like this,

distance(Chicago, Champaign, 100)

one sentence for every direct connection between two stations. In order to derive the distance from, say, San Francisco to Ann Arbor, the system would have to consider every sentence that mentions San Francisco to locate adjacent cities and associated distances, take each of those adjacent stations and look up stations that are adjacent to them and so on, summing as it goes. Eventually it would find a set of paths converging on Ann Arbor and it would return the shortest such path. The number of paths searched would be enormous.

Dreyfus's alternative is to represent the railroad system analogically with a kind of mesh constructed out of knotted strings. The knots represent the stations, the length of a string between two knots corresponds to the length of a direct connection between the corresponding stations. To determine the shortest path between two stations and its distance, simply hold the corresponding knots one in each hand and pull them apart until the string between them becomes taut. The taut part of the string represents the shortest path. There could be nothing simpler.

This example is not intended a realistic model of human representation, but nevertheless illustrates clearly the way in which differences in the structures of representations correspond to differences in the efficiency of reasoning. Such a model would have to show that those inferences which humans make naturally are those which are easy to derive in the model. Where humans spontaneously fill implicit information into the internal representation of a specific instance of a sequence of events, the system of mental representation should also support the ability to derive the same inferences in an efficient way. We have seen that it is in such respects that the advantages of scripts, frames and schemas as compared with logic-based representations show up. Note that elements of efficiency are particularly subject to experimental verification; this element of functionality is probably of most interest to experimental psychology.

Calling for particular attention is the informal observation that human reasoning in complex domains, such as those of fiction, hypotheticals, generalizations and beliefs, is, one would expect, as fast or almost as fast as reasoning about concrete real situations. Also important is the ability to shift between alternative perspectives and make use of inferences generated by these alternatives. These observations will be of particular concern in this book.

Rationality

Humans are extremely well adapted to function successfully in a very uncertain environment. Humans are, in other words, what Dennett (1978) describes as an *intentional system* with goals, awareness of the environment and *rationality*. To paraphrase Dennett, the capacity to believe has no survival value unless it is the capacity to believe truths, the capacity to communicate has no function unless it is the capacity to communicate truths and the capacity to infer has no value if it is not the capacity to infer truths. Dennett suggests, for example, that even a mouse can be expected to reason in a manner consistent with a logical rule of inference, like *modus ponens*, even if it does not actually *possess* the rule, e.g., "there is a cat at the left; if there is a cat at X then I had better not go to X; therefore, I had better not go to the left." It is the responsibility of a theory of mental representation to explain how that rationality arises. A theory that does so will, in general, all else being equal, be a better motivated theory.

Of course, humans are not perfectly rational. In fact it might surprise some readers that rationality might be considered a criterion for assessing theories of representation at all, especially in light of the importance many psychologists have attached to *irrationality*. Tversky and Kahneman (1973), for instance, demonstrate that under certain conditions humans make judgements about probabilities that defy the mathematics of probability, for instance, judging that it is more likely that an earthquake in California will trigger a massive flood than simply that a massive flood will occur. Johnson-Laird (1983) motivates his theory of *mental models* primarily on the basis of inconsistencies between human reasoning and logical syllogisms. Nevertheless, it is because we accept rationality as the norm that such observations are so striking. And making such observations forces us to ask why rationality fails at particular points, and thus leads to insights about underlying mechanisms.

An analogy might be helpful. In vision humans are very good a perceiving depth, and this ability has obvious functionality. A theory of visual processing is all the stronger for being able to account for the correctness of depth perception, all else being equal. On the other hand, depth perception fails under certain circumstances, for instance when the subject is presented with a row of closely equidistant, identical objects in the visual field. Such an observation that contrasts with the expected norm of rationality can be especially revealing of underlying mechanisms implementing visual perception, in this case the role of binocular vision. Yet, in the absence of such observations, if a theory fails to account for, or is inconsistent with, the existence of accurate depth perception, then the plausibility of that theory is considerably weakened. Rationality and irrationality must *both* be accounted for. But, as Dennett argues, rationality is the norm; it can generally be assumed in the *absence* of counterevidence. Irrationality must be *demonstrated.*

Another pitfall in assessing rationality is to accept deductive reasoning, achieved reliably in traditional logics, as an ideal. The problem with this is that in an uncertain world there may be few strictly deductive inferences available; a system should be capable of jumping to conclusions in the absence of complete information where this is heuristically justified. Essentially, a system that makes lots of correct inferences and goofs only occasionally should be regarded as more rational than a system that only makes correct inferences, but very few of them. This is why Captain Kerk is the captain rather than Spock. This also agrees with trends in applied AI, for instance in expert systems, where the ability to reason *nonmonotonically,* basically, to jump to conclusions, has become an asset.

Linguistic Evidence

Language has played an especially prominent role in many subfields of cognitive science. Linguistic structures mirror general underlying cognitive structures. Likewise language processing is tightly integrated with virtually every form of cognitive processing. AI researchers and psychologists have long been aware of the roles that mental representations play in determining the ease with which linguistic processing occurs, the possibility of resolving subtle ambiguities, and the functional basis for applying common-sense reasoning to language understanding. If a theory of language built on such a set of assumptions about mental representations can in itself be justified on independent grounds, then this is good evidence that the assumptions are correct. In this sense any evidence for a theory of language understanding is strong evidence for the theory of mental representation that it presupposes.

Speaker intuitions about correct grammatical forms, entailments of sentences, appropriate uses of linguistic expressions, and so on, have given rise to most of the ideas in theoretical linguistics and to much of the work in the philosophies of language and mind. Such linguistic data play much the same role as experimental data in the empirical grounding of theories of mental representation.

Because linguistic evidence plays such a strong role in motivating the theory of partitioned representations, I devote Chapter 3 to a separate discussion of language processing and the role of linguistic data is assessing theories of mental representation.

Adequate Justification

Most of the subfields of cognitive science focus on justification in terms of one kind of criterion, often with unfortunate consequences. For instance, in AI, with its particular emphasis on functionality, it is hard to distinguish proposals that are marvels of engineering from those that exhibit scientific insight. In linguistics, the failure, in fact the systematic refusal, to accept independent criteria for assessing linguistic theories has been, I feel, disastrous (see Chapter 3).

Justification of theories from all perspectives is an ideal illustrated in Figure 1.6. I submit, however, that where justification from

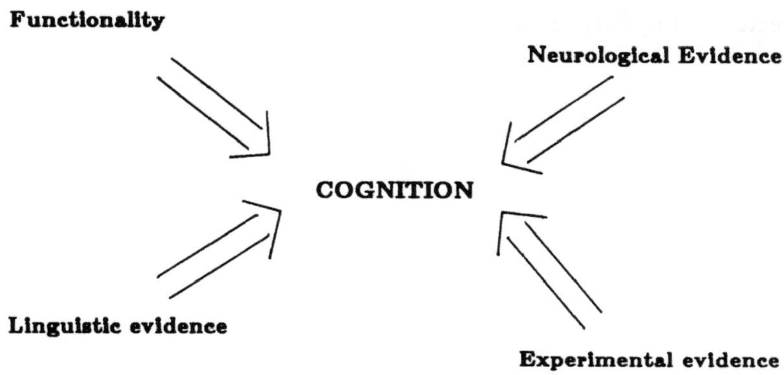

Figure 1.6. Cross-justification, the coincidence of evidence from multiple sources.

two of the three major perspectives—experimental evidence, functionality and linguistic evidence (recall that only weak neurological evidence is forthcoming)—coincide one has built a strong case for the theory at hand. This is what I dub *cross-justification.*

There have been pioneers in cross-justification. Some theories of mental representation, such as schema theory and associative networks, have their origins in psychology, where they have been motivated experimentally, and then taken up in artificial intelligence, where they have been discovered to have a functionality that has been exploited in practical expert systems and natural language understanding systems. Johnson-Laird's *mental models* are similarly motivated both experimentally and functionally. Lakoff's (1987) *idealized cognitive models* are motivated simultaneously by the results of experimental work in conceptual categorization and by linguistic evidence, both structural and semantic.

The present book will also seek cross-justification in motivating the theory of partitioned representations, most especially in terms of functionality and linguistic evidence. The next chapter presents the theory, focusing at the same time informally on its functional justification, with some suggestions of linguistic and experimental evidence that supports the theory. Chapter 3 introduces language and language processing in broad strokes. Chapter 4 will develop the *three-level theory,* which is a direct extension of partitioned representations to language processing. The second part of the book explores the way partitioned representations and the three-level model are reflected in linguistic data.

CHAPTER TWO

Partitioned Representations

Functionally, partitioned representations illustrate the principle *divide and conquer* in mental representation. Rather than a large homogeneous representation or set of representations with unmanageable possibilities for synthesis in reasoning, partitioned representations make use of many isolated context-dependent representations with locally circumscribed by effective inference opportunities. In this chapter my concern will be with describing and motivating partitioned representations initially as a *functional* system of mental representation and in the fourth chapter as a principled basis for language understanding.

GENERAL OVERVIEW

In partitioned representations the information communicated in a discourse or acquired by other means is distributed in a principled way over a large set of *spaces*, each of which defines a local, or *parochial*, domain of reasoning. Examples are belief spaces; hope and wish spaces; possibility spaces; fictional, dream and pretense spaces; spaces representing specific places, times and situations; spaces representing the scope of certain existential assumptions, spaces expressing generalizations; and spaces representing the implications of certain propositional assumptions, either conditional or counterfactual. There are belief spaces within fictional spaces; temporal spaces within belief spaces; and so on. We will see that spaces individually tend to be simple, but an appropriate distribution of information over multiple spaces allows the most complex information to be encoded and processed concretely.

Some Examples

One space might represent what the world looks like *now* (at a point in 1991):

sp_1	**Bif has a pet goldfish** **George Bush is the U.S. President** **The Democrats control the Senate** **Earth is the third planet from the sun**

I've tagged the space with an arbitrary name **sp_1** to make it easy to refer to. **sp_1** functions as a small knowledge base in which certain propositions are *satisfied*, that is, regarded as true, and certain objects are *situated*, that is, regarded as existing. The totality of information satisfied or situated in a space is called the *content* of that space.

Another separate space, say **sp_2**, might be used to represent what Bif *now thinks* the world looks like:

sp_2	**George Bush is President** **The Libertarians control the Senate** **Extraterrestrials live among us** **Beer is good for you**

sp_2 is likely to be much less fully specified than **sp_1**.

The fact of Bif's believing certain things now is a complex part of what the world is like now. We can show this by *embedding* Bif's belief space within the *now* space as follows.

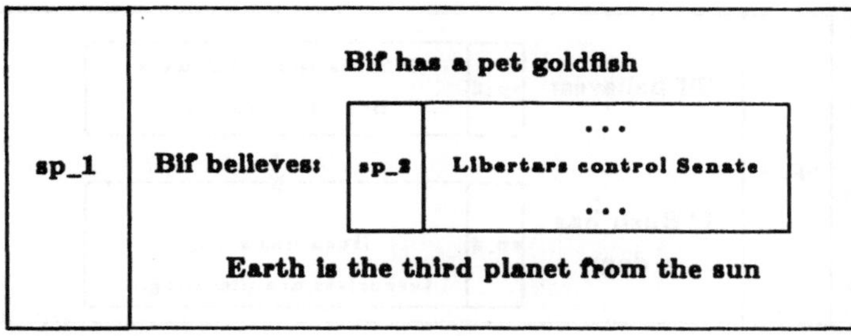

In this diagram, **Bif believes:** is known as the *context* of **sp_2** and serves to define the role of **sp_2** with respect to **sp_1**. Within **sp_2** reasoning processes can function locally, just as they do in **sp_1** to predict additional beliefs of Bif. This can be done concretely since reasoning in **sp_2** does not require explicit reference to the fact that we are dealing with Bif's beliefs. Because of the license to ignore information external to a space in reasoning within that space, I call this localized reasoning *parochial.* Reasoning in **sp_1** is also parochial in this sense, but the presence of the context allows **sp_1** to pull the results of **sp_2**'s parochial reasoning into **sp_1**, as we will see.

Still another space might represent what is true of the world now *if* George Bush has a dog, which may or may not be the case.

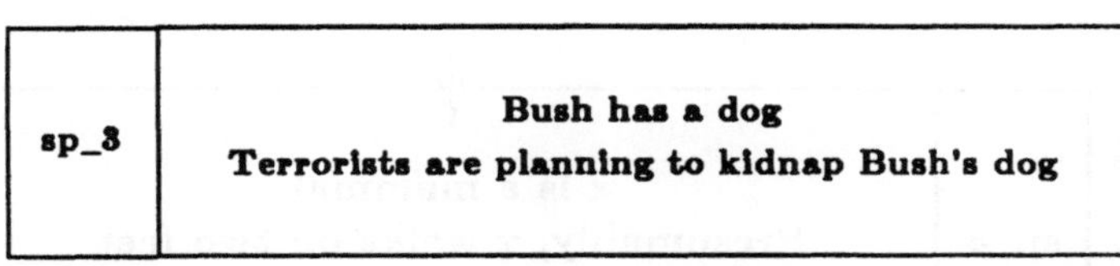

Like **sp_2**, **sp_3** is used to represent a complex component of the contents of **sp_1**. Accordingly a context tells us what role **sp_3** plays in **sp_1**.

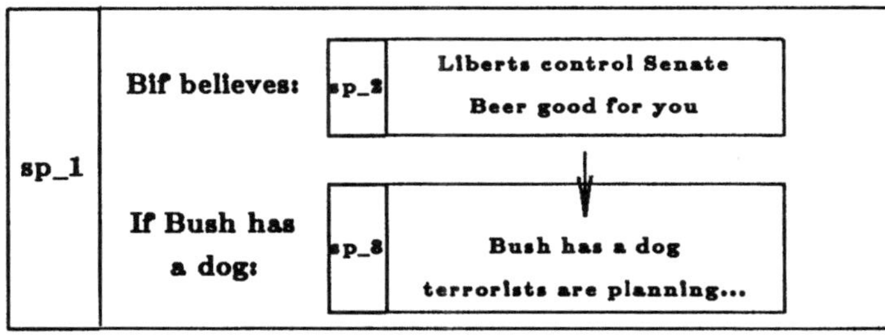

The space **sp_3** is used to reason about a *candidate reality*, how the world is now *if* George Bush turns out to own a dog. This means that everything satisfied the world now, **sp_1**, should also belong to the contents of **sp_3**, for instance, that George Bush is president. Unlike **sp_2**, **sp_3** is *more fully specified* than **sp_1**. In this sense I say that **sp_3** *inherits* from **sp_1**. Inheritance is indicated in the last sketch by the arrow. Inheritance is one of the most basic structural properties determining how a space will be used in the framework of partitioned representations. In fact, inheritance is regarded as a kind of context, since it also pulls information from one space into another.

Still another space would represent what is true now *for every human* **x**:

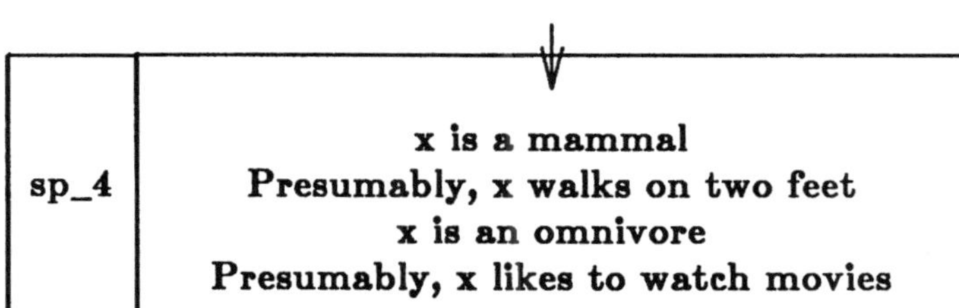

In **sp_4** an object **x** would be situated and treated parochially as a normal object, even though it has no unique existence outside of **sp_4**. Like **sp_3**, **sp_4**, it can be argued, inherits from **sp_1**.

Another space would represent what *would* be true now *if* Dukakis (remember the liberal hope of 1988?) were president:

sp_5	**Mike Dukakis is President** **Kitty is First Lady** **Peace in Central America is imminent**

sp_5 is constructed to look as close to **sp_1** as possible while maintaining the satisfaction of the *counterfactual antecedent*. This entails a kind of inheritance from **sp_1**, albeit one that is much more lax than the inheritance relation found for **sp_3** or for **sp_4**.

Another space might represent what the world looked like at some point in 1900:

sp_6	**Bif's great grandfather has a pet goldfish** **McKinley is the U.S. President** **Top hats are in style**

And finally, another space might represent what is true in the fictional Hornbower saga:

sp_7	**Horatio is a British naval officer** **Horatio becomes easily seasick** **Horatio's best friend is Bush**

Motivation

In short, each space represents some logically coherent situation or potential reality, in which various propositions are treated as true, objects are assumed to exist, and relations between objects are supposed to hold. The people and things that Warren believe to exist are represented as existing in Warren's belief space; the properties that Horatio Hornblower has, such as intelligence and clumsiness, are represented as real within the Hornblower fiction space; and so on.

Partitioned representations are functional: Complex knowledge can be represented successfully by an appropriate distribution of knowledge over multiple spaces. Still, the full semantics of the contents of spaces is preserved in the contexts of spaces. The knowledge in each space tends to be simple and concrete, and to form a natural domain for parochial reasoning processes. Thus parochial reasoning replaces the convoluted reasoning processes associated with non-partitioned representations of complex knowledge. Beyond functionality, partitioned representations provide support critical in language understanding.

Related Models

Models of representation and of natural language processing which bear a strong resemblance to the theory of partitioned representations developed here have arisen in artificial intelligence, logic, psychology and linguistics. Some of these models have been motivated functionally in terms of their computational efficiency, and conceptual simplicity. Among these are *belief spaces* and *context-layered data bases* and *mental models*. Other models have been motivated in terms of their support of language processing along with the account they provide for problems in linguistic structure. Among these are *discourse representations*, and *mental spaces*. We will have the opportunity to look at these in the course of this book.

A number of knowledge representation systems in artificial intelligence support very general mechanisms for creating separate data bases for representing belief systems, fictional stories, times, and so forth. Among these are *KL-ONE* (Brachman and Schmolze 1985) and *NETL* (Fahlman 1979). Perhaps the most general of these systems is Hendrix' *Partitioned Semantic Networks* (Walker 1978, Hendrix 1979) that is the source of some of the terminology used in this book. In partitioned semantic networks the knowledge base is partitioned into overlapping *spaces*. Spaces are used to delimit the scopes of logical connectives, quantifiers and higher-order predicates. They are used for maintaining alternative hypotheses and intermediate results of computation, for representing *discourse focus* in language understanding and maintaining a boundary between old and new information.*

In this book I will develop partitioned representations explicitly as a general framework characterized by a common set of principles, study the general function and computational properties of this framework and trace out the consequences of the framework, which turn out to be profound.

THE CONTENTS OF SPACES

The theory of partitioned representations imposes a *higher-level* organization on representations. It makes no specific commitment to how the content is structured within spaces, nor to the nature of the reasoning processes that might occur locally within a space. I will call the representation scheme used within spaces as the *parochial medium* of representation As far as the theory of partitioned representations per se is concerned, virtually any kind of parochial medium might be used. For instance, I have developed two computational implementations that model partitioned representations. The first of these, the *Lisp* version of Spaceprobe, uses a semantic network/schema based representation within spaces. The second of these, the *Prolog* version of Spaceprobe described in Chapter 12, supports a logic-based representation. Some kind of analogical medium could just as well be used. Whatever parochial representation is used, the principles of partitioned representations serve the same function in terms of expressiveness efficiency and rationality, and, as we will see, serve to support language understanding in the same way. But these principles of

* Although Hendrix' model has many similarities to partitioned representation, I should point out that his model is both more general and at a lower-level that partitioned representations. First, Hendrix' spaces may, but do not have to, bear semantic significance. Spaces in partitioned representations must. For instance, Grosz (1981) defines *focus spaces* to represent the focus of attention of the discourse participants. These are used for disambiguation (generally referents for definite noun phrases and pronouns will be found within a focus space), but do not themselves contribute to semantic interpretation. In the theory of understanding based on partitioned representations the focus space may be chosen, its choice will aid in disambiguation—as in Grosz' model—but its choice *must* contribute a critical part of the complete semantic interpretation of the discourse—through its context. In sum, spaces in partitioned semantic networks are not equivalent to spaces in partitioned representations, although their uses may overlap.

partitioned representations cannot be expected to account for everything. A proper parochial representation must be motivated, to a large extent independently, by its ability to support common-sense reasoning within spaces and by its ability to support the many parochial processes of language understanding, some of which were described in the introductory chapter.

For the most part I will model the contents of spaces as *propositional*, using English-like sentences like **Dan Quayle is the president**. These propositional representations are the most familiar to most readers. Often I will use in propositional representations simple elements of logical notation and other symbols to more concisely represent and explicitly identify relevant structures in the representation while at the same time maintaining readability. For instance, I will use the symbols $\rightarrow$ and $\Box\!\!\rightarrow$ to represent two senses of "*if*". The first of these represents respectively the normal (material) implication ("*if ... is true then ...*") while the second represents the counterfactual implication ("*if ... were true then ...*"), as in

> **Dukakis wins the election** $\Box\!\!\rightarrow$
> **Kitty paints the White House green.**

This means that if Dukakis *had* won the election then Kitty would paint the White House green.

A linear notation will be convenient to show that a proposition **P** is part of the content of a space **S**, i.e., that **P** is *satisfied* in **S**. Stylizing the box notation used above gives us something like this:*

> **sp_1 | Dan Quayle is the president**

I call such an expression a *statement*, the subexpression **sp_1** the *space tag*, or simply *tag*, of the statement, and the subexpression **Dan Quayle is the president** the *content* of the statement.

In different spaces different objects might be represented as existing, or *situated*. Since the situation of an object in a certain space is one of the most common kinds of things I want to represent, a concise notation for that will also be convenient. A dot notation as in

---

* **sp_1** here is not the **sp_1** mentioned in the previous set of examples. I will make a habit of reusing the same low numbered space tags in distinct examples for readability. Of course, in an actual partitioning system we would expect thousands of distinct spaces.

sp_2 | • Santa

adapted from Kamp's (1980) discourse representations discussed in the next chapter, will represent that the object referred to by the name is situated in the tag space. For instance, if **sp_2** is Little Freddy's belief space, then this last statement would mean that Little Freddy believes in Santa Clause.

PAROCHIAL REASONING

Although partitioned representations entail no particular parochial representation scheme, the converse, that certain representation schemes entail some sort of partitioned representation, is probably true for theories of representation that otherwise have no principled way to represent complex knowledge. Analogical representations, for instance, of the kind Johnson-Laird (1983) advocates, discussed briefly in Chapter 1, are difficult if not impossible to realize with any generality *without* making use of partitioned representations. Thus, his theory and the experimental evidence that supports it can be taken indirectly to motivate the theory of partitioned representations.

A space consolidates information that belongs together in one place, to model a coherent possible "reality" or situation. This ensures that conventional reasoning processes will work effectively within a space. A space is, in AI terms, a small knowledge base in its own right. For instance, if we have a situation space like **sp_3** and we know about **sp_3**:

sp_3 | block_1 is on block_2.
sp_3 | block_2 is on block_3.

we can reason within **sp_3** to infer parochially

sp_3 | block_1 is above block_3.

to learn more about **sp_3**.

Similarly a belief space **sp_4** for Warren is useful because its presumed coherence allows the inference of additional beliefs for Warren. It is useful to infer **sp_4 | P** parochially, because **sp_1 | Warren believes that P** might be useful to know. Similarly, an *if P then* space **sp_5** is useful because it allows us to derive more things that are true if P is true. It is useful to infer **sp_5 | Q**, because **sp_1**

I P → Q might be useful to know.

Existing Models of Parochial Reasoning

Something like our *belief spaces* are often used in artificial intelligence systems to consolidate in one place the set of propositions some *agent* believes to be true. This allows for the representation of the belief system of the agent as a coherent model that can be viewed and reasoned about as a self-contained unit. Cohen and Perrault (1979), and Allen and Perrault (1980) show the usefulness of belief spaces in a system which infers the intentions of participants in natural language discourse in order to interpret their utterances and plan its own. Martins (1983) describes a further application in a system which coordinates planning among several people, for instance in the planning of a meeting in which different participants have different beliefs relevant to an appropriate time to hold the meeting.

Creary (1979) explains the utility of belief spaces as follows: Once a separate knowledge base has been set up for a particular agent, say Bif, and any propositions explicitly known to be believed by Bif are added to that knowledge base, the system can *simulate* Bif's thinking by using its own reasoning facilities to derive further beliefs of Bif. Since the system's reasoning capacity presumably matches Bif's, more or less, any inferences derived in the system's model of Bif's beliefs are likely to reflect inferences Bif actually derives in his belief system. Thus we have a means of reasoning about Bif's beliefs. If the system knows that Bif believes that Harry ate a sandwich the system readily infers that Bif believes that Harry is not very hungry.

Moore (1976) describes how efficiently queries are answered in a system using belief spaces as separate data bases. To answer a query like my example,

What does Mabel believe the unicorn ate?

the system automatically shifts to Mabel's belief space and issues the simpler query

What did the unicorn eat?

which should be easily answered. Ballim and Wilks (forthcoming) present an elaborate model for setting up and using belief spaces dynamically.

Reasoning about action and change is a central problem in artificial intelligence. It shows up most particularly in *planning* systems, systems that try to formulate a reasonable sequence of actions beginning with some *state* of the world and ending in some new state which satisfies some goal description. In order to know if a goal is achieved it is important to be able to trace how the world will evolve if a particular sequence actions is executed. A means of computing changes from state to state as well as of reasoning about the state itself, is provided in a couple of short-lived A.I. programming languages. CONNIVER and QA4 (McDermott and Sussman 1972; Bobrow and Raphael 1974) make use of a *context-layered data base*, as set of separate but hierarchically organized data bases that can be used to represent individual states that might occur as stages in the execution of a potential plan.

Psychologists (Kahneman and Tversky 1982; Wells and Gavanski 1989) have studied the use of mental simulations about counterfactual scenarios. Experimental evidence suggests that subjects process counterfactual events cognitively in exactly the same way they manipulate factual events. Rips and Marcus (1977) motivate a similar model of representation for conditionals. These results seem to confirm experimentally the use of at least a couple of kinds of spaces in human cognition.

Also Johnson-Laird's (1983) psychological theory of mental models emphasizes the functional role of his system in supporting efficient common-sense reasoning as well as in representing the conditional existence of objects. He introduces multiple mental models as a means of expressing complex knowledge in the concrete terms dictated by his proposal that humans use analogical representations as the basis of reasoning. For instance, the representation of possibility or permission depends on the capacity to construct models of situations that are alternatives to reality and to determine what is true or false in them.

Sanctioned Inferences

Just as I am using propositional or language-like representations to model the parochial medium, I will use what I call *sanctioned inferences* to model parochial reasoning processes. Sanctioned inferences will have roughly the form of *meaning postulates* in logic, and are intended to express simple common-sense reasoning steps that people are capable of. For example, in any space in which **above** makes sense, we expect people to use this sanctioned inference:

(above) if **S | A is above B** and **S | B is above C** then **S | A is above C.**

Keep in mind that such sanctioned inferences are only intended here as convenient approximations. Johnson-Laird's (1983) criticisms of the adequacy of meaning postulates should ultimately be taken seriously.

PRIMARY CONTEXTS

We have seen that a context expresses an embedding of one space in another as in

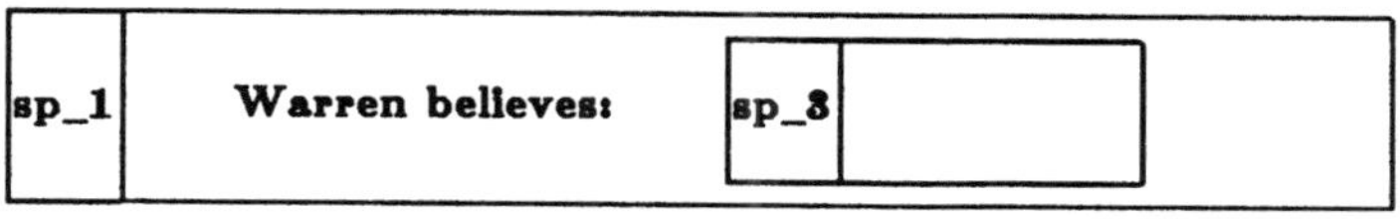

The examples I have given of such embeddings are of *primary contexts*. Our snazzy linear notation can be extended to contexts by stylizing the boxes a little more. This gives us, for the current example, the following:

sp_1 | Warren believes that ⟦sp_3⟧

A primary context looks like an ordinary statement, but contains a *space term* of the form **⟦S⟧**, where **S** is the name of some space. The space term stands for the contents of the whole space.

A primary context gives a necessary criterion for a proposition to be satisfied in the associated space, in other words, what the satisfaction of a proposition in a space means. For instance, we have **sp_3 | Penguins fly**, because it is *true* (relative to **sp_1**), i.e., satisfied, that Warren believes Penguins fly. The primary context should tell us this.

Observe that in general spaces tend to exhibit high levels of embedding. For instance, there might be one belief space for Warren in the *now* space, and another for Warren in a particular fiction space.

There might be one *If penguins could fly* space in the *now* space, and another in Warren's belief space in the *now* space, representing what Warren believes would be true if penguins could fly. In other words, a context can serve more generally to relate the content of one space to the content of another rather than directly to the real world. Figure 2.1 illustrates this. The contexts represented in Figure 2.1 are the following:

sp_0 | At the present time: ⟦sp_1⟧
sp_0 | At some time in 1900: ⟦sp_2⟧
sp_1 | Warren believes that ⟦sp_3⟧
sp_1 | Dukakis is President □→ ⟦sp_5⟧
sp_3 | There is a frog in Alma's pocket → ⟦sp_9⟧

Given a context of the form **S0 | X ⟦S1⟧ Y**, I say that this is the *primary context of* **S1**, say that **S0** is the *parent* of **S1** and say that **S1** is a *child* of **S0**.

This idea of contexts in our sense as representations of the semantic roles of spaces is found in some of the other related representation schemes, though under different names. Johnson-Laird (1983) develops a partitioning scheme in introducing multiple mental models built as an essential part of the construction of the internal representation. For instance, embedded mental models are constructed as part of the interpretation of discourse when words like *believes* or *hopes* are

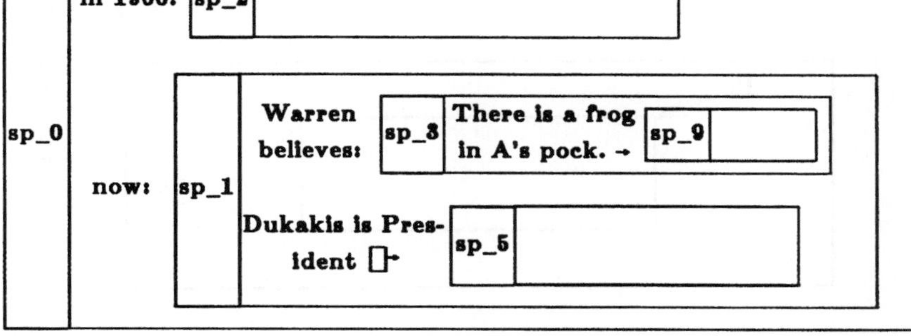

Fig. 2.1. Embedding of spaces.

encountered. A propositional attitude, e.g., a belief, is represented in one mental model as an abstract relation between an individual and some other mental model. For instance, Johnson-Laird's sentence

The police chief believes that the hijackers are in the plane.

is represented by modeling the proposition that the hijackers are in the plane in a mental model embedded within a model in which the belief relation is represented between the police chief and the embedded model. This would look like Figure 2.2. To represent a conditional, $P \rightarrow Q$, a mental model is constructed in which the truth of the antecedent, P, is realized, and with respect to which the consequent, Q, is then interpreted. This representation captures our concept of *context* since the semantic role of the inner model is made explicit. For Kamp's discourse representations, a *discourse representation structure* is imposed on sets of discourse representations to ensure that a full semantics can be defined. This effectively represents all of the embedded contexts in one big expression.

Context Climbing

The remarks about the role of primary contexts can be captured in the following sanctioned inference, which I call *context climbing*:

(Context Climbing)

If S0 | X [[S1]] Y and S1 | P then S0 | X P Y

This says that anything P satisfied in the child space S1 can be lifted out of the child space and embedded in the primary context S0 | X ...

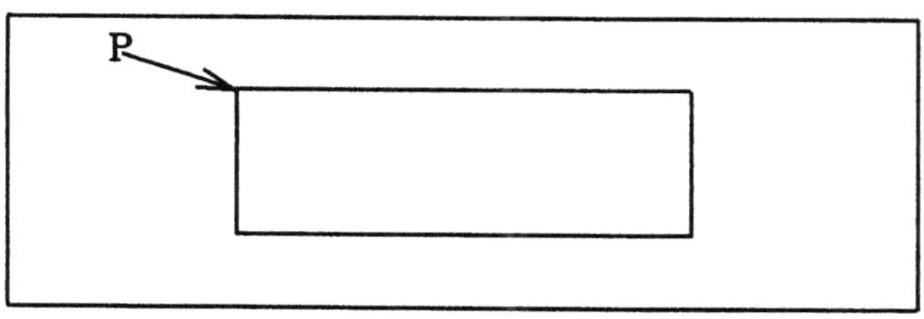

Fig. 2.2. Embedding of a mental model to represent "*The police chief believes that the hijackers are in the plane,*" where P = the police chief.

Y of the child space, deriving **S0 | X P Y**. For instance, if we have **sp_1 | Warren believes that [[sp_8]]** and **sp_8 | oranges make good baseballs** then we can conclude **sp_1 | Warren believes that oranges make good baseballs.**

PARTITIONED SEMANTICS

Spaces are a structural construct use in composing representations of complex information. They belong to syntax, not to semantics. In particular, they should not be confused, as they often have been in presentations of this work, with *possible worlds.* As Lakoff (1987, pp. 281-2) puts it with reference to Fauconnier's closely related mental spaces, spaces "have no ontological status outside of the mind." The differences and similarities of spaces and possible worlds are discussed further toward the end of this chapter. In general spaces cannot be given a semantics directly; they are more like parentheses in logical notation than like predicates or constants. But the structures in which they occur are meaningful.

The Role of Contexts

The content of a space is not in general taken to be a direct representation of the real world, but indirectly as an aspect of the real world subject to the assumptions or conditions specified by the primary context of the space. The primary context tells us how the entire contents *or any subpart thereof* is to be interpreted. To use a logical analogy, a space term is treated as a kind of variable that stands for any of a set of sentences embedded within a larger sentence, which are found in the space named in the space term. Still another way to look at contexts is as representations of functions that map the satisfaction of a proposition in one space onto the satisfaction of a (more complex) proposition in another space. For instance, Figure 2.1 tells us that the statement

sp_9 | frog_1 is asleep

maps implicitly into

sp_8 | frog_1 is in Alma's pocket → frog_1 is asleep

which in turn maps into

sp_1 | Warren believes that (frog_1 is in Alma's pocket → frog_1 is asleep)

This theoretical mapping process is what sanctions the inference that I called *context climbing* in the last section. Context climbing tells us what the content of a child space actually says about the content of the parent space from which the child spaces are carved.

An Objectivist Semantics

Abstractly, if we carry this process far enough we should discover what the content of a space says ultimately about objective reality, if we accept this possibility. For purposes of modeling a complete objectivist semantics we can postulated the existence of a space which I call **base** as the outermost space in the embedding hierarchy, the great grandfather of all spaces where context climbing bottoms out. **base** can be thought of the space that represents things as unconditionally true, i.e., not relative to some context, and so **base** is assumed not to have a primary context. By repeated applications of context climbing, the satisfaction of a proposition in a given space should ultimately map onto the satisfaction of a proposition in **base**, an thus onto truth conditions. A proposition is satisfied in **base** if and only if that proposition is true. **base** is thus conceived of as the non-temporal, non-situational, totally objective repository of universal truth. The space **base** is used in Chapter 10 where a logic-based model of partitioned representations, along with an objectivist-style semantics, is discussed.

Contributions to Folk Theories

To return to the debate between *objectivist semantics* and *internal realism* brought up in Chapter 1, we can see the difference between the two reflected in the question whether we can ever reach **base** or, equivalently I suppose, whether **base** can have ever have any content. The highest-level spaces to which we might attribute content would be those whose contents represent interpretations of, perspectives on, or folk theories about reality. Happily, spaces are ideally suited for representing such folk theories, in fact for representing multiple alternative folk theories, since each space is treated as representing a coherent "reality" and is therefore an independent domain for parochial reasoning.

Beyond this, the partitioned framework undoubtedly contributes to the way we interpret, or even create, reality conceptually. For instance, without spaces there probably could not be such a thing as an hypothesis. The idea would be conceptually vacuous without the ability to consider a "reality" in which the hypothesis is true and to explore the consequents. There probably could be no such a thing as a counterfactual proposition without the ability to construct counterfactual spaces. Furthermore, without counterfactual propositions, many *physical* properties could not exist. For instance, we can classify a particular piece of copper as a *conductor*, whether or not it is *actually* conducting electricity. We do so by recognizing in an imaginary "reality" in which we have hooked the copper into an electrical circuit that it is conduction electricity. Probably the most convincing example of the point to which I have devoted this paragraph is fiction. There would certainly be no such thing as fiction without the ability to treat fiction as reality and keep it separated from reality. An extraterrestrial without out scheme for structuring mental representations would be as confused by fiction as this alien tourist in *Black Suits from Outer Space*:

> *"What are these people doing," he asked...*
>
> *I looked at the TV set. ... It was one of those crime movies...*
>
> *"They're getting ready to rob a bank," I said.*
>
> *"That is what I thought. But why are they letting someone take their pictures and broadcast them? ... It would seem that such plans should be kept secret."*
>
> *"They* are *being kept secret"* ...
>
> '*I know. Anyone who is watching this broadcast knows."*
>
> ...
>
> *"It's just a story," I said. "It's not real."*
>
> *"Not real? In what way is it 'not real'?" (DeWeese 1985, 58-59)*

COHERENCE

The functionality of spaces is realized only if spaces are properly configured. The guiding principles in the successful configuration of spaces are *coherence* and *consolidation.*

Coherence is the property of a space for which parochial reasoning makes sense. This means that for a coherent space the results of parochial reasoning are *appropriate* to the primary context of the space. Thereby, a coherent space is assured of supporting inferences that make more global sense, that is, make more sense from the perspective of the parent space. For instance, we have seen that a sentence like

If Warren ate a bug then Warren is a Bulgarian spy.

would be represented internally as something like

sp_1 | Warren ate a bug → [[sp_2]]
sp_2 | Warren is a Bulgarian spy

This representation is functionally useful, since any inference made in **sp_2** is appropriate to the context. Observe that we should be immediately able to make the simple inference

sp_2 | Warren is from Bulgaria

We now have the internal representation corresponding to the English sentence

If Warren ate a bug then Warren is from Bulgaria.

This is indicative of the coherence of **sp_2**, since the internal representation of the original English sentence *should* entail the internal representation of this one.

I assume coherence to be criterial for spaces. This means that, as a working assumption, I take it that the principle of coherence tells us what spaces *can* exist as well as what spaces *cannot* exist. Of course, to return to an issue of Chapter 1, this idealization may well need qualification somewhere along the line. It may be that some spaces do not exist that would be coherent, but we need experimental or linguistic evidence to discover them. Although for now I am relying primarily on functional arguments, we will find later that the linguistic evidence fits this assumption of idealized rationality remarkably well.

Suppose that we were (incorrectly, as I will show) to represent

If Warren ate a bug then Warren is a Bulgarian spy.

internally as something like

sp_1 | ⟦sp_3⟧ → Warren is a Bulgarian spy
sp_3 | Warren ate a bug

We would see immediately that **sp_3** would *not* be coherent. Within **sp_3** we should easily infer

sp_3 | Warren ate something

but this time the inference is *not* appropriate to the primary context. We now, presumably, would have derived the representation corresponding the sentence

If Warren ate something then Warren is a Bulgarian spy.

But this should *not* be inferred; it doesn't follow from the original sentence. We want to *exclude* contexts like **sp_1 | ⟦sp_3⟧ → Warren is a Bulgarian spy** because they would not define coherent spaces.

Using similar arguments I could show that the following *do* support coherent spaces,

sp_1 | George believes that ⟦...⟧
sp_1 | it is possible that ⟦...⟧
sp_1 | in 19th century America, ⟦...⟧
sp_1 | in *Black Suits from Outer Space*, ⟦...⟧
sp_1 | every paleontologist is such that ⟦...⟧

while contexts like the following would not (and are therefore illegal).

sp_1 | George hopes that ⟦...⟧
sp_1 | it is not the case that ⟦...⟧

Chapter 10 will provide an explicit analysis, in terms of a logical model, of the semantic property shared by contexts that ensures coherent spaces, the ability to ***preserve entailments.*** There a formal proof is presented that imposing the requirement of entailment preservation supports a *sound* logical system, in less technical terms, one that leads only to correct inferences as long as the premises are correct.*

---

* It should be noted that coherence is a feature in which spaces in partitioned representations differ from spaces in Hendrix' partitioned semantic networks or from Kamp's (1980) discourse representations. These do not have to be internally coherent. For instance, these latter are used to represent the antecedents of conditionals as well as negation. This is not, I hasten to add, a point of dispute; it only means that spaces as defined in partitioned representations only partially (but substantially, it turns out) overlap with spaces

CONSOLIDATION

Secondarily to coherence, we want to provide *consolidation*. *Consolidation* is achieved in a space that brings together as much coherent information relevant to parochial processing as possible in order to acquire maximal benefit from the partitioning framework. It is achieved in a number of ways, and motivates some natural consequences for the forms of representation.

Non-duplicate Spaces

Suppose we know each of the following facts (with respect to sp_0),

Bif is a monarchist.
Bif believes that the Austrian head of state is a king.
Every monarchist believes that kings are benevolent rulers.
Bif thinks that benevolent rulers guarantee a happy populace.

We would like to be able to infer that Bif believes that Austria has a happy populace. This is inferred easily in partitioned representations only if we bring the appropriate set of propositions together in one space, as in

sp_0 | Bif believes that ⟦sp_1⟧
sp_1 | the Austrian head of state is a king
sp_1 | kings are benevolent rulers
sp_1 | benevolent rulers guarantee a happy populace

We do not want, by any means, *two* separate belief spaces for Bif within sp_0 with Bif's beliefs divided between them. Although such spaces would be coherent, they would fail to treat Bif's belief system as a single model of a possible "reality."

I call a context like **sp_0 | Bif believes that ⟦sp_1⟧** *unique*, meaning that we do not have a context of the form **sp_0 | Bif believes that ⟦sp_2⟧**, where sp_2 is different from sp_1. I should not give the impression that all contexts are unique. **sp_0 | it is possible that ⟦sp_3⟧** would not be unique, because of the existence of multiple, mutually inconsistent possibilities. I will return to this

in partitioned semantic networks or discourse representations. These systems do not impose coherence because they do not envision parochial reasoning as a general process in all spaces.

point below.

The functionality of consolidation is justified in terms of its support of efficiency of reasoning. It in turn can be used to justify a variety of structures and constraints. Again, as in the case of coherence, our idealized functionality should be tempered by experimental and linguistic evidence.

Inheritance

Consolidation is to a large degree a matter of avoiding the creation redundant spaces, although it manifests itself in other ways too. In addition to collapsing otherwise equivalent spaces, I assume that consolidation is also realized by *inheritance*. For instance, continuing the current example, we *do* want a separate space to represent common beliefs of monarchists, in the interests of coherence, as in

sp_0 | every monarchist believes that ⟦sp_2⟧
sp_2 | kings are benevolent rulers

Notice that **kings are benevolent rulers** occurs in both **sp_1** and **sp_2**. More generally, everything satisfied in **sp_2** is satisfied in **sp_1**, since Bif is a monarchist. Consolidation is achieved if everything in **sp_2** is copied into **sp_1**. Consolidation is also achieved, but without this redundancy, if instead we have some way to inherit this content from **sp_2** to **sp_1**. We will see momentarily how *secondary contexts* provide us with this capability.

Aspects and Ambient Representations

In general, in the interests of consolidation, we will often want to look at the same content from the perspective of different spaces. An interesting feature of *temporal* spaces, for instance, is that what is satisfied in a given space is likely to have effects in other temporal spaces. For instance, if we have **sp_1 | Fred dies**, then any space **sp_2** ordered temporally *after* **sp_1** (e.g., **sp_0 | at time_1: ⟦sp_1⟧**, **sp_0 | at time_2: ⟦sp_2⟧** and **sp_0 | time_1 < time_2**), we will have **sp_2 | Fred is dead** or **sp_2 | Fred has died**. The differences in perspective explain the existence of many parallel co-occurring concepts like dying and being dead, traveling and arriving, looking at and spotting, cracking and being cracked and so on: The same event or situation may be relevant to the contents of more than one temporal space; therefore we require a way to view the same event or situation from the perspective of more than one space. *Temporal aspects* like the English perfect (e.g., *it has occurred*) are provided by natural languages as a productive way of defining these different perspectives. I will devote a whole chapter to temporal aspects later.

We will commonly find in partitioned representations that we have an option for expressing the same information either by means of a representation in a parent space or by means of a representation in a child space. For instance, if we have

sp_0 | at time tm_3: [[sp_3]]

to express that **tm_3** is in 1945 we might say either

sp_0 | tm_3 is during 1945

or

sp_3 | it is 1945

The second representation consolidates more information in **sp_3**. The representation in the child space will generally be simpler, without predicating anything of certain times or events. Since this representation characterizes the whole of the space, I will refer to the more local representation as an *ambient* representation.

Where such alternative representations are possible, we require a means of deriving one alternative from the other, to provide for consolidation in either space. The following sanctioned inference does this for us in the current example.

(It is) S | at time T1: it is T2 iff S | T1 during T2.

Ambient representations are important in partitioned representations, but the compositionally closest representations in *non*-partitioned representations must seem cumbersome and unnatural. Thus,

In 1946 World War Two had occurred.

seems from the perspective of non-partitioned representations a round-about way of saying

World War Two occurred before 1946.

Language understanders based on traditional logic-based systems, for instance, will tend to translate the first onto a representation that looks more like the second. For this reason I do well to stress the importance of ambient representations, which make more sense from the perspective of partitioned representations.

SECONDARY CONTEXTS

A primary context is necessary and sufficient for representing the role or function of a space. Every space (except **base**) is assumed to have a single primary context. The interests of consolidation often call for additional means of accessing the contents of other spaces. A *secondary context* provides a kind of mapping from the content of one space to the contents of another that is a consequence of the semantics of the primary contexts involved.

Inheritance Contexts

For instance, **sp_9** in Figure 2.1 (p. 57) is a conditional space and as such is intended to represent a candidate "reality" relative to **sp_3**. Therefore, if something is satisfied in **sp_3** it should be satisfied even if there is a frog in Alma's pocket in **sp_3**. Therefore, **sp_9** should *inherit* the contents of **sp_3**. In this case I talk of an *inheritance context.*

Something like our linear notation for primary contexts is used for secondary contexts as well. The secondary context in this case looks like this

sp_9 | [sp_3]

Notice the convention that a space term in a secondary context uses simple square brackets, [S] instead of ⟦S⟧. But, as is the case with primary contexts, *context climbing* gives secondary contexts their functionality. For instance, we can replace the space term in **sp_9 | [sp_3]** by the content of **sp_3 | Alma likes frogs** to derive **sp_9 | Alma likes frogs.** All of the contents of **sp_3** are similarly inherited into **sp_9**. In this way, a secondary context opens a channel of communication between two spaces.

A couple of frameworks that posit such inheritance from one space-like domain to another occur in the literature. One of these is the *context-layered data base,* which I discussed briefly above.

Although these data bases are called *contexts* in the terminology of the time, I will call them *spaces* to underscore their relevance to partitioned representations and to avoid the conflict with the specific meaning of *context* used in this book. Spaces in this scheme are arranged in a hierarchy. In the hierarchy each space can have a set of *successor* spaces. Generally each space represents a set of conditions that are true in the corresponding situation. The contents of a successor space should be derived from the contents of its predecessor in a way predicted by the application of some alternative action such as moving, lifting or putting down some object. Most conditions will not change from the predecessor to the successor. Rather than modeling the maintenance of those conditions that do not change with the transition from a predecessor to a successor by copying most of the contents of the predecessor to the successor, an *inheritance* link is used instead. Positive and negative assertions are made in the successor in correspondence to the particular action hypothetically performed. The biggest problem encountered here is not that of identifying the effects of a particular action, but rather that of identifying what conditions are *not* affected by a particular action. This is the very well-known *frame problem* (Hayes 1973) in artificial intelligence. In reasoning about the successor space in a context-layered data base any assertions visible in the predecessor can be used in the successor, *as long as they do not conflict with the explicit contents of the successor.* Thus we have inheritance by *default* which avoids the prohibitive redundancy of copying.

Another framework in which inheritance is described is that of *mental spaces* (Fauconnier 1985), which we will encounter frequently in the course of this book. Mental spaces are likewise organized so that one space may be nested within another, such as a belief space within a story space. Beyond this, one space always inherits from its embedding space. The principle of *space optimization* states that if space **S2** is nested in space **S1**, then **S2** should be structured so that it is maximally similar to **S1**, while inconsistencies are avoided with what is explicitly known about **S2**.*

* Fauconnier modifies space optimization to deal with a specific problem with the assumption that the hope space of a particular individual inherits from the belief space of the same individual when the two spaces are nested as *siblings* in the nesting hierarchy. Later we will see reason to reject the principle that a space

Inheritance is also found, we have seen in Chapter 1, in frames, schemas and scripts. In fact, these structures can actually be viewed as specific kinds of spaces, which I call *generalization spaces* later. Inheritance of this kind, however, also critically involves associating, binding or linking up certain objects in the generalization space with certain objects in the space in which the instance is represented.

Other Secondary Contexts

A more complex but also useful example of a secondary context involves two temporally ordered spaces, **sp_2** and **sp_4**:

sp_0 | at time tm_2: ⟦sp_2⟧
sp_0 | at time tm_4: ⟦sp_4⟧
sp_0 | tm_2 < tm_4

As discussed above, if **P** is satisfied at some time **T**, then it has occurred that **T** is satisfied at any time after **T**. For instance, if it is true at noon May 18 that Fred graduates from college, then it is true on June 18 that Fred *has* graduated from college. It follows that we can introduce the secondary context

sp_4 | it has occurred that [sp_2]

to map the satisfaction of *any* proposition in **sp_2** onto a related proposition in **sp_4**.

In summary, a secondary context is useful when one space wants to have a view of the contents of another space. It is like a window, a one-way window, between two rooms. If the information from one space carries over with no or little alteration, then it is appropriate to talk of an inheritance context. Often the information is viewed from another perspective; the window is tinted.

A TYPOLOGY OF SPACES

Some questions that naturally remain are: How many different kinds of spaces are there? What are they? How are they similar and how do they differ?

---

always inherits from its parent in favor of the principle stated above that secondary contexts result from the semantics of primary contexts.

I have identified a number of representative schemes from the literature as instances of partitioned representations. Actually, each of these is generally limited to a single kind of space, e.g., a situational space in context-layered data bases or a belief space in various frameworks. I assume a maximally promiscuous working model of partitioned representations consistent with the principles of coherence and consolidation.* At this point we can justify this position in terms of functionality. Beyond this, we will see this assumption cross-justified when we later see that this provides the most general and uniform account of a wide variety of linguistic phenomena.

In looking at the various types of spaces we will be particularly interested in the following aspects of structure.

(1) The properties of the primary contexts. Of particular interest is whether a primary context is *unique*, or whether there are other contexts of the same form.

(2) Secondary contexts they contain. Of particular interest are the *inheritance contexts* that might exist between spaces.

(3) The contents of spaces. Of particular interest is what is *essentially satisfied* in the spaces, i.e., what must be satisfied in the space *by definition*, as opposed to what is *accidentally satisfied.*

(4) Any *specialized inference procedures* that might be used for particular spaces, beyond normal parochial reasoning and context climbing.

This typology is not meant to be exhaustive, and the discussion of many kinds of spaces will be preliminary.

---

* Johnson-Laird (1983) would disagree with me in one instance: He specifically argues against the use of a mental model in the representation of a universal quantification, as in

Every man owns a car.

He rules out the use of a model to represent the generic man on the grounds that it would conflict with an essential structural constraint on mental models: the representation would not correspond structurally to the situation that the sentence describes, since the situation described has a set of men, each owning a car, not a single generic man. Nevertheless, we will see that linguistic evidence suggests otherwise.

Conditional Spaces

A *conditional space* is involved in the representation of an English sentence like

If Warren ate a bug, he will soon be sick.

This sentence would be represented with a pair of statements something like

sp_0 | Warren ate a bug → [[sp_1]]
sp_1 | Warren will soon be sick

Functionally, a conditional space is used to explore the consequences of some proposition which the system speculates to be true. That is, a conditional space represents some *coherent candidate "reality"* in which the antecedent of the conditional is satisfied. Three properties of **sp_1** follow. First, all consequences of Warren eating a bug will be true *together*; we don't need a separate "what if Warren ate a bug" space for each consequence. This means that, in the interests of consolidation, there will be only one primary context of the form **sp_0 | Warren ate a bug → [[...]]**. Second, everything satisfied in **sp_0** will be satisfied in **sp_1**. For instance, if Alma likes frogs, then she still likes frogs if Warren ate a bug. This means that we have the secondary context:

sp_1 | [sp_0].

Third, the *antecedent* proposition **Warren ate a bug** of the primary context must necessarily be satisfied in **sp_1**, such that

sp_1 | Warren ate a bug.

This statement is therefore essentially satisfied, that is, as part of the definition of the space. In contrast, the content **Warren will soon be sick** is *accidentally* satisfied.

More generally, given a context of the form,

S0 | P → [[S1]]

the following hold:

(1) There is no other context of the form **S0 | P → [[...]]**.

(2) **S1 | [S0]**

(3) **S1 | P**

A ***specialized inference technique*** might be used for conditional spaces to establish that something ***fails to be satisfied*** in the parent space. To show that **sp_0 | not P** we create a space **sp_2** with the context

sp_0 | P → [[sp_2]]

then show that a ***contradiction*** **false** can be derived in **sp_2**. **sp_0 | P → false** allows the inference **sp_0 | not P**. This is analogous to ***reductio ad absurdum*** or ***proof by contradiction*** well-known in logic systems of ***natural deduction.***

Possibility Spaces

These are involved in the representation of English sentences like

Maybe George spilled the beans.
It is possible that Bif is a tiddly-winks wizard.

The second sentence, for instance, might be represented internally as

sp_1 | it is possible that [[sp_2]]
sp_2 | Bif is a tiddly-winks wizard

Like conditional spaces, possibility spaces are a kind of speculation space, i.e., they represent coherent candidate "realities." Unlike conditional spaces, the primary contexts of possibility spaces do not specify *which* candidate realities are under consideration. For this reason, nothing is specifically essentially satisfied in a possibility space. We must permit more than one context of the form **sp_1 | it is possible that [[S]]**. For instance, the following might be true together

It is possible that Bif is a tiddly-winks wizard.
It is possible that Bif is a tiddly-winks neophyte.

but this does not mean that it is possible that both *individually* possible propositions are true *together*. We do not, for instance, want the representations

sp_2 | Bif is a tiddly-winks wizard
sp_2 | Bif is a tiddly-winks neophyte

instead, the second sentence is represented as

sp_1 | it is possible that [[sp_3]]

sp_3 | Bif is a tiddly-winks neophyte

Consolidating **sp_2** and **sp_3** would degrade coherence. Contexts of the form **sp_1 | it is possible that ⟦...⟧** are *not* unique. Since **sp_2** represents a candidate reality, we have,

sp_2 | [sp_1]

in analogy to conditional spaces.

More generally, given a context of the form,

S0 | it is possible that ⟦S1⟧

the following hold:

(1) There may be other contexts of the form **S0 | it is possible that ⟦...⟧**.

(2) **S1 | [S0]**

Counterfactual Spaces

These are involved in the representation of English sentences like

If George had won the Illinois lottery, he would have repaid all of his debts.

This would be represented internally as something like

sp_0 | George has won the Illinois lottery $\Box\!\!\rightarrow$ ⟦sp_1⟧
sp_1 | George has repaid all of his debts

Counterfactual spaces are like conditional spaces in many respects. Functionally, they are each a type of ***hypothesis*** or *what if* space, based on the assumption of some antecedent proposition. Structurally, they are each unique: There is no other space with a primary context of the form **sp_0 | George has won the Illinois lottery $\Box\!\!\rightarrow$ ⟦...⟧**. Second, the antecedent of the primary context is essentially satisfied in the counterfactual space, that is,

sp_1 | George has won the Illinois lottery

The main difference between counterfactual and conditional spaces is that the former do not represent *candidate "realities"* or speculations but rather coherent *alternative* "realities" that are similar in most respects to "reality." Thus, virtually all of the things that are satisfied in **sp_0** are satisfied in **sp_1**: If we assume that George has a brown dog named Puff then George would presumably *still* have a brown dog named Puff *if* he had won the Illinois lottery. On the other hand, certain things related to the antecedent of the counterfactual will be satisfied in **sp_0** but not in **sp_1**: the fact that George did *not* win the Illinois lottery, or that George is a short-order cook of modest means. In brief, anything satisfied in **sp_0** can be presumed satisfied in **sp_1** unless its negation can be derived from satisfied propositions that are in some sense more basic.* We can express this rule of *default inheritance* with the secondary context:

sp_1 | presumably: [sp_0]

It has been observed (Lewis 1973) that the counterfactual behaves differently than standard material implication. If

$$P \rightarrow Q$$
$$Q \rightarrow R$$

then it follows that

$$P \rightarrow R$$

But if it is true that

$$P \;\Box\!\!\rightarrow Q$$
$$Q \;\Box\!\!\rightarrow R$$

it does not follow that

$$P \;\Box\!\!\rightarrow R$$

For example, the following (from Lewis 1973),

If J. Edgar Hoover had been born a Russian, then he would have been a Communist.
If J. Edgar Hoover had been a Communist, he would have been a traitor.

together do not entail

If J. Edgar Hoover had been born a Russian, then he

* This is at least roughly the rule of inheritance used in context layered data bases discussed. Exactly which propositions win out is not a trivial problem. Work in nonmonotonic reasoning and reason maintenance in AI (McDermott and Doyle 1980) would be relevant to modeling determination of the appropriate contents of counterfactual spaces. The literature on counterfactuals suggests the importance of a variety of subtle factors, which are, however, beyond the scope of

would have been a traitor.

The difference between material implication and the counterfactual seems to be captured precisely in the two kinds of inheritance contexts. For instance, the first of these sentences would be represented as something like

sp_2 | J_Edgar_Hoover is born Russian □→ ⟦sp_3⟧
sp_3 | J_Edgar_Hoover is born Russian
sp_3 | presumably: [sp_2]
sp_3 | J_Edgar_Hoover is Communist.

The second would would be represented as something like

sp_2 | J_Edgar_Hoover has been Communist □→ ⟦sp_4⟧
sp_4 | J_Edgar_Hoover has been Communist
sp_4 | presumably: [sp_2]
sp_4 | J_Edgar_Hoover is traitor.

These together do *not* allow the derivation of

sp_3 | J_Edgar_Hoover is traitor.

We observe that the truth of the first sentence above in the real world is at least partially a consequence of the fact that J. Edgar Hoover was born in a strongly anti-communist country. But in **sp_3** he would be born in a Communist country, so **sp_3 | J_Edgar_Hoover is traitor** would be incompatible with the antecedent proposition **sp_3 | J_Edgar_Hoover is born Russian** used to define that space; it would have to be one of the propositions that is *not* inherited.

More generally, given a context of the form,

S0 | P □→ ⟦S1⟧

the following hold:

(1) There is no other context of the form **S0 | P □→ ⟦...⟧**.

(2) **S1 | presumably: [S0]**

(3) **S1 | P**

There is probably a lot to say about specialized inference procedures used with counterfactual spaces. For instance, counterfactual

---

this book.

sentences are generally used to make concise usually incisive comments about the *real world*. The sentences cited above,

> *If J. Edgar Hoover had been born a Russian, then he would have been a Communist.*

is generally taken to mean that J. Edgar Hoover was very conservative and pro-establishment rather than a strong advocate of democratic principles. Fauconnier's (personal communication) sentence

> *In France, Watergate wouldn't have done Nixon any harm.*

supports a wide variety of conclusions about the French political system in the real world. Now, the account above says something about how these counterfactual spaces are set up, by injecting an antecedent proposition into the space and allowing the space to inherit by default from the parent space. It does not tell us how unconditional inferences are derived in the parent space. The specialized inferences that counterfactual spaces support call for further investigation.*

Generalization Spaces

These are involved in the representation of English sentences like

> *Each of Farmer Bob's chickens lays an egg a day.*
> *Every fireman has a red helmet.*

The second of these would be represented as something like:

sp_0 | any fireman, obj_2, is such that ⟦sp_1⟧
sp_1 | • obj_2
sp_1 | obj_2 is a fireman
sp_1 | • obj_3
sp_1 | obj_3 is a red helmet

---

* These inferences may depend on something like *regression* discussed (Weyhrauch 1980), which deals with reasoning backwards from plan goals. Given that **S2** is derived from the previous situation **S1** by action **A** such that **S2** inherits the conditions of **S1** that do not contradict effects of **A**, regression answers the question, what must be satisfied in situation **S1** to ensure that **P** is satisfied in situation **S2**? Regression applied to the counterfactual J. Edgar Hoover case discussed above might answer the question, given **sp_3 | J_Edgar_Hoover is born Russian** and **sp_3 | presumably: [sp_2]** what must be satisfied in **sp_2** to warrant the inference **sp_3 | J_Edgar_Hoover is Communist.**

sp_1 | obj_2 has obj_3
sp_1 | [sp_0]

This quantification space is based on the existential assumption of a unique typical fireman. More generally, given a context of the form,

S0 | every P, X, is such that ⟦S1⟧

the following hold:

- **S1 | [S0]**
- **S1 | • X**
- There is no other context of the form **S0 | every P X is such that ⟦...⟧**.

Such generalization spaces are discussed further in Chapter 11, in which the similarity of these spaces to *frames* is developed.

Belief Spaces

These are involved in the representation of English sentences like

Skip thinks that Mabel is a marginal tiddly-winker but a great cook.

This sentence might involve an internal representation like

sp_0 | Skip believes that ⟦sp_1⟧
sp_1 | Mabel is a marginal tiddly-winker but a great cook.

There seems to be much utility in representing *common beliefs* of all people or of particular sets of people, such as cognitive scientists, spectators at a particular football game, Troskyites, and so on. For instance,

Every American kid believes in Santa Claus.

might be represented as

sp_0 | every American child believes that ⟦sp_2⟧
sp_2 | • Santa

Actually the context here could be decomposed into a belief context embedded in a generalization space. A large part of reasoning about Skip's beliefs might consist of categorizing Skip as a member of certain groups for which common belief spaces exist, and then inheriting the contents of those belief spaces. Thus, if Skip is an American kid we might derive

sp_1 | presumably: [sp_2]

Ballim and Wilks' (forthcoming) concept of *personae* seems to be related to the idea of spaces of common beliefs. A persona may be used in their system to ascribe beliefs typical of some class of people to individual people as long as no contradictions arise in the individual's belief system.

Like conditional spaces and quantification spaces, belief spaces are *unique*. Everything Skip believes to be true he believes to be true *together*.

More generally, given a context of the form,

S0 | X believes that ⟦S1⟧

for some constant **X**, the following hold:

- There is no other context of the form **S0 | X believes that** ⟦...⟧.
- There is the potential for many secondary inheritance contexts from common belief spaces.

Belief spaces, more than most other kinds of spaces, are probably subject to specialized and possibly complex inference procedures. For one thing, the functionality of belief spaces is somewhat unusual in that belief spaces are not strictly coherent. In particular, if **P** is satisfied in a belief space **sp_1** then it is not necessarily the case that every consequence of **P** is satisfied in **sp_1**. This would mean that people would be aware of all logical consequences of their beliefs. Moreover, this is true of any space embedded, even indirectly, in a belief space. Still, as Creary (1979) argues, there is a clear *heuristic motivation* in treating belief spaces as coherent domains and pursuing logical consequences of the represented contents of belief spaces and as almost all of the applications of belief spaces in artificial intelligence demonstrate. Ballim and Wilks (forthcoming) discuss the kind of modifications to normal reasoning processes that might be required for localized reasoning in spaces.

Wilks and Bien (1983) and Ballim and Wilks (forthcoming), working in a belief space framework (they call such spaces *environments*) see *belief ascription* as a central problem in reasoning about beliefs. Essentially, interactions with other agents requires that people have rich models of the belief systems of these other agents. However, only limited explicit evidence of the beliefs of others is generally available. They discuss a number of strategies to support belief ascription. These would be still other means of achieving consolidation, that is, of getting as much relevant information into spaces as possible. One strategy, which Ballim and Wilks call the *default rule*, says roughly that if you have embedding of belief environments expressed in the linear notation of partitioned representations as follows,

S0 | X believes ⟦S1⟧
S1 | P
S1 | Y believes ⟦S2⟧

we can *push down* the environment S1 into the environment S2 to derive

S2 | P

as long as P does not meet explicit contradictory information in S2. Alternative strategies are defined for *atypical beliefs*, such as technical expertise or secrets, which cannot be so easily pushed down. The *percolation* strategy allows information to be moved out from nested belief environments. Barnden (1989), in an alternative account, argues that beliefs are actually represented in a variety of ways, each an alternative common sense *metaphorical* model of belief. He calls the representation as a space the *AGENT'S-WORLD metaphor* and regards it as the default metaphor. Alternative metaphors, such as the *BATTLEGROUND metaphor* are required to avoid the consequences of logical omniscience.

These specialized supplemental inference strategies that are specific to belief spaces will not be given much attention here, since my concern is with the more general properties of partitioned representations that can be observed in all spaces or in large classes of spaces. In should be noted, though, that such specialized strategies critically depend on partitioned representations for beliefs. Ballim and Wilks, for instance, further point out the importance of belief spaces (environments) in supporting comparisons of sets of beliefs and in detecting contradictions within a set of beliefs.

Fictional Spaces

These are involved in the representation of sentences occurring within the setting of a fictional story, movie, theatrical production, or picture. Parochial reasoning in fiction spaces results in an ability to process fiction much like we process information about the real world, and at the same time to keep it separate. Because we have spaces like **sp_3**

sp_0 | in *the War of the Worlds*: ⟦**sp_3**⟧

we can read *the War of the Worlds*, come to a deep understanding of what is going on in the story *and*, amazingly, not go into a complete panic.

The ways in which fictions are processed certainly exhibit a lot of variation that is not entirely predicted from the partitioning framework alone. Inheritance from other spaces undoubtedly plays an important role. Fictions with a modern or clear historical setting should inherit from real temporal or situational spaces, much like a counterfactual space inherits from its parent space. For instance, in a modern detective novel one would expect a real-world backdrop, such as Los Angeles, with is hispanic communities, beaches, smog, drugs and gangs.

Likewise, fictions are classified into *genres* with common non-real-world background assumptions. Generic fiction spaces may represent the common contents of typical instances of particular genres, for instance, a generic fairy tale space in which dragons and fairies are situated, or a generic Western space, in which people engage in show-downs. This would allow fiction spaces to be categorized by genre much as belief spaces are categorized by common belief spaces. Categorizing a fiction as belonging to a certain genre would allow the contents of the associated spaces to be inherited.

Spaces for Other Propositional Attitudes

These are involved in the representation of English sentences like

Warren hopes that the dog has eaten his steamed carrots.
Kymrie is worried that there will not be enough spaghetti.
Warren wishes that he were Superman.

If we might engage in some philosophical speculation, most propositional attitudes seem to be closely related to belief in that they arise when some agent considers either some alternative to what he believes "reality" to be, or come candidate "reality" consistent with what he believes reality to be. Intuitively, in formulating a wish or hope, Warren makes a comparison between what he believes to be the state of the world and what the world would be like *if* some proposition, in the current example that his dog has eaten his steamed carrots, *is* true or if some proposition, in the current example that he is Superman, *were* true. He then concludes that such a space compares favorably to to the real world. Thus this representation is appropriate.

sp_0 | Warren believes that ⟦sp_1⟧
sp_1 | the dog has eaten Warren's steamed carrots → ⟦sp_2⟧
sp_2 | [sp_1]
sp_2 | the dog has eaten Warren's steamed carrots
sp_1 | Warren is superman □→ ⟦sp_3⟧
sp_3 | presumably: [sp_1]
sp_3 | Warren is superman

Observe that there are no hope or wish spaces *as such*. That is, there are no primary contexts like

sp_0 | Warren hopes that ⟦sp_4⟧
sp_0 | Warren wishes that ⟦sp_5⟧

Such spaces would not be coherent. For example, *Fred's dumb cat has fleas* entails that Fred's cat is dumb, but *Fred hopes that his dumb cat has fleas* does not entail that Fred hopes that his cat is dumb. What we might call a "hope space" is actually a conditional space embedded in a belief space. What we might call a "wish space" is actually a counterfactual space embedded in a belief space.*

---

* Notice that the *subjunctive mood*, often expressed by *were*, is used with *wish*. The subjunctive is otherwise used in English in counterfactuals, in fact in the antecedents of counterfactuals, as discussed in Chapter 6. This is independent evidence from language understanding that the analysis of wish spaces as counterfactual spaces embedded in belief spaces is correct.

The analysis of hope and wish outlined above immediately and explicitly captures the inheritance to hope and wish spaces from belief spaces that Fauconnier attributes to the unanalyzed *mentor relation*. In the present account, inheritance is simply a consequence of the inheritance contexts associated with conditional and counterfactual spaces. In the Warren example, these are **sp_2** |

Temporal Spaces

These are involved in the representation of English sentences like

> *At three o'clock Bif was driving to work.*
> *Mortimer had eaten a whole pizza and snored loudly.*

The second sentence might project onto the following.

> **sp_0 | at time time_4: [[sp_4]]**
> **sp_4 | it has occurred that [sp_8]**
> **sp_4 | Mortimer snores loudly**
> **sp_8 | Mortimer eats a whole pizza**

A temporal space serves to consolidate everything true at some particular time within some "reality." Therefore a temporal space is unique for a given time.

Alongside temporal spaces are *positional spaces*, which are used in the representation of sentences like

> *In Slurbovia the populace is happy even though it is constantly raining.*

Actually, pure temporal spaces and pure positional spaces may be relatively rare. *Situational spaces* specifying both temporal and spatial extent at the same time might be more useful. All of the preceding examples of temporal spaces might actually be situational spaces.

Perspective Spaces

Many things may described from one perspective or another. To describe events or objects located in space, for instance, we have to establish spatial coordinates. Each of the following makes sense only with respect to such coordinates.

> *The sun is rising.*
> *The earth is turning.*
> *The trees were whizzing by.*
> *The train is whizzing by.*
> *Bif's kitchen is to the right of Bif's living room.*
> *Bif's kitchen is to the left of Bif's living room.*

[sp_1] and **sp_3 | presumably: [sp_1]**.

Statements that take alternative perspectives should not be mixed because they would together be incoherent. Statements that take the same perspective should be consolidated. Accordingly, we have spaces like sp_4 and sp_5,

> **sp_0 | as viewed from the Earth: ⟦sp_4⟧**
> **sp_0 | as viewed from the North: ⟦sp_5⟧**

each of which is internally coherent and can be used to make inferences that are valid from the same perspective.

If the arguments for *internal realism* (Putnam 1988), discussed in Chapter 1, are valid, then it is never possible to have a "God's eye view" that is independent of a certain perspective. Thus, the decision to carve the world up into one set of objects rather than another, or to impose a certain institutionalized interpretation on the events one observed involves entering some perspective space or another.

WHERE PARTITIONED REPRESENTATIONS GET THEIR POWER

The functional advantages of partitioned representations over non-partitioned representation systems result from two factors. First, the information relevant to parochial reasoning is strongly delimited. Rather than considering the entire knowledge base in drawing inferences, only the contents of a specific space are considered. This helps control combinatorial problems, well-known in artificial intelligence. Second, inferences themselves are made simpler, and accordingly require fewer computational steps.

It is useful to contrast partitioned representations with the two better established representation schemes current in logic and artificial intelligence that are also capable of representation and reasoning in complex domains. These are *possible world* representations and what I call *Fregean* representations. Contrasting these will underscore partitioned representations' advantages in providing a concise representation of complex knowledge that supports efficient reasoning about that knowledge.

Fregean Representations and Possible Worlds

The first of these approaches uses a higher-order or intentional language in which terms can denote propositions, and relies heavily on axioms to make appropriate inferences. Maida (1985), making a similar contrast, calls this the *Fregean* approach. The Fregean approach can be recognized in modal and intentional logics (e.g., Hughes and Cresswell 1968), in adaptations of such logics to artificial intelligence (e.g., McCarthy 1979), and in specific knowledge representation systems in artificial intelligence (e.g., Shapiro 1979).

The second approach generally uses a lower-order representation but derives a lot of power from terms which may denote things like possible worlds or potential situations. Possible worlds are often introduced in a metalanguage to define a model-theoretic semantics for a higher-order or intentional language like one used in the Fregean approach (Kripke 1963, Hintikka 1962, Montague 1974). Such a semantic metalanguage, itself usually a first-order language, can be used directly to make the same inferences as the Fregean object language (Moore 1985).

Contrasts

The two approaches can be contrasted with partitioned representations by considering how each represents and derives an intuitively simple inference. From the two premises

> *George believes that Fred's phone number is 123-4567.*
> *George believes that Mary's phone number is the same as Fred's phone number.*

we would expect the following to be easily derived in any adequate model of mental representation:

> *George believes that Mary's phone number is 123-4567.*

The Fregean approach. In the Fregean approach, the two premises of our example might be represented as something like the following:

> **George believes (Fred's phone number = 123-4567)**
> **George believes (Fred's phone number = Mary's phone number)**

In order to derive the conclusion, additional knowledge about the logical properties of belief might be made available in the form of what logicians call *axioms* or *meaning postulates*, such as the following (which are actually only approximately correct).

> **(X believes P & X believes Q) → X believes (P & Q)**
> **(X believes P & P ⊩ Q) → X believes Q**

Here **P ⊩ Q** means that **P** *logically entails* **Q**. Using these as additional premises along with some axioms about ⊩, *logical entailment*, the conclusion we want can be derived.

The Fregean approach provides a simple, uniform but expressive system of representation and inference. Much progress has been made in providing an appropriate objectivist semantics for languages representing the Fregean approach. The main weakness of this approach as compared to the other two approaches is in its support of reasoning: It is relatively inefficient in deriving higher-order inferences. Such derivations require repeated reapplication of the rather cumbersome meaning postulates. This results in long inferences with associated problems in controlling the direction of inference. For instance, the reader who works through the complete derivation for the sentence above will find that an axiom for **believes** must be applied at each stage to unpack beliefs from a larger sentence each time.

What seems to be called for is a representation of the totality of George's beliefs as a coherent system that can be reasoned about internally. The possible worlds approach and especially partitioned representations each provide such a representation.

The possible worlds approach. The meanings of the two premises about George's beliefs above might be expressed in the possible worlds approach as follows,

> **W is consistent with George's beliefs → it is true in W that Fred's phone number = 123-4567**
> **W is consistent with George's beliefs → it is true in W that Fred's phone number = Mary's phone number**

The derivation of the inference that George believes that Mary's phone number is 123-4567 can be made under the assumption that normal rules of inference, such as *substitution of equals*, are applicable in individual possible worlds, such as in any arbitrary world which is consistent with George's beliefs. The possible worlds approach is powerful, general, and relatively well-understood. It manages to effectively consolidate knowledge into embedded models through indexing by universally quantified variables, thereby avoiding the cumbersome inferences via the explicit meaning postulates necessary in the Fregean approach.

However, since the possible worlds approach involves reference to entities not referred to in the Fregean and partitioning approaches, it entails additional *ontological* commitments. Commitments to possible worlds have been attacked by philosophers (Quine 1953), and have received virtually no support in the cognitive science community. What is more, the possible worlds approach really doesn't work *in principle* (Moore and Hendrix 1979): In reasoning about beliefs, in particular, it is often necessary to discriminate between logically equivalent propositions. Bif could well believe **P** and disbelieve **Q** even though **P** and **Q** are logically equivalent, as long as Bif is unable to recognize their logical equivalence. However, if **P** and **Q** have different representations in Bif's belief space they can be discriminated differently in terms of what inferences they most readily give rise to. Representing beliefs as a set of possible worlds is incompatible with the fact that beliefs are not strictly closed under entailment, i.e., that people are incapable of recognizing all of the logical consequences of their beliefs, because it is in the nature of possible worlds that they are closed under entailment. There have been attempts to overcome this discrepancy by introducing *impossible worlds* (e.g., Cresswell 1972), but these entail even more problematic ontological commitments.

Partitioned representations. In partitioned representations the premises of our *George believes* example might be represented by making the following assertions parochially in a space, call it **sp_8**, representing George's beliefs like this:

sp_8	**Fred's phone number = 123-4567** **F's phone number = M's phone number**

Within this space, the conclusion **Mary's phone number = 123-**

4567 can be derived parochially without difficulty. That's it!

The advantage in reasoning in multiple knowledge bases is found in the efficiency of reasoning parochially once information is appropriately consolidated into coherent and concrete models of possible realities. It is accordingly possible to reason about beliefs without reference to propositions of belief, to reason about conditionals without reference to conditional propositions, to reason about fictions without reference to the fact that we are not dealing with reality. In short, partitioned representations avoid repeated direct use of modal, temporal, or hypothetical structures and the associated cumbersome meaning postulates or equivalent reasoning processes.

The effects of partitioned representations are often similar to those of the possible worlds approach, but it turns out that these effects are more general. Although a space often corresponds to a delimited *set* of possible worlds, there are some contexts that resist this correspondence. Quantificational contexts must be handled somewhat differently in the possible worlds approach. More critically, spaces of perspective, with contexts like sp_1 | as viewed from the-north, [[sp_4]], have no possible worlds correspondent.

Natural Deduction

This demonstration is probably best underscored by observing the similarity of the parochial reasoning processes in partitioned representations to the logical methods of constructing *subordinate proofs* (Fitch 1952) in *natural deduction* as alternatives to the use of axioms in Fregean type representations. These techniques include *conditional proof*, the related *proof by contradiction* (*reductio ad absurdum*), *proof by cases*, and proofs using *universal instantiation* followed later by *universal generalization* on the corresponding term. It also includes some less well known techniques of inference for modal logics. Such a subproof generally begins with the provisional introduction of a propositional or existential *assumption*. It continues with a sequence of deductive steps in the *scope* of the assumption. Generally, but not always, any item in a superordinate proof may be *reiterated*, that is copied, into the subproof. Finally it concludes by *discharging* the assumption to generate some global consequence as an item in the superordinate proof.

...

Bulgarian(Bif) *assumption*

...

...

spy(Bif)

Bulgarian(Bif) → spy(Bif) *discharge assumption*

...

Fig. 2.3. A conditional proof, illustrating the analogy between spaces and subproofs in natural deduction.

For instance, a conditional proof might have the form exemplified in Figure 2.3. The inner bracket represents the scope of the assumption **Bulgarian(Bif)**. Any sentences derived within this scope are by no means proven or assumed to follow logically from the premises, but make sense only in a *context-dependent* way. However, anything preceding in the outer box can be reiterated in the inner box to help the subproof along. If **spy(Bif)** occurs in the inner box, it means that **Bulgarian(Bif) → spy(Bif)** can be derived in the outer bracket by discharging the assumption **Bulgarian(Bif)**.

A proof using *universal instantiation*, then *universal generalization* typically has the form exemplified in Figure 2.4 Any inferences made in the inner box, introduced by the assumption **cloud(X) → nebulous(x)** can not necessarily be regarded as true in an absolute sense (in fact the assumption itself is meaningless in an absolute sense, since the term **x** doe not refer to anything specific). If **cloud(x) → silver_lined(x)** occurs in the inner box, it means that **∀x cloud(x) → silver_lined(x)** is inferable in the outer box by discharging the assumption **P**. However, any premise or inference that occurs before the assumption, i.e., in the outer box, may again be reiterated in the inner box. Within the inner box a conditional proof could well occur, giving the proof structure another level of embedding.

...
∀x cloud(x) → nebulous(x)

  cloud(x) → nebulous(x) *universal instantiation*
  ...
  ...
  cloud(x) → silver_lined(x)

∀x cloud(x) → silver_lined(x) *universal generalization*
...

Fig. 2.4. A proof using universal instantiation and universal generalization.

These techniques of natural deduction utilizing subproofs have the following critical features in common with partitioned representations:

(1) The *semantic intents* of sentences in the scope of an assumption can only be defined in a *context-dependent* way. Sentences within the scope cannot be attributed truth conditions directly, but only relative to the assumption. A subproof, or the scope of an assumption, corresponds to a *space*. A sentence occurring within a subproof corresponds to part of the *contents* of that space.

(2) Inferences can be derived locally within the scope of an assumption in the normal way. This corresponds to parochial processing. Reiteration of an element into a subproof corresponds to *inheritance.*

(3) Inferences derived within the scope of an assumption are mapped onto some more global consequence outside of the scope of that assumption. The way a sentence derived in a subproof is mapped onto a global consequence when the assumption is discharged corresponds to the primary *context* of the space.

(4) The usefulness of these proof techniques lies in the relative simplicity of the proofs they provide vis-a-vis the axiomatic proofs otherwise required in a Fregean type of system. In essence, we avoid, in these techniques, the repeated direct use of modal, temporal, or hypothetical structures and the associated cumbersome meaning postulates or equivalent rules of inference.

Partitioned representations in effect maximize the advantages of the methods of constructing subproofs in natural deduction. In fact, in Chapter 11 I show that all of the uses of subordinate proofs in natural deduction are consequences of the logical model of partitioned representations discussed in Chapter 10, but beyond this, partitioned representations effectively find new applications for those techniques in reasoning about beliefs, possibilities, counterfactuals and so on. In summary, of the formal methods for dealing with complex knowledge subproofs in natural deduction are by far closest to partitioned representations. No wonder they call it *natural deduction.*

SUMMARY AND CONCLUSIONS

In this chapter I have described the structural elements of partitioned representations (spaces, primary and secondary contexts and contents), the principles that determine how spaces are actually configured (coherence and consolidation) and the basic principles directing reasoning (parochial reasoning and context climbing). The primary motivation throughout has been in terms of functionality: Partitioned representations provide an effective means of representing complex information. By localizing reasoning processes in restricted context-dependent domains, reasoning becomes concrete and efficient.

Partitioned representations are not intended as a complete theory of mental representation, only about its highest-level organization. The further details of mental representation—the choice between propositional, analogical and procedural representations, the mechanisms of associative memory, and so on—should be developed for the most part parochially, i.e., in terms of the structures found *within* spaces. In the course of this book, I will speculate about the nature of such additional aspects of mental representation and how these additional aspects interact with the partitioned representations framework, but these additional mechanisms are not part of the theory of partitioned representations per se.

On the other hand, a commitment to a certain basic medium of representation can make the functionality of the partitioning framework even more striking. Consider, for instance, an analogical representation. In Chapter 1 I described Dreyfus' analogical representation for a railroad system. Although this was not intended as a serious model of human cognition, it will be instructive to see how it can be naturally embedded in a partitioned representation. Partitioned representations do nothing to help us represent a single railroad system but are indispensable in representing multiple systems, for instance George's beliefs about the railroad system, the railroad system at different times in American history, what the railroad system would look like if additional lines were added and so on. In a partitioned framework we would use a set of spaces to represent such information and place separate string net in each space. Each space would carry a label to tell us what possible reality the space represents. Within each space inferring optimal routes can be achieved parochially by grabbing knots and pulling, as before. Accordingly we might derive what the easiest route from New York to Chicago would be *if* a line were added between Akron and Gary, what George believes to be the easiest route, what the easiest route was *in 1950* and so on. Without partitioned representations these inferences would be impossible, at least by string pulling. In brief, for an analogical representation no other alternative means of representing complex information, analogous to the Fregean or possible worlds approach for instance, would be available.

In the introductory chapter I suggested four criteria for justifying a theory of mental representation. This chapter has stressed functionality (expressiveness, efficiency and rationality). Most of the rest of this book will evaluate the theory of partitioned representations with respect to linguistic evidence. It is here where cross-justification will be primarily established.

CHAPTER THREE

Language: Process and Structure

Language is the most direct window we have into the mind.

In this chapter I will suggest how a theory of mental representation ties in with the study of language, outline a framework for talking about linguistic processes and elaborate our criteria for assessing theories of mental representation on the basis of linguistic evidence. In discussing language, let me again begin from a very broad perspective in order to frame the approach taken in this book.

A SIMPLE PHILOSOPHY OF LANGUAGE

What is language? What is grammar? What is the relationship of grammar to actual language processing? If the answer to the last question is a matter of *competence* vs. *performance*, what are competence and performance, anyhow? Do we need separate theories for these? Many researchers have addressed these questions, but as a rule I rarely find the answers adequate. For this reason I will begin with these fundamental issues in this short section. If nothing else, this will give these researchers the opportunity to complain about *my* answers to these questions.

My answer contradicts, say, Chomsky's (1965), but is, I think, much in the spirit of de Saussure's (1959). It recalls the discussion of *levels of description* of Chapter 1, in particular with respect to the distinction between *individual cognition* and *social cognition*, as well as of the somewhat befuddled distinctions often found between different levels of description. *Language* per se belongs—along with games, laws and other systems of *conventions*—at the level of social cognition.

Language can be identified with grammar, as understood by many linguists, although the term *grammar* has a tendency to be applied specifically to syntax, to the exclusion of semantics and such. *Language processing* belongs at the level of individual cognition. The distinction is important and necessary, and actually reflects de Saussure's *langue* and *langage* or Chomsky's *competence* and *performance.* On the other hand, it gets confused for two reasons. First, language processing, as one would expect, presupposes a language to process. Second, and more importantly, the rules of language presuppose the cognitive processes and structures involved in language processing.

Language as Social Cognition

What it means for language to belong to social cognition will become clearer if we consider analogous systems: games and laws. A game like chess is a product of human individual cognition (someone invented it, or rather many individuals invented it through minor modifications over time). Playing the game is a task for individual cognition. Yet the game itself consists in abstract rules that can be completely described without reference to the cognitive process that would be involved in actually playing the game. Similar things can be said about traffic laws.

Language has in common with games and traffic laws the following three properties. First, each is normative. Second, the function of each is found in interpersonal intercourse. Third, knowledge of each is distributed within the language community, and is not generally necessary for individuals to have complete knowledge.

Normativeness. Physical constraints on driving, moving pieces on a board or speaking and attributing interpretations are relatively liberal. But most of the things that one could possibly do physically are in the relevant sense *wrong*; knowing a game, traffic laws or a language is the same as knowing what is *right.* A *normative* system is imposed in each case on behavior. Cicourel (1974), Itkonen (1976), Anttila (1973) discuss norms and conventions and their relation to language.

Interpersonal intercourse. Games, traffic laws and language control behavior to realize functional interpersonal cooperative interaction.

The function of games (excluding solitaire) is, I suppose, something like entertainment through competition. The function of traffic laws is to provide fast average traffic flow while minimizing accidents (also to provide revenues for local governments). The primary function of language is *communication.* Lewis (1969) analyzes the functionality of systems of conventions, including language, in this regard.

Speech act theory focuses on the properties of language that follow from the function of language in interpersonal intercourse. Grice (1975) points out what he calls the *cooperative principle,* that people have an obligation to work with others effectively and efficiently in human interaction and shows how speakers' consequential obligation to communicate effectively and efficiently leads to predictions about many observed properties of language. According to Searle (1969) communication occurs because an utterance is generally associated with certain commitments, obligations or responsibilities on the part of the speaker, hearer or both. The *type* of obligation, i.e., who takes on or is given a responsibility, how that commitment is to be fulfilled, etc., is the *illocutionary force* of the statement. Some statements, for instance, commit the speaker to a future action, or the hearer to a verbal response.

The distribution of knowledge. People often play games without individually knowing all of the rules, with disagreements arbitrated by consulting either instructions or some expert. Few people know all of the traffic laws they are supposed to observe (some people seem to know very few). Likewise, much of a language is unknown to the individual. This is especially true of the lexicon. Putnam's (1988) thesis of the *division of linguistic labor* makes this point. Observe that people are also very good at behaving in a manner consistent with the normative system in spite of incomplete knowledge, by exercising more care where knowledge is incomplete. The individual who doesn't know the conditions under which one can castle in chess will probably avoid castling (at least if unable to ask for a clarification at the critical point); the individual who doesn't know if turning right on red is legal when driving will (annoyingly to others) often simply not turn when the opportunity presents itself, assuming that not turning right is certainly legal.

All of this suggests that language, from the individual's perspective, exists "out there" as something that the individual can know about, but not as something that is reducible to the individual's own cognitive structures and processes. The fact of language acquisition underscores this point: If language existed in individual cognition there would be nothing to learn.

Some apparent consequences of language as social cognition. The idea that language belongs to social cognition would seem to support the traditional view of natural language meaning that linguistic expressions themselves *denote* things out there in the world, as depicted in Figure 3.1. I call this the *semanticist view*, using *semantics* in the technical sense it has in formal logic, in which this view predominates. The semanticist view is especially fundamental to the school of *Montague grammar* (e.g., Montague 1974, Dowty 1979). The semanticist view is often criticized because it seems to attribute meaning without reference to people. However, this is what we might expect if we view language as a normative system at the level of social cognition. Chess moves, for instance, are described without reference to real people.

On the other hand, the idea that language belongs to social cognition would seem to undermine the traditional Chomskian view of linguistics as concerned with finding the grammatical formalism, such as *government and binding* or *generalized phrase structure grammar*, that accounts for language in the simplest way. It would seem that, beyond sufficient generative power, there could be no empirical basis for distinguishing one descriptive formalism from another at the level of social cognition. For instance, there are probably a lot of ways to correctly describe the rules of chess, some pretty opaque, others more convenient. But there is not interesting theoretical distinction there.

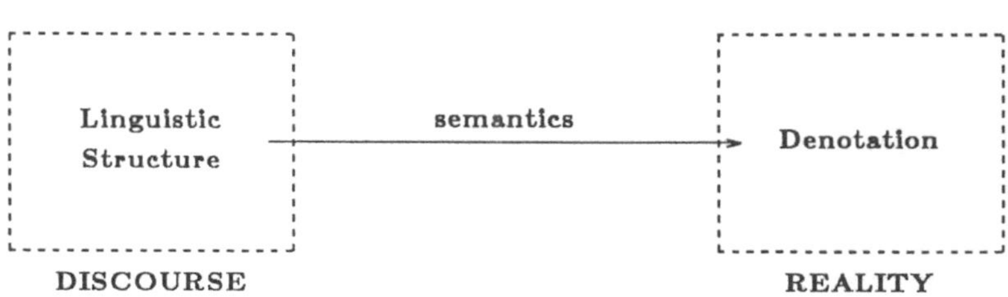

Fig. 3.1. The semanticist view of meaning.

In spite of the case for language as social cognition, closer inspection reveals that it is difficult to confine linguistic description to a single level of either language or language processing. This point is analogous to the point of Chapter 1 that it is difficult to neatly separate out symbolic and connectionist levels.

Language and Individual Cognition

Although language is, like the rules of chess, a set of socially defined conventions, language is, like chess, used by individuals and is therefore a proper topic for the study of *individual* cognition. This is the level at which *natural language processing* occurs. In exploring the distinction between language and language processing, it will be noticed that language processing presupposes language, just as expert reasoning presupposes the expert domain that is being reasoned about. Language processing without language is otiose.

What is more surprising than the dependence of language processing on language is the dependence of language on language processing. This is in contrast to the rules of games. There are at least two ways in which the rules of language presuppose features of language processing: shared structures of individual cognition, and monitoring of others cognitive states.

Monitoring of cognitive states. What makes language particularly interesting when compared to things like traffic laws and games is that language assumes that states of individual cognition be monitored very carefully by the participants as a discourse unfolds. These cognitive states, belonging to what I will call the *pragmatic setting,* provide a background which together with actual utterances determine meaning.

For instance, the cooperative principle requires that the speaker shape the discourse in a way in which the hearer can most efficiently assimilate the communicative contribution of each statement. Keenan and Schieffer (1976) call this *recipient design.* Recipient design includes balancing old and new information (Clark and Haviland 1977; Chafe 1970) and centering the discourse around an established *topic.*

Furthermore, the way in which meanings are attached to language expressions depend critically on the ability to monitor the cognitive states of other discourse participants. For instance, definite descriptions (usually beginning with *the* in English) must be interpreted to refer to a most cognitively salient object satisfying the description. If I use the phrase *the doorknob* in a discourse, I mean some particular doorknob, and intend for the hearer to have some doorknob in mind or close at hand so that will be recognized as the one I mean. An adequate description of the meaning of *the* at the level of language would have to refer to some performance-level concept like focus of attention.

Commonalities of individual cognition. Certain features of language could well be individually innate, belonging therefore to individual cognition, but showing up in language in a form difficult to differentiate from those features acquired under social influence. Bees, for instance, are apparently pre-wired to perform different forms of dances in response to different conditions in the environment. Sharing the same code, they are able to communicate. Humans, likewise, share common folk theories that largely constrain possible meanings. A Chomskian response to the argument that language belongs to social cognition would almost certainly be that a substantial part of human language reflects commonalities of individual cognition. The important point about commonalities is that they help determine the nature of language, so macrostructure is emerging from microstructure, yet do not require monitoring.

The constructivist view of meaning. If linguistic meaning cannot be described independently of mechanisms of individual cognition, then the semanticist view of meaning depicted in Figure 3.1 seems too

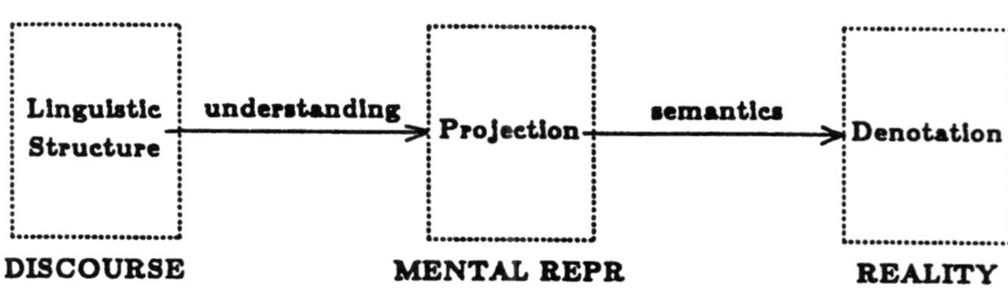

Fig. 3.2. The constructivist view of meaning.

simplistic. Notice that, as we have seen, a semantics, a relationship between a representation and what is being represented or could be represented in the external world, is a requirement of any functional system of *mental representation.* Since understanding must result in a mental representation of the content of the discourse defining a separate semantics for linguistic structures seems rather redundant. As long as surface structures can be systematically related to mental representations, it is also unnecessary. This is what I call the *constructivist* view of meaning, shown in Figure 3.2.

The constructivist view is adopted also by Fauconnier (1978), who talks of *meaning construction* and regards the meanings of linguistic constructions as directions for building mental representations. Johnson-Laird (1983) and Kamp (1980) also adopt a similar view, showing that this leads to a much more systematic account of meaning. Guenthner (1987) articulates the position very well. The constructivist view is also implicit in almost all work in language understanding in artificial intelligence.

LINGUISTIC EXPLANATION

Linguistic data. Linguistic data are full of patterns, recurring syntactic structures, and regular correspondences between syntactic and semantic structures. These patterns manifest themselves primarily in judgements of *grammaticality*, and of *truth conditions* or *entailment.* They also manifest themselves in the discourse use of certain constructions. For instance, most speakers judge that the following

The man that the dog bit is a mailman.
I have been to France.

are grammatically well-formed, while the following

* *The man that I saw the dog that bit is a mailman.*
* *I am to France.*

are not. Most speakers feel that the following, differing only in sentence stress (indicated by capitalization) mean something different.

Fred even gave Bif a BICYCLE.
Fred even gave BIF *a bicycle.*

The first seems to entail that Fred also gave Bif things other than a bicycle and the second that Fred also gave someone else a bicycle. The following seem to paraphrase these sentences respectively.

Fred gave even Bif a bicycle.
Fred gave Bif even a bicycle.

Most speakers judge intuitively that the following sequence of sentences

The Lone Ranger broke the window. He fired his gun.

mean that the breaking occurred immediately *before* the shooting, while the following sequence has the complementary interpretation.

The Lone Ranger fired his gun. He broke the window.

Observations such as these are the rich fund of data on which both theoretical linguistics and the philosophy of language are built. These data raise many fascinating theoretical questions: Why should certain sequences of words be grammatical while others are not? Why should changes in stress sometimes affect the truth conditions of sentences? Why are some sentences presuppositional? How does the ordering of sentences determine the sequencing of actions entailed in a discourse? Observations about linguistic structures constitute a massive set of data that can be used, as we will see, also to motivate theories of mental representation.

It is interesting to contrast linguistic data with the experimental data that also can be used to motivate theories of representation. In contrast to experimental evidence, linguistic data can be elicited easily—from one's armchair—and are extremely abundant. On the other hand, experimental evidence is generally painstakingly acquired, only after clever experiments have been designed and subjects have spent many hours in the lab. On the other hand, experimental evidence tends to get at cognitive processes *as they occur*, while linguistic evidence, as I now argue, tends to reflect less immediate results of those processes.

Explaining linguistic data. Data such as these, especially intuitions about grammatical well-formedness, and so on, are often taken to directly reflect the *grammar* of a language, i.e., competence or language. Nevertheless, such intuitions are judgements that arise in individual cognition and as such could well result such things as the processes and strategies of language understanding, i.e., performance, the way knowledge is structured and applied in human cognition, the way the world we use language to talk about is structured, the conceptual categories we impose on the world, rules of cooperative human interaction, the historical evolution of language, the structure of goal-directed behavior, and so on, factors which are subject, in principle at least, to independent investigation. Something like this view is found in Langacker (1987), Givon (1980) and Dinsmore (1979).

The realization of the many factors underlying linguistic data provides many opportunities for explaining linguistic structure and, of relevance to general cognitive science, for motivating theories of representation and processing in terms of the predictions they make. Nevertheless, linguists have traditionally rarely exploited such opportunities for explaining linguistic data; linguistics has been one of the most isolated of the cognitive sciences. Certainly one reason for this is the wide acceptance of Chomsky's (1965) idea of an *innate language faculty*, that much linguistic structure *cannot* be explained in terms of factors external to language itself. The problem with this idea is not that it is a priori wrong, but that there is no a priori way of knowing whether a particular linguistic structure can be explained in terms of external factors or must be attributed to the innate language faculty. In practice proponents of the theory almost always try to explain a linguistic structure by first finding the simplest set of rules that describe that structure, then attributing those rules either to the innate language faculty or to the grammar of the specific language involved, thus eschewing any attempt to account for linguistic data in terms of outside factors.

However, this fails to appreciate that whenever an explanation exists in terms of external factors the explanation in terms of the innate language faculty is entirely vacuous. To draw an analogy, if the fact that planets have elliptical orbits is a consequence of the independently motivated laws of inertia and of gravity, then attributing the shapes of the planetary orbits to some other mysterious force is not only redundant, but misleading. If the laws of inertia and gravity are correct, then the planets *must* have these orbits.

For example, the two views can be illustrated in accounting for the fact that noun phrases like

the man that I saw the dog that bit

meaning *the man that is such that I saw the dog that bit him,* are judged to be ill-formed. The traditional Chomskian account of this structure, due to Ross (1967), posits an explicit constraint, the *Complex Noun Phrase Constraint,* on relativization of a noun phrase, in this case the object of *bit,* in a deeply embedded clause. Rather than regarding the Complex Noun Phrase Constraint as a fairly accurate descriptive generalization based on observations of a large number of similar sentences, generative grammarians take it to *explain* the observations. On the other hand, a non-Chomskian account of this structure, suggested by Givon (1980), among others, proposes that perceptual strategies in language understanding make it much more difficult for a language understander to reconstruct the correct subject and object relations in a deeply embedded clause than in a less deeply embedded clause. The ill-formedness is due to an inability of the hearer to understand what the noun phrase means. Marcus (1980) has developed a computational model of language processing which *implicitly* obeys the Complex Noun Phrase Constraint because of such inherent limitations built into the model.

In summary, cognitive scientists should take linguistic data seriously as clues to the underlying cognitive structures and processes of mental representation and language processing. Many of the linguistic structures that can be recognized in such data may be direct consequences of theories of mental representation and language processing or may belong to the grammatical structure of language whose analysis requires reference to concepts defined within such theories.

THE PROCESS OF LANGUAGE UNDERSTANDING

My focus here will be that of most work in natural language processing: the mental encoding of propositional contents. While *generation* is concerned with mapping mental representations onto sentences or other structures in a natural language, language *understanding* is concerned with the process of mapping from surface language structures onto mental representations of the meanings of those sentences. Let's look at what is required of a theory of language understanding with special regard to the role of mental representation.

The input to language understanding is what I will call *surface structures*, occurring in phonetic or orthographic form (the distinction will generally not be important here). The output of language understanding is a set of internal mental representations, which I will call *internal representations* or *projections* of the surface structures.

Understanding natural language involves a number of interacting processes, highly constrained by the rules of language and operating on structures at many different levels: phonetic, lexical, syntactic, semantic and so on. Syntactic processes, for instance, deal with how the words (or morphemes) that occur in the surface discourse are grouped together to form larger structures. They should therefore tell us for a sentence like

The hobo dialed up his rich Uncle Seymour.

that the adjective *rich* goes with *Uncle Seymour*, that the noun phrase *the hobo* is the subject of the verb *dial up*, and so on.

Many processes in understanding are, we will see, tightly bound to mental representations, such as those that find specific projections for definite descriptions, those that integrate incoming knowledge with given information, and those that make high-level inferences necessary for recognizing a coherent interpretation. Following Dinsmore and Moehle (1990) I will call these *knowledge-based* processes. An example of a knowledge-based process is involved in understanding the phrase *the hobo* in *The hobo dialed his rich Uncle Seymour*, which will require that a *unique* mental representation satisfying the description as being a *hobo* be identified within existing knowledge structures. This may involve inference in addition to direct access of existing knowledge, as well as some basis within the mental representation of *discriminating* one hobo representation from all others. At an even higher level, understanding the sentence as a whole should trigger inferences about the purpose of the hobo's call. Probably a significant factor in these inferences will be the difference in wealth between the two people mentioned. Such inferences may be necessary to make the rest of the story coherent.

It is critical to keep in mind that processes involved in understanding are conditioned strongly not only by the long-term knowledge of the discourse participants, but also by numerous transient factors in the *pragmatic setting* such as which objects are present, who the discourse participants are, what time it is, etc.; speaker's and hearer's intentions and the current states of the mental representations of the discourse participants, including common background knowledge, discourse representations already built in processing the current discourse, the focus of attention or activation of certain mental representations, and so on. What I am calling pragmatic setting is more often referred to as *speech context*, but I am already using the word *context* to refer to one of the components of partitioned representations. Changes in pragmatic setting over time or from discourse to discourse cause the same sentence to project onto a different internal representation in virtually every use: Names, pronouns and definite descriptions find different referents, individual morphemes assume different readings, metaphorical and metonymous extensions are constantly at play, and so on. For instance, the phrase *the hobo* may be projected differently even at different times within a single discourse, as the pragmatic setting evolves.

Constructive Rules

It is useful and innocuous to think of natural language understanding as a transductive process whereby surface discourse is *projected* through a series of *intermediate structures*. I will follow the lead of the many computational systems and models of cognition that take *production rules* as the basic units of processing.*

A production rule has two parts, a set of *conditions* and a set of *actions*. The conditions look for certain kinds of intermediate structures as well as features of the pragmatic setting. When the conditions are satisfied then the rule *may fire*, which means that the actions are performed, usually to build some new intermediate structure. I say *may fire* because production rules are generally in *competition* with other production rules which may try to carry the projection in a different direction. More about this in a moment. One of the

* Some relevant references on what are known as *production systems* or simply *rule-based systems* are Anderson (1983), Schank and Riesbeck (1981), Waterman and Hayes-Roth (1978), Newell and Simon (1972), Buchanan and Shortliffe (1984), and Holland, et. al (1986). The *restructuring rules* of *Spaceprobe*, the computational realization of partitioned representations described in Chapter 12, are production rules that have been used to model constructive processes in language understanding in roughly the way described here.

advantages of thinking of processing in terms of production rules is that we separate the processing options from the decisions about which options to evoke. Each step in the path from the surface sentence to the internal representation can be seen as the effect of a modular production rule.

We will focus exclusively on the rules that suggest intermediate structures closer to the internal representations rather than those that retract candidate intermediate structures or make high-level processing decisions. In view of their specific function, I will do two things for you. First, I will call these *constructive rules*, since they support a constructivist view of meaning. Second, I will adopt what I hope is a clear notation for these rules. For instance, simple versions of the rules used in interpreting indefinite and definite descriptions respectively are as follows.

Conditions: X "$(_{NP}$ a D $)_{NP}$" Y

Actions: create an object, W
W is D
X W Y

Conditions: *X* "$(_{NP}$ the D $)_{NP}$" *Y*
? U is " D "

Actions: X U Y

In these rules, the condition part always begins with a surface or intermediate, in these cases X "$(_{NP}$ a D $)_{NP}$" Y and X "$(_{NP}$ the D $)_{NP}$" Y. We call this the *posted condition.* A posted condition will contain at least one *linguistic structure* whose projection the rule is working on. The linguistic structure is contained in quotes. Of course, a structure with a linguistic structure is not a meaningful representation itself, since it has not been fully interpreted. Capitalized terms indicate variables, i.e., they match arbitrary parts of intermediate structures. Subscripted parentheses are used to convey syntactic information. Thus S | X $(_{NP}$ a D $)_{NP}$ Y indicates that a D must form an *noun phrase.* NP means *noun phrase* and S means *sentence.* For instance "a dog bit Fred" matches the condition of the rule for indefinites (a compound linguistic structure has linguistic structures as parts, it is assumed).

The posted statement is followed by zero or more *preconditions* marked with ?, in this case **? U is " D "**. Preconditions potentially match information that is already *given* in the discourse representation, i.e., information explicitly represented or easily inferable. It is not necessary that a precondition contain a linguistic structure, but if it does, as "D" in this case, the linguistic structure has to be projected before any match with given representations is possible. For instance, in **"Fred bit the dog"**, **"dog"** is projected onto a representation, which I would probably just call the predicate **dog**, then an object **U** is located such that **U is dog** is given.

Each constructive rule serves to restructure the posted statement of the conditions. Statements in the action part are posted by the rule when it fires and may then be further restructured by subsequent processing. Commands, like **create an object, W**, are procedures that are executed when the rule fires.

Thus the rule for indefinite descriptions simply creates a new constant as the projection of the noun phrase and predicates the constant with **D**. For instance, in **"a dog bit Fred"** this rule creates an object representation, say **obj_6**, and predicates it with **"dog"**, which projects onto **dog** to yield the representations **obj_6 is dog** and **obj_6 "bit Fred"**. The rule for definite descriptions fires if the representation of an object already exists that satisfies the description. In this case, that object simply becomes the projection of the definite noun phrase. For instance, in **"Fred bit the dog"** this rule finds an object representation, **obj_6**, for which **"dog"**, i.e., **dog** is predicated, to yield the representation **"Fred bit" obj_6**. The rule for definites is inadequate, by the way, since it will not distinguish one object satisfying the description from another. A constructive rule tries to model a process in a purely symbolic vocabulary. However, the literature on definite descriptions suggests that the process here is mysterious in the sense of Chapter 1. This means that a complete analysis would probably require dropping down to the connectionist level of description. We will see later that a somewhat more adequate rule is nevertheless available in a partitioned framework.

Interactive Processing with Constructive Rules

One of the advantages of thinking of processing in terms of production rules is that we separate the processing options from the decisions about which options to evoke. If a particular rule fires it produces structures that make it possible for other rules to fire. In this way we proceed through intermediate levels in the direction of the final internal representation. For instance, ***Fred thinks he saw the unicorn in his garden*** could pass through the following intermediate and final forms (based on a partitioned representation).

"Fred thinks $(_S$ he saw the unicorn in his garden $)_S$"
sp_0 | "Fred thinks
$(_S$ he saw the unicorn in his garden $)_S$"
sp_0 | Fred_7 "thinks
$(_S$ he saw the unicorn in his garden$)_S$"
sp_0 | Fred_7 believes ⟦sp_10⟧
sp_10 | "he saw the unicorn in his garden"
sp_10 | Fred_7 "saw the unicorn" in garden_4
sp_10 | Fred_7 owns garden-4
sp_10 | Fred_7 saw unicorn_4 in garden_4

The knowledge structures that remain after all constructive rules have applied belong to the internal representation, and are said to be *interned.*

However, processing is not as deterministic as this example suggests. Choices are constantly being made about which way to disambiguate a word or syntactic structure, how one piece of knowledge combines with another, and so on. Even if a particular production rule fires its results may be mistaken. For instance, a decision made at the syntactic level might yield representations at the conceptual level that really don't make much sense. In such cases, it is often necessary to retract the results of firing production rules. Eventually the understander should find a unified analysis that is optimally correct at all levels. A classic example is the processing of the *garden-path* sentence

The horse raced past the barn fell.

which initially gives rise to an analysis with *raced* as the main verb. However, with the realization that this does not make syntactic sense, an analysis with *raced* as a past participle modifying *horse* and with *fell* as the main verb emerges.

Our purpose will not be to establish what kind of computational mechanisms are required to find the set of rules that ultimately result in the correct analysis. Much research has been devoted to such problems in artificial intelligence. But, in any case, it is proper to think of language processing as *interactive* rather than *serial*, with processing occurring at all levels of analysis simultaneously, in effect talking among themselves until this globally coherent analysis is agreed on, producing the final projection for the discourse sentence. For instance, conditions satisfied at one level may trigger actions that produce *candidate* representations at a higher level or actions that *eliminate* candidate representations at a lower level. Computational architectures for language processing designed around this principle include the *blackboard* architecture of *Hearsay-II* (Erman and Lesser 1980), and a variety of neural architectures (e.g., Cottrell and Small 1983).

LINGUISTIC EVIDENCE FOR MENTAL REPRESENTATIONS

Because of the prevalence of knowledge-based processes, a theory of mental representations is an integral part of any adequate theory of language understanding. I wish to underscore four properties directly related to mental representation that we expect to find in a theory of language or of language processing. These are listed in Figure 3.3, which elaborates Figure 1.5 (p. 35).

We have seen the functionality as a critical feature of a theory of mental representation per se, important in a variety of cognitive tasks. We do well to emphasize that functionality is critical in language understanding as well: It is important that internal

(4) Linguistic Evidence
- Functionality
- Proximity
- Discrimination
- Explanation for Constraints

Fig. 3.3. Linguistic evidence for mental representation.

structures exist onto which surface structures can be projected, that is, that the mental representation scheme be expressive enough for natural language. It is also important that the system be able to make the kinds of common-sense inferences that humans do in fact make during discourse understanding.

Proximity entails that the distance between discourse sentences and internal representations is reasonably small, i.e., that the process of projecting surface structures onto internal representations is as simple as possible. *Discrimination* is important because conceptual distinctions found in the internal representation are rarely sufficient to totally disambiguate surface structures or to determine unique projections. The language understanding system therefore requires in such cases that the internal representation provide a *structural* basis for discriminating candidate interpretations for linguistic structures where no conceptual basis is at hand. The ability to explain linguistic constraints has to do with linguistic data, that is, with grammaticality judgements, intuitions about semantic entailment, and so on, exemplified earlier. Since these factors are so important, let's look at each in a little more detail.

Functionality Again

Many processes in understanding work hand-in-hand with general common-sense reasoning. For instance, when viewed independently of pragmatic setting, natural language is highly ambiguous. Yet a basic common-sense understanding of the situations and relations described in natural language discourse can remove much of the ambiguity. For instance, English syntax allows that in the sentence,

I shot the man in the hall with a gun.

either I or the man could have the gun. Reasoning about the specific situation described is likely to identify the more plausible interpretation. In each of the following, the word *Chomsky* refers to a person, a set of books or a theoretical framework.

Chomsky gave a talk on Central America.
Chomsky fills up eight inches on my bookshelf.
Chomsky is finding his way into George's thinking.

Common-sense reasoning is necessary to avoid unfortunate

interpretations, such as that of a talking book or of a person condensed to a eight-inch width and placed on a bookshelf.

Aside from lexical and syntactic disambiguation, processes of common-sense reasoning, sometimes at a very high level of sophistication, are called upon to identify *referents* for linguistic structures, such as definite noun phrases. Consider what must be involved in finding a referent for *the robbery* in

Chris was broke. He got out his pistol. After the robbery, he had lots of money.

A language understander, in order to form a coherent internal representation, must make the inference that Chris planned to commit a robbery. In summary, the ability of the representation to support common-sense inferencing is necessary for successfully projecting surface structures onto internal representations.

Proximity

Proximity is, roughly, the closeness of a model of mental representation to natural language structures. I submit that a fairly direct projection of surface discourse structures onto a given system of mental representation is strong evidence for the appropriateness of that system.

Some examples. Let's consider how two alternative theories of mental representation might internalize the information conveyed in an indefinite description used in a discourse sentence and see what our language understander must do to process the following discourse on the basis of each of these theories of representation.

Fred's dog bit a mailman. He is suing Fred.

The first of our hypothetical theories uses a logic-like representation in which an indefinite description is projected onto a structure including a variable bound by an indefinite quantifier. Accordingly the first sentence of the example discourse, will be projected onto something like

$$\exists x\ (\text{bite}(\text{Fido}, x)\ \&\ \text{mailman}(x))$$

where **Fido** is a constant assigned to Fred's dog (presuming something like **dog(Fido)** and **owns(Fred, Fido)** is already represented).

The second, alternative, theory about the internal representation of indefinite descriptions simply uses a unique constant created to refer to the object being described (in logic, this would be called a *Skolem constant*). Accordingly the first sentence of our example discourse is projected onto something like

bite(Fido, obj_4) & mailman(obj_4)

where **obj_4** is a newly generated constant with no previous occurrences in the knowledge base.

The difference in the proximity provided in the two alternative theories of mental representation becomes very evident when the second sentence of the discourse is interpreted. In the first theory, the representation just assimilated into the knowledge base must be *restructured* in order to allow the intended meaning of the second sentence to be represented fully. The representation resulting after the second sentence is processed would be something like

∃x (bite(Fido, x) & mailman(x) & sue(x, Fred))

In the second theory, on the other hand, the projection of the first sentence would remain fully intact. The representation resulting after the second sentence is processed would be something like

bite(Fido, obj_4) & mailman(obj_4)
sue(obj_4, Fred)

We see that the projection from surface structure to internal representation is more proximate for the second theory. First, a simple discrete representation is constructed for each simple sentence. Second, little or no restructuring of existing knowledge is required when new knowledge is assimilated. Finally, projections are easy to compute: Observe that a uniform interpretive rule can be attributed to the word *he* in the second theory, but not in the first. In the first theory *he* must sometimes be projected onto an existing constant, as when *he* is used to refer to Fred, but must at other times condition the embedding of a larger representation into the scope of an existing existential quantifier, as in the example here. In the second theory, on the other hand, *he* is consistently projected onto an existing constant described as a male. We conclude that the concerns of proximity in language understanding provide much better motivation for the second theory of mental representation. The second theory provides a more *natural* basis for language understanding than the first.

Of course, illustrating the relative proximity of one logic-based representation over another is not a blanket endorsement of the more proximate representation. A more realistic example would be the proximity afforded by scripts (see Chapter 1) in interpreting a discourse like the following.

Fred staggered into the doctor's office. The receptionist asked him if he had an appointment.

Script theory makes the representation of a receptionist immediately accessible, even though he or she has not yet been explicitly mentioned in the discourse. A traditional logic-based representation would require a lot of work to identify what receptionist is being referred to. The relative proximity provided by script theory in this case is a strong argument in favor of that theory.

Motivation for proximity. Why should proximity between surface structures and their projections count as evidence for a theory of language understanding and its associated theory of mental representation?

Actually proximity is a special case of the functional criterion of efficiency used to motivate mental representations. Although we have no clear a priori expectation of *how* proximate surface structures and internal representations should be, we know that language is a sophisticated and finely tuned tool, one which we would expect, like other tools, to optimize efficiency and at the same time to be as easy to learn as possible. A reduction of proximity would tend to entail a decrease both in computational efficiency and learnability.*

Historical forces also reinforce proximity. Martinet (1962) in his linguistic theory of *functionality* describes the tendency of languages to adapt to external changes in a way that ensures efficiency (for instance, as a new concept like *video cassette recorder* becomes more common, a shorter surface expression, like *VCR* will be adopted to refer to the concept). Grice (1975) in his theory of cooperative behavior in conversation describes how speakers deliberately choose

* Keep in mind, of course, that maximal proximity, whereby the surface expressions of language are identical to the internal representations, would be impossible, largely due to the differences in media and durability of the two kinds of structures.

linguistic expressions to maximize communicative efficiency, avoiding, for instance, excess processing on the part of the hearer. Structures that are difficult to process would accordingly fall into disuse. Therefore, a theory in which the distance between surface structure and internal representation is excessive must be suspect, because it would leave unexplained why the the language tolerates the associated additional computational effort, why speakers do not avoid the expressions that most violate the concerns of proximity and why the language has not evolved to remove the excess distance.

Discrimination

Surface forms underdetermine their projections. The greatest problems in language understanding very often involve reducing the ambiguity and vagueness permitted in surface structures. *What* is already represented often is not a sufficient basis for making these choices. *How* things are represented must be taken into account. Two alternative schemes of mental representation might be able to represent exactly the same knowledge faithfully, yet because of alternative means of structuring that knowledge, one might have a nonconceptual basis for making discriminations necessary to language understanding that the other cannot. Discrimination might be considered just a critical form of proximity. It is often the case that a model of representation provides *no* principled and correct way to compute a projection for a surface expression. In this case the lack of proximity proves fatal.

For example, a definite description like *the book* should project onto a unique book in the internal representation, distinguished from all other books. Yet many objects might be represented internally, each of which satisfies the description *book*. The model of representation must therefore support a procedure that distinguishes, at least in a particular pragmatic setting, a unique object from all other objects in the knowledge base that might match the description *book* on other than conceptual grounds.

Discrimination in such cases is a primary motivation for the *associative network* (discussed above), in which different representations of books might be distinguished in a given pragmatic setting in terms of varying levels of *activation* (Sidner 1983, Grosz 1981).

Essentially, in a given discourse setting certain regions of a associative network will be activated. These will be the representations of concepts recently accessed or closely associated with those concepts. These regions form a *focus of attention* which distinguished likely referents and interpretations from unlikely. For instance, the first sentence in

> *Warren has trouble drinking without slurping. So, he decided to try using a straw.*

brings **Warren** into the focus of attention. This makes **Warren** a prime candidate for the referent of *he* in the second sentence, which otherwise could refer to any of a multitude of male entities. It seems to be the case that discrimination is mysterious in the sense of Chapter 1. I suspect, therefore, that discrimination may be particularly useful in motivating theories at a connectionist level.

Linguistic Constraints

The example of the observed Complex Noun Phrase Constraint on relative clauses discussed above illustrates how cognitive factors result in linguistic constraints. There is not much previous work that shows how the underlying structures of mental representation are reflected in linguistic structure. This will be a major contribution of this book.

In summary, the contribution of a theory of representation to a model of language understanding is found in its *functionality* in providing expressive richness and in supporting common-sense reasoning, in its *proximity* to surface expressions, in the non-conceptual *discriminations* it makes and in their ability to explain linguistic constraints. We will see that the constraints found in surface discourse structures themselves actually reflect the ways in which these structures are projected onto mental representations in language understanding and the structure of mental representations onto which they are projected.

CHAPTER FOUR

Three Levels of Language Processing

The *three-level theory* of language processing is almost a direct consequence of the theory of partitioned representations. It makes three basic claims:

(1) In discourse understanding communicated information is distributed over spaces as the internal representation evolves. This means that at various points in language understanding a decision is made that some particular *intermediate structure* (or part thereof) will *project into* some particular space.

(2) There are two kinds of processes responsible for these decisions. One implants an intermediate structure in some space in which further processing can begin. The other distributes an intermediate structure between a parent and a child space. I will call these *contextualization* and *distribution* respectively.

(3) Most linguistic processing is completed with reference to the contents of a particular space. This includes most of the familiar processes. I will call such processes *parochial.*

Contextualization, distribution and parochial processing are the three levels of processing referred to in the title of this chapter. Figure 4.1 illustrates, by way of example, the processing of the sentence *Bif believes that the unicorn ate his cat.*

In the process of *contextualization* the highest level decisions are made about projections into spaces. Contextualization is very underdetermined by surface structures and is therefore particularly dependent on features of the pragmatic setting. In step (a) of the figure the sentence as a whole is contextualized into the space sp_0, perhaps

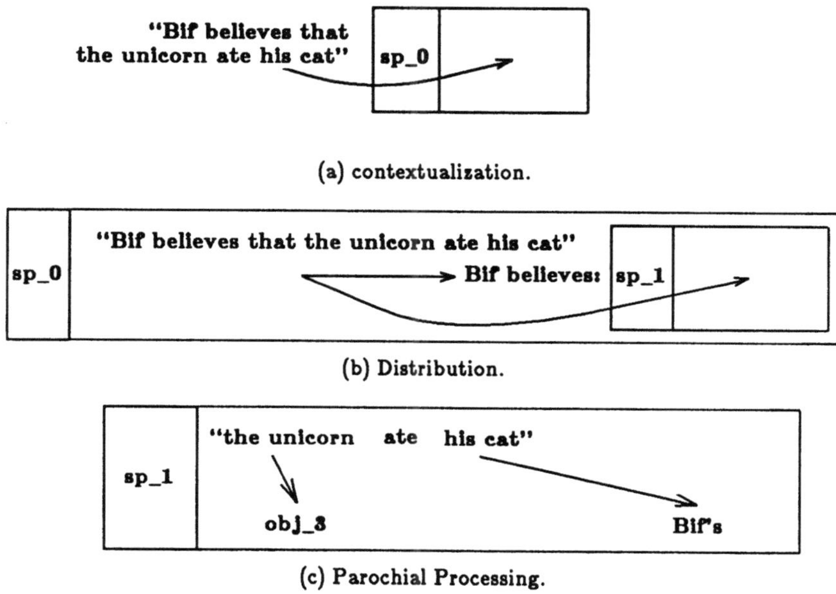

Fig. 4.1. An Example of 3 Processing Stages.

some fiction space. Some additional processing might occur within **sp_0**, for instance the understander might make a decision about which Bif is referred to.

In the process of *distribution* decisions are made about how structures and processing already localized in one space are allocated to additional spaces. In step (b) the understander either locates Bif's belief space, **sp_1**, or creates it, and projects the embedded clause into that space.

In *parochial processing* decisions are made about what representations to project onto, but not about which spaces to project into. In step (c) parochial processing occurs within **sp_1**. This might include additional syntactic processing, but will have to include finding a projection for *the unicorn* and *his*.

Contextualization and distribution are unique to partitioning models; they only make sense in terms of partitioned representations.

Although each makes decisions about projections into spaces, they work very differently, and must accordingly be distinguished in our theory. The third, we will see, includes the kinds of processes discussed in many systems based on non-partitioned representations. However, their domain of operation is generally localized to a particular space, in which all of the representations relevant to their success can generally be found. For this reason I call them parochial.

I should stress that what I present here is a *partial* theory of language understanding, one that focuses on the role of multiple spaces in language understanding. Many interesting properties result from the interaction of other processes, some of which are subtle and complex in themselves. All of the processes that will be mentioned are well motivated and discusses in the literature. Just as extensions of the theory of mental representation are achieved primarily by developing parochial representations within spaces, extensions of the three-level model of language processing are achieved primarily by specifying the nature of parochial processing.

Among the claims made about the theory of language understanding based on partitioned representations are the following: First, it promotes a very *proximate* projection from surface discourse sentence to internal representation. Second, it supports *functional* representation, reasoning and retrieval over that internal representation. Third, it makes many *discriminations* required for successful understanding that are not available in non-partitioning models. Finally, it underlies a uniform account of an extremely diverse variety of *linguistic constraints* in terms of a small set of general principles.

Let's look at each of the parts of the theory—contextualization, distribution and parochial processing—in more detail.

PAROCHIAL PROCESSING

Once projected into a particular space, intermediate structures can be further processed such that information given in the space provides the preconditions that direct the processing, and the processing builds internal representations within that space. Such parochial processes include integrating new information with existing internal representations, determining referents for definite descriptions, satisfying the presuppositions of certain grammatical constructions, disambiguating lexically and syntactically ambiguous structure, and computing metonymous and metaphorical interpretations. Parochial processing works hand-in-hand with parochial reasoning, which, as we saw in Chapter 2, effectively performs many of the common-sense inferences that are necessary in making sense of discourse. For the most part, parochial processes occur internally in spaces, but, as we will see, may spill over the boundaries of spaces when certain associations arise between the objects and relations in separate spaces.

Parochial processes are for the most part familiar processes that have been studied by other researchers independently of the theory of partitioned representations. For instance, in Chapter 3 we looked at a way of modeling the interpretation of indefinite and definite descriptions using constructive rules. The same rules are adapted as parochial rules in partitioned representations by tagging the sentences with a common space variable, to give:

Conditions: S | X "($_{NP}$ a D)$_{NP}$" Y

Actions: create an object, W
S | W is "D"
S | X W Y

Conditions: S | X "($_{NP}$ the D)$_{NP}$" Y
? S | U is "D"

Actions: S | X U Y

The second rule, for instance, makes a query ? S | U is "D" to the existing knowledge base to see if the existence of an object U is represented explicitly or can be inferred. This rule locates an object *in the local space* that satisfies the definite description "D" and posts the assertion about that object in the local space.

Although familiar from non-partitioning frameworks, parochial processes assume a different character in the partitioning framework, for three reasons. First, the partitioned representations serve to constrain parochial processes to the very restricted domains delimited by spaces. For instance, the projection of *the unicorn* is probably easy to compute for the sentence *Fred thinks he saw the unicorn in his garden* because it is projected into a specific space, Fred's belief space, where probably not many unicorns are situated. In this case, the partitioning model plays a *discriminatory* role.

Second, in addition to this discriminating function, the partitioned representations serve to *consolidate* all of the information relevant to the success of the parochial processes together in a common space. Continuing the example above, Fred's belief space might accumulate all the knowledge about Fred's beliefs conveyed over time to ensure that the representation of a unicorn can be located when needed in order to interpret the definite description *the unicorn.* The result is that the partitioning model improves the *proximity* of a surface structure to its internal representation.

Third, partitioned representations allow the representations over which the parochial processes operate to assume forms different from those found in non-partitioning models. For instance, a projection can be found for *the unicorn* in *Fred thinks he saw the unicorn into his garden* without providing special rules or conditions that refer to *intensional objects* or that depend on particular *semantic scopes* to account for the irreality of the unicorn. We simply look for the unicorn situated in the space into which *the unicorn* is projected. In this sense, the partitioning model is providing both discrimination and proximity to simplify the understanding of definite descriptions.

Also we find that parochial processing interacts with distribution in some interesting and telling ways, ways that have important consequences for linguistic structure. We will explore these in Part Two, but first, let's look more closely at distribution.

DISTRIBUTION

Instead, once projected into a space a part of an intermediate representation may be projected into a child space. A new space and its associated context needs to be set up, or an existing context needs to be used to access an old space. A representation or intermediate structure is then built in this space. Distribution is conditioned, for the most part, by the occurrence of certain morphemes and syntactic constructions that Fauconnier (1985) calls *space builders*, such as *Fred believes that ..., In 1929, ..., If clams have eyes then ....* Johnson-Laird (1983) and Kamp (1980) also describe a similar process of constructing space-like structures in language understanding.

Distribution builds up spaces according to the principles of *coherence* and *consolidation* discussed in Chapter 2. For instance, the space builder *possibly* will condition the construction of a new possibility space that inherits from its parent. The space builder *believes* will condition the projection of the sentential complement into an old belief space, if the appropriate old belief space already exists, or the construction of a new belief space if one does not already exist.

The following production rule describes how an intermediate structure expressing possibility might be distributed over two spaces. A new space with a primary context and an inheritance context is set up and the object of the possibility projected into that space.

Conditions: **S0 | "it is possible that" P**

Actions: **create a new space, S1**
S0 | it is possible that ⟦S1⟧
S1 | [S0]
S1 | P

Thus, the sentence

It is possible that Hamlet actually saw his father

contextualized into the fiction space **sp_1** might ultimately project onto the internal representation

sp_1 | it is possible that ⟦sp_2⟧
sp_2 | [sp_1]
sp_2 | Hamlet saw Hamlet's father

The following two production rules describe how an intermediate structure expressing belief might be distributed over two spaces. A new space with a primary context is set up *if* no such belief space already exists. If one does exist, then it is used.

Conditions: **S0 | X "believes" P**
? **S0 | X believes that ⟦S1⟧**

Actions: **S1 | P**

Conditions: **S0 | X "believes" P**

Actions: **create a space, S1**
S0 | X believes that ⟦S1⟧
S1 | P

Recall that the ? in the first rule marks a *precondition* that must be satisfied for the rule to fire. It is assumed that the first rule is given priority to ensure consolidation. Thus, the following two sentences in sequence,

Hamlet believes his father is a ghost.
Hamlet believes his uncle is a murderer.

might result in the following internal representation:

sp_1 | Hamlet believes that ⟦sp_3⟧
sp_3 | Hamlet's father is a ghost.
sp_3 | Hamlet's uncle is a murderer.

If the precondition fails for the first sentence, the space **sp_3** with its context **sp_1 | Hamlet believes that ⟦sp_3⟧** will be created. In any case, the precondition must be satisfied for the second sentence, ensuring projection into the existing **sp_3**. This achieves consolidation for *believes.*

Distribution tends to be fairly deterministic in comparison with contextualization. For instance, every occurrence of the word *believes* in a discourse sentence is likely to trigger distribution. Whether distribution occurs or what direction it assumes may depend on the direction of lexical or syntactic disambiguation or on the projection of referring expressions. For instance, *feels* in the discourse sentence *Fred feels that, too* might project ambiguously onto the concept **believes** or onto the concept **senses**. Only in the first case will it function as a space builder. If it is a space builder, the name *Fred* must be projected onto the representation of a particular person before the context can be successfully created in distribution.

Some additional examples and discussion of distribution are provided in Part Two.

CONTEXTUALIZATION

A parochial or distributive process assumes that an intermediate structure has been projected into a space in which an internal representation is still to be completed (in the case of distribution the representation will involve the further embedding of a space). Contextualization, on the other hand, determines in which space to begin the construction. For a discourse sentence like

Watson was reading the newspaper.

contextualization determines the space, that the sentence as a whole is intended to say something about. In this case, the sentence probably says something about a particular situational space embedded within a fictional space. However, depending on the pragmatic setting, it might be interpreted as saying something about a situational space within the real world, or even within Bif's belief space. The space that a discourse sentence as a whole is intended to say something about, that is, the space into which the sentence is contextualized, is known as the *focus space* for the sentence.

Johnson-Laird (1983) in describing language processing in his theory of mental models touches on a simple case of contextualization when he describes a circumstance under which a new model might be created: that in which new objects are mentioned in the discourse. Each discourse sentence should refer (possibly implicitly) to objects already introduced into the current model in previous discourse in order that a coherent integrated model be developed. If this condition fails, then a new model must be introduced. For instance, the speaker might have begun a fictional narration and might no longer be talking about the real world. Fauconnier (1985) describes an example of what I am calling contextualization in the sequence

I wish Lucky had won. I would be rich.

Here the first sentence sets up a wish space, and the second makes an assertion relative to that wish space. For Fauconnier, the conditional mood, *would*, helps indicate the shift, as do tenses. Roberts (1986) identifies a similar process within the theory of discourse representations. She calls the process *modal subordination.*

Apparently the focus space can be identified on the basis of a variety of factors, both pragmatic and grammatical. These include the following:

- The current *activation* of various spaces. Spaces are *active* to a degree dependent on how recently or how often they have been used in recent discourse processing or on how closely they are associated with spaces that have been recently used.
- The grammatical *space cues* that occur in the discourse. *Space cues* are generally, in English anyway, verb forms, like the past tense or the conditional mood, and certain adverbials, like *once upon a time*, that restrict the set of focus space candidates for contextualization.
- The potential *communicative function* of the current discourse sentence in various spaces. Communicative function has to do with the broader role of language in effective and cooperative communication. The projection of a discourse sentence into a space is generally communicatively functional if the pragmatic preconditions for its successful interpretation are satisfied there, if the objects it mentions are situated there, if it does not conflict with knowledge that is already given there and if it says something relevant about that space. For instance, the focus space in the Watson sentence might be readily identified as a fictional *Sherlock Holmes* space if an object named *Watson* is situated only there.

I will return to these factors influencing contextualization below.

The contextualization process supplies, though the primary context of the focus space, a lot of information that is only implicit in natural language discourse, but that is essential in the construction of a complete internal representation of the semantic intent. Notice that the full intent of the Watson sentence, which must include its fictional basis, is *only* realized after contextualization. Contextualization supports proximity in opening up a generally elaborate context (including possibly many levels of embedding) to meet the relatively simple incoming sentence half-way, or more likely better than half-way.

Contextualization and Recontextualization

Contextualization is a process that applies generally to a discourse sentence *as a whole* in order to begin constructing an internal representation. To a large extent, the space into which an *embedded sentence* is projected is determined through distribution by the syntactic environment in which it is embedded. Thus,

> *Bif believes that the Big Bang theory is correct.*

is projected into some space by contextualization, whereupon

> *The Big Bang theory is correct.*

is projected fairly deterministically in response to the space builder *believes* into another space (Bif's belief space) by distribution. Nevertheless, contextualization continues to play a role in the projections of embedded sentences as well as whole sentences. For instance, in

> *If Fred had broken his arm, he would be in the hospital. Bif believes that Fred would sue.*

Fred would sue is projected not strictly into Bif's belief space, but into a *what if Fred had broken his arm* space within Bif's belief space. Similar observations can be made about the following, in which *he would have become more popular* is projected into a counterfactual space within a positional (*in France*) space and *Sherlock was a homosexual* is projected into a fictional space within Bif's belief space.

> *In Sweden, the president would have resigned, while in France he would have become more popular.*

> *Bif believes that Sherlock was a homosexual.*

Recontextualization is this process I have exemplified, that locating the space into which an *embedded* sentence is projected. Recontextualization is similar to contextualization, but is much more narrowly constrained. In particular, the examples above suggest that the *parent* of the recipient space is identified prior to recontextualization by grammatical means (distribution) but the specific space into which the embedded sentence is projected during recontextualization is identified only as some space embedded in that parent space.

Tracking the Focus Space

The most difficult aspect of contextualization to get a handle on is tracking the focus space as it shifts during discourse. Like many processes in language understanding, tracking the focus space seems to involve a wide range of poorly understood factors.

As we have seen it seems to be generally the case that the focus space is a space:

- that is *active*,
- that is consistent with the *space cues* of the current discourse sentence, and
- in which the discourse sentence is *communicatively functional.*

We will look at these factors a little more closely.

Activation. I submit that spaces are *active* to a degree generally dependent on how recently or how often they have been used in recent discourse processing, or, for that matter, in other types of cognitive processes. Spaces thus become more active as they are created and/or referenced during distribution. One would expect that a space representing the *current speech situation*, independently of what is actually communicated, would always maintain a certain degree of activation. Also, the activation of one space may spread to associated spaces.

We observe a tendency to return to a previous focus space, or to use the same focus space in successive contextualizations. For instance, we find this in the following.

> *At 12 o'clock, Bif was munching lunch. He was dressed in a tasteful hawaiian shirt with flowers and palm trees. He also wore plaid shorts and was listening to the news. He was about to go out on one of the hottest of dates.*

Here each sentence in succession is contextualized into a common situational space. Let's call this tendency to maintain the existing focus space *inertia.*

Another typical pattern is for a new space to be created in processing one sentence that serves as a focus space for another shortly thereafter, as in the following.

> *If Little Freddy would clean his room everybody would be much happier. I, for one, would be very pleased.*

Here the first sentence is projected into a focus space in which a context is constructed for a new conditional space. The new space then serves as the focus space of the second sentence. Let's call this the *construct and then contextualize* pattern.

Probably related to activation is the tendency for a series of spaces to form a *trajectory*. For instance, a common type of trajectory is through a temporally ordered set of temporal spaces. In the following, each sentence is contextualized into a separate focus space, but the time of one focus space is slightly later than the time of the previous focus space.

> *The Lone Ranger pulled out his gun. He aimed. He fired. Tonto fell down dead. Tonto could no longer insult Trigger.*

Here the first sentence is projected into one temporal space, the second into a slightly later temporal space and so on.

Activation of spaces is almost certainly not a unique phenomenon. We find similar processes in focus of attention and semantic priming, which *associative networks* are used for modeling, as discussed in Chapter 1. Spreading activation and associations are characteristic of connectionist models, also as discussed in Chapter 1. Finally, *pragmatic functions*, to be discussed in Chapter 5, which play a role in metonymy, can be viewed as associative relations that allow activation to be passed from one concept, identified at one stage of processing as a likely candidate projection, to another concept. Therefore, it is not surprising to find similar processes of activation involved in contextualization.

Space cues. Space cues are inflectional morphemes and other syntactic structures occurring in discourse sentences that explicitly restrict the set of spaces into which the sentence can be projected. Space cues are generally verb forms, like the past tense or the conditional verb form, and certain adverbials, like *once upon a time*.

For instance, a sentence using the conditional verb form (*would*) consistently projects into a counterfactual space, i.e., one with a primary context of the form **S0 | P □→ ⟦S1⟧**. The following sentence,

> *The senator would offer a rebuttal.*

might be projected into a space like **sp_1**, with the context

> **sp_0 | the senator is awake □→ ⟦sp_1⟧**

This will yield the observed semantic intent that if the senator were

awake the senator would offer a rebuttal.*

I will consider more examples of the role of space cues in contextualization momentarily.

Communicative function. **Ultimately, the current intermediate structure should be meaningful in the focus space. First, it should be *interpretable*. That is, all preconditions necessary for interpretation should be satisfied in the focus space and its projection should be minimally ambiguous. Second, it should be *relevant* to the content of the focus space. That is, it should say something that leads to useful inferences about the content of the focus space. Third, it should make sense conceptually. That is, it should be *plausible* given what is already known about the focus space.**

For instance, the sentence

The man of steel can fly around the world in less than a minute.

will be contextualized into a fiction space but hardly into a space representing the real world, or into a temporal space representing a real situation, or into a normal belief space embedded in such a reality space. In none of these latter spaces will a projection for *the man of steel* be found. Nor is the predication made about the man of steel plausible for any person situated in any of these spaces. In any of these spaces, the sentence is not fully interpretable, and, to the extent that it is interpretable, it is not plausible. This helps direct the contextualization process to the fiction space.

What I call *communicative function* has to do with *cooperative principles* of human interaction finding application in discourse, as Grice (1975) describes. These principles require that what is communicated is truthful, easy to interpret, informative for the hearer, and

---

*** It should be mentioned that space cues actually restrict projection during distribution as well as during contextualization. For instance, observe that the consequent of a counterfactual *if* sentence also uses the conditional verb form. So does the sentential complement of *wish*, as in:**

Fred wishes his dog were a cat.

Recall from Chapter 2 that this sentence would project onto something like

sp_1 | Fred believes that [sp_2]
sp_2 | Fred's dog is a cat □→ [sp_3]
sp_3 | Fred's dog is a cat
sp_3 | Fred is fortunate

relevant to the goals of the discourse. These principles have been widely studied, aside from in the philosophy of language, in linguistics (e.g., Cole and Morgan 1975), and in artificial intelligence (e.g., Cohen and Perrault 1979).

In the theory of partitioned representations I assume that these principles are relevant to what is communicated about the contents of spaces. Since spaces function to model individual coherent "realities," it is at this level that judgements of truthfulness, informativeness, relevance and plausibility are most effectively realized. In contextualization these judgements are directed toward candidate focus spaces. The violation of cooperative principles forces the choice of an alternative focus space. Let's look at some examples that highlight particular components of communicative function.

Communicative function: interpretability. The focus space in a sentence that mentions *Sherlock Holmes* is likely to be identified as fictional since Sherlock Holmes is generally known not to exist in reality. Similarly,

The horse is an herbivore.

requires that a unique horse be identified in the focus space. If no more appropriate candidate focus space is suggested for other means, the space **sp_3** such that

sp_0 | For any horse obj_8: ⟦sp_3⟧

will work, since we have

sp_3 | • obj_8
sp_3 | • obj_8 is a horse

Hence, the *generic reading* of *the horse.*

Communicative function: plausibility. The effects of plausibility in the choice of focus space can be demonstrated in a discourse in which Bif describes himself as watching a cowboy movie starring Clint Eastwood, while he is accompanied by Clint Eastwood himself, who happens to be Bif's friend. In this case, the focus space could well switch back and forth between **sp_4**, representing the *real* situation in the theater, and **sp_5**, the *fictional* situation depicted in the movie, since both spaces certainly enjoy a certain level of activation. Because of the *identity principle*, to be discussed in Chapter 5, *Clint Eastwood* might refer to one object, the actor, when **sp_4** is in focus, and to another object, the cow poke, when **sp_5** is in focus, so interpretability is not an issue. In the course of the discourse each of these sentences might occur.

Clint spilled his popcorn.
Clint got on his horse.

The first of these sentences will almost certainly project into **sp_4**. The reason is that Clint Eastwood's spilling popcorn is *plausible* in **sp_4** but not in **sp_5**. On the other hand, the second of these sentences will almost certainly project into **sp_5**. Clint Eastwood is not likely to have a horse in the movie theater.

Communicative function: relevance. Another sentence that might occur in Bif's movie discourse is the following.

Clint hadn't reloaded his gun.

The satisfaction of this sentence could be entirely plausible in either **sp_4** or **sp_5** (Clint might have a gun at home and might have failed to reload it before he met Bif to go to the movie). However, this sentence is much more likely to be projected into **sp_5**, the fictional space, because it is relevant to what we know about **sp_5** but, in the absence of some special circumstances, such as an earlier assassination attempt on the mayor of Carmel, it is not relevant to watching a movie.

When all else fails. The alert reader may have recognized that the role of communicative function in identifying focus spaces entails that at least some parochial processing must occur within candidate focus spaces *before* the contextualization process can be completed. This is another clear instance of the need for an *interactive* model of language processing as described in Chapter 3. In effect, it may be necessary to test the communicative consequences of contextualization into each of several candidate focus spaces before the intended focus space is identified.

If no space can be located which is consistent with the space cues, and in which the content of the sentence is reasonably communicatively functional, a new space might on occasion actually be *created* that satisfies these deficiencies. For instance, the following sentence might be used in the absence of an active counterfactual space in which the sentence will make sense or be relevant.

A president who cared about people would be a welcome change.

In this case, a new counterfactual space would probably be constructed. Its primary context would be one that makes the content plausible, for instance,

sp_0 | a president cares about people □→ ⟦sp_2⟧

Roberts (1987) points out a similar discourse.

A wolf might walk into the house. It would eat you first.

The first sentence sets up a possibility space, say **sp_4**. The second cannot be contextualized into **sp_4**. This would fail to entail that if a wolf were to walk into the house it would eat you first. Rather it must be contextualized into a space **sp_5** with a context something like **sp_0 | a wolf walks into the house □→ ⟦sp_5⟧**. Roberts independently calls the normal construct and contextualize pattern of contextualization the *insertion approach* to modal subordination, and the construction of a new space the *accommodation of the missing antecedent approach.*

AN EXAMPLE DISCOURSE

To get a better idea of how contextualization, distribution, and parochial processes work together to yield a proximate, semantically complete, partitioned internal representation of complex discourse structures, let's look at how the story of Figure 4.2. is processed in the proposed theory. It will be observed that this story appears rather

Once upon a time, there was a tailor named Siegfried.

Siegfried had once consulted a famous wizard. The wizard mistakenly thought Siegfried was an alcoholic. Still, if Siegfried would work hard, he would be very successful. The wizard assumed that anyone who was rich was happy. Well, Siegfried would be rich, and would even stop drinking.

Now the tailor Siegfried did work hard and had in fact become rich. But he was not happy, and he had actually become an alcoholic.

Figure 4.2. The Siegfried story.

contrived. Nevertheless it manages to illustrate most aspects of the three-level model in a minimal amount of space.

Processing the Siegfried story will build the context structure shown in Figure 4.3 and build up contents of the spaces shown in Figure 4.4. Before considering the process of understanding itself, we observe the advantages of this internal representation over alternative representations. First, knowledge conveyed in the discourse is consolidated in this internal representation into coherent spaces, each of which supports parochial reasoning processes that optimize commonsense inferencing. Second, the full semantic intent of the discourse is realized (sp_0 will have a context, omitted in Figure 4.3, to tell us that we are dealing with a fiction).

For each sentence in turn we will consider what interesting things happen at each of the levels of contextualization, distribution and parochial processing to produce this internal representation in an accurate and proximate way.

(1) ***Once upon a time, there was a tailor named Siegfried.***

Contextualization. In order to contextualize this sentence a fiction space sp_0 must be set up, as well as a new temporal space sp_1 within that fiction space. The adverbial ***once upon a time,*** **is a cue to set up this configuration of spaces. This results in the contexts**

base | in the Siegfried story: ⟦sp_0⟧

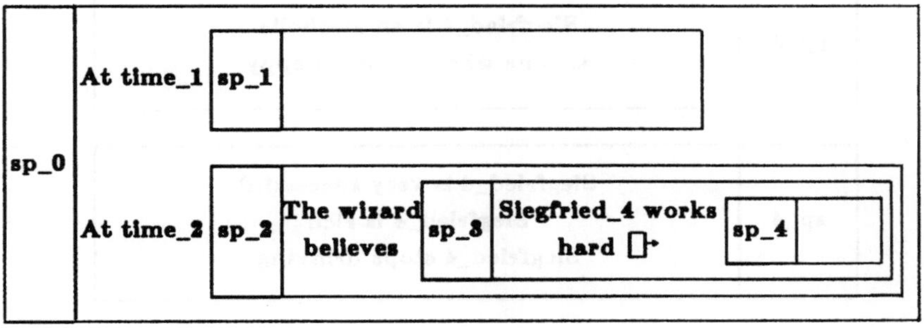

Fig. 4.3. The contexts used in representing the Siegfried story.

sp_0 | At time_1: ⟦sp_1⟧

sp_0 is defined to represent the entire contents of the fictional story. sp_1 represents the situation at time_1 a time within the fiction in which there is a tailor named Siegfried. We will see, by the end of the story, that at time_1 Siegfried is represented as a rich, hard-working, but unhappy and alcoholic tailor. sp_1 now serves as the focus space into which the sentence is projected to produce the intermediate structure

sp_1 | "there is a tailor named Siegfried"

This is the only case in this story where a focus space does not exist prior to the processing of a sentence to receive the contents of that sentence.

sp_1	there is a tailor named Siegfried Siegfried_4 works hard Siegfried_4 has become rich Siegfried_4 is not happy Siegfried_4 has become an alcoholic
sp_2	Siegfried_4 consults a famous wizard
sp_3	Siegfried_4 is an alcoholic anyone who is rich is happy
sp_4	Siegfried_4 is very successful Siegfried_4 is rich Siegfried_4 stops drinking

Fig. 4.4. Contents of Spaces in the Siegfried story.

Distribution. Aside from the spaces necessary for contextualization, no new spaces are created and no old spaces are accessed.

Parochial Processing. Within **sp_1** some simple assimilation of the intermediate structure takes place. For instance, a new object **Siegfried_4** will be situated and then some predications made about that object, giving us the internal representations

sp_1 | • Siegfried_4
sp_1 | Siegfried_4 is named "Siegfried"
sp_1 | Siegfried_4 is tailor

(2) *Siegfried had once consulted a famous wizard.*

Contextualization. The focus space stays fixed at **sp_1**. This illustrates the importance of *activation*, in fact of *inertia*, the tendency to stay with the same focus space unless directed otherwise. As we proceed with the Siegfried story we will see that the focus space for every sentence starting at this point is a space used or created shortly before the the current sentence was processed.

Distribution. The construction of its internal representation involves creating another temporal space **sp_2** with the context

sp_1 | it has occurred that ⟦sp_2⟧

and the intermediate structure

sp_2 | "Siegfried consults a famous wizard"

is created. The creation of **sp_2** is in response to the use of the perfect *had*, which we will look at in Chapter 8. **sp_2** is actually another *temporal/situational* space embedded within the fiction space **sp_0**, as shown by the secondary context

sp_0 | at time time_2: [sp_2].
sp_0 | time_2 < time_1

time_2 represents the time at which Siegfried visits a wizard and at which, as we find out by the end of the story, the wizard has the various beliefs mentioned.

Parochial Processing. Within **sp_2** the existence of Siegfried must be asserted, and a representation for the wizard created.

sp_2 | • Siegfried_4

sp_2 | • wizard_8
sp_2 | wizard_8 is a wizard
sp_2 | Siegfried_4 consults wizard_8

Some disambiguation may occur for the word *consult* (consulting a person is different than consulting a book). Also some parochial inferences, such as that Siegfried and the wizard talked to one another, might occur.

(3) *The wizard mistakenly thought Siegfried was an alcoholic.*

Contextualization. At this point **sp_1** and the newly created **sp_2** are active. However, *the wizard* is *interpretable* in **sp_2** but not in **sp_1**, since

sp_2 | wizard-8 is a wizard

is given. Therefore, the focus space shifts to **sp_2**. This, we have seen, is the common pattern, *construct then contextualize.*

Distribution. Understanding this sentence involves creating a belief space, **sp_3**, for **wizard_8**, and embedding it within the temporal/situational space **sp_2**. This represents the wizard's set of beliefs at **time_2**.

sp_2 | "the wizard" believes that ⟦sp_3⟧.
sp_3 | "Siegfried is an alcoholic"

Parochial Processing. Within **sp_2** a referent for definite description *the wizard* must be found, that is a constant X satisfying the description

sp_2 | X is a wizard

Notice that a unique referent is immediately available even if other wizards, perhaps characters in other stories like Merlin in the story of King Arthur, are already represented in the knowledge base. This exemplifies the role of partitioned representations in *discrimination.* Notice also that finding the referent for *the wizard* must go hand in hand with the identification of the focus space, as described above. This kind of interaction between contextualization and parochial processing will be investigated in Part Two.

(4) *Still, if Siegfried would work hard, he would be very successful.*

Contextualization. The focus space now shifts to sp_3. The adverb *still* acts as a cue for this shift by indicating that the content of the sentence leads to implications that contrast with the existing content of the focus space. Here the contrast is between Siegfried's being an alcoholic and his working hard. No similar contrast can be found in another active space.

Distribution. A *counterfactual* space sp_4 embedded within the wizard's belief space sp_3 is constructed. This represents the hypothesis that Siegfried is working hard, along with all consequences that that hypothesis has in the wizard's belief system. The full representation created is something like

sp_3 | Siegfried_4 works hard □→ ⟦sp_4⟧.
sp_4 | Siegfried_4 works hard
sp_4 | presumably: [sp_3]
sp_4 | he is very successful

Parochial Processing. A referent for *he* must be located, which is found in sp_3, Siegfried_4.

(5) *The wizard assumed that anyone who was rich was happy.*

Contextualization. The focus space for this sentence actually returns to sp_2. This is due to the fact that there is no explicit representation of a wizard in sp_3, and to the fact that this sentence has a content parallel to that of (3) (both are about the wizard's beliefs), which was also contextualized into sp_2.

Distribution. No new space or context needs to be set up. Since, as discussed in the last chapter, belief spaces are unique, the wizard's existing belief space, sp_3 is accessed and the following intermediate statement derived.

sp_3 | "anyone who is rich is happy"

A quantification space for rich people will be set up for this statement and knowledge further distributed, but we will forego discussion of this further processing at this point in order to get on to the next sentence.

Parochial Processing. This is fairly straight-forward.

(6) *Well, Siegfried would be rich, and would even stop drinking.*

Contextualization. The focus space shifts to sp_4. This is conditioned by the space cue *would* which always requires contextualization into a active counterfactual space. Since there is only one counterfactual space, identification of the focus space is unambiguous.

Distribution. No additional spaces or contexts are created.

Parochial Processing. Presumably the conjunction can be eliminated to derive a simpler representation within sp_4.

sp_4 | Siegfried_4 is rich
sp_4 | Siegfried_4 stops drinking

For each of these two statements some instructive additional parochial reasoning and processing can be identified. The following inference could and probably would be made on the basis of the first statement.

sp_4 | Siegfried_4 is happy.

This would be made by first *inheriting* the statement **sp_4 | everybody who is rich is happy** from **sp_3** using the context **sp_4 | presumably: [sp_3]** and by then completing the inference parochially in **sp_4**.

sp_4 | Siegfried_4 stops drinking contains the presuppositional construction **stops** and therefore requires that the statement **sp_4 | Siegfried_4 has drunk** be given as old information (We will look at presupposition in greater detail in Chapter 6). Again, by inheritance from **sp_3** we see that **sp_3 | Siegfried_4 is an alcoholic** is derived, from which the satisfaction of the presupposition follows.

(7) *Now the tailor Siegfried did work hard and had in fact become rich.*

Contextualization. Finally, the focus space returns to the temporal space **sp_1** introduced at the beginning of the story. This is conditioned by the space cue *now* which indicates specifically the return to a temporal space subsequent to the current focus space. *Now* obviously cannot mean "at the present time," since the sentence is in past tense. *the tailor* also helps to condition this shift—again exemplifying the influence of *interpretability*—since there is no explicit representation of Siegfried *as a tailor* in any other active space.

Distribution. The use of the perfect aspectual form conditions the creation of an additional temporal space into which the Siegfried_4 becomes rich is projected. This is analogous to what happens in (2). This space will not be accessed in subsequent discourse.

Parochial Processing. This is straight-forward.

(8) *But he was not happy, and he had actually become an alcoholic.*

Contextualization. The focus space stays fixed at sp_1 by inertia, since there is no reason to change it.

Distribution. Another temporal space is created for representing the perfect aspectual form in *had .. become.*

Parochial Processing. This is straight-forward.

In summary, we get an idea of how contextualization, distribution, and parochial processing work together to project information conveyed in the discourse sentences into spaces, such that the full semantic intent of the discourse is reconstructed, and the information required by knowledge-based processes is both correctly delimited and correctly consolidated in spaces. The result is a discourse representation in which information is appropriately consolidated into small spaces, each of which concretely and coherently represents a possible reality or situation. Parochial reasoning in the individual spaces produces the common-sense inferences needed to fully comprehend the discourse.

CONCLUSIONS

The following claims are made about discourse processing involving such partitioned internal representations: First, the model provides *proximity*. The mapping from surface discourse structure to unambiguous internal representations is relatively simple. One reason for this is that the explicit, that is, grammatically encoded, content of the discourse sentences tends to correspond to the contents of spaces in the internal representations, while much of the implicit content, that is, the remaining parts of the semantic intent, corresponds to the contexts of those spaces. Thus, much of the semantic intent is recovered simply by locating the appropriate spaces as recipients of the explicit discourse content.

Second, this model provides *discrimination*, the structural distinctions in the internal representation that are most critical to language processing. Notice how processes that find referents for definite descriptions are naturally allocated to the small domains in which those referents are likely to be found. Similarly, presuppositions are naturally satisfied simply within the appropriate spaces. In general, this model constrains in appropriate ways each of a variety of semantic processes that have been studied independently of the partitioned representations framework. The underlying assumption here is that these processes operate for the most part parochially *within* spaces.

Third, the partitioned internal representations support very well the types of common-sense inferences that human natural language understanders make so readily. Recalling sentence (6) of the Siegfried story, the reader can determine by way of contrast that the inference **sp_2 | wizard_8 believes that Siegfried_4 works hard □→ Siegfried_4 is happy** would not be easy to derive logically in a system that did not employ something like partitioned representations. This inference would require the use of several complicated meaning postulates about the predicates **in**, **at**, **believe**, and □→ in a rather long derivation. In partitioned representations a one-step parochial inference suffices.

And fourth, this model of language understanding with partitioned representations leads to an explanation of an extremely wide variety of otherwise very puzzling linguistic data.

Part Two of this book will demonstrate these points in detail and explore some of the amazing consequences of the three-level scheme of processing language with partitioned representations.

PART TWO

STUDIES IN LANGUAGE

CHAPTER FIVE

Pedro's Donkey and Oedipus's Mother

In this chapter I undertake to look closer at parochial processing, at distribution, and at the interaction of the two.

Let's assume that we have made the decision to contextualize the discourse sentence

the quarterback wishes his dog were a cat.

into the focus space **sp_0**, perhaps some fictional space. Simply by identifying the focus space we have recovered the outer layer of the full semantic intent of the sentence that the content belongs to a particular fiction. However, to finish processing the sentence we need to build a representation within **sp_0**. This will involve finding existing or inferable projections for *the quarterback* and *his*, but also will involve creating or accessing at least two spaces, a belief space embedded within **sp_0** and a counterfactual space embedded within the belief space. Processes of this last kind, *distribution*, are the primary focus of this chapter, but distribution is best studied in light of how it influences processes of the first kind, *parochial processes.*

SOME COMMON PAROCHIAL LINGUISTIC PROCESSES

Parochial processing is that which affects the contents of a single space, that is without distribution of knowledge over multiple spaces. Parochial rules are recognized by the use of the same space tag for the posted condition and all of the actions of the rule. Most of the examples of parochial processes that I will refer to are generally processes that have been studied in models of representation and language understanding independent of partitioned representations. Some of these processes are the determination of projections for definite descriptions; structural disambiguation; semantic disambiguation; the computation of so-called extensions of meaning, such as metaphorical and metonymous interpretations; model building and common-sense inferencing; and checking to see if presuppositions are appropriately satisfied. Although the existence of these processes does not depend on, and is not explained by, the theory of partitioned representations, they do assume a different character in the partitioning framework, as we will see in more detail below. This is because a parochial process is assigned to a specific space whose very restricted content provides a degree of discrimination unknown in non-partitioning models.

In this section we look at some examples of parochial processes. This is undertaken purely for illustration; except when considering temporal adverbs, no serious new claims are made about the specific mechanisms involved in these processes, nor are old claims defended, although we will assume that they are at least approximately correct. Actually, many of these processes are certainly mysterious in the sense of Chapter 1, probably ultimately requiring a connectionist teatment. Our interest will be mainly to model a general idea of the kinds of results these processes produce, so that we can look at the *interaction* of these processes with the partitioning framework later.

Definite Descriptions

The interpretation of definite descriptions like *the donkey* or pronouns like *it* in discourse processing models generally involves locating an object that already exists (implicitly or explicitly) in the internal representation of the preceding discourse appropriate to the description or gender of the syntactic structure. We can approximate this process with the following simple constructive rule.

(Def)

Conditions: S | X "$(_{NP}$ the D $)_{NP}$" Y
? S | U is "D"

Actions: S | X U Y

This rule locates an object in the local space that satisfies the definite description "D" and posts the assertion about that object in the local space. The rule makes a query **? S | U is "D"** to the existing knowledge base to see if the existence of an object U satisfying the description is represented explicitly or can be inferred. I assume that (Def) can be supplemented in a straight-forward way to account for pronouns as well as noun phrases that begin with *the*. Kamp's (1980) rule for definite descriptions and pronouns is similar to (Def). An example occurs below.

It is normally assumed that the biggest problem in interpreting definite descriptions is not in identifying an object that satisfies the description, but in identifying a *unique* object to satisfy the description. Usually some representation of focus of attention is proposed to provide the necessary discrimination to do this (Grosz 1981, Sidner 1983). Notice, however, that in partitioned representations the spaces themselves tend to provide substantial discrimination, greatly reducing the number of candidate projections: Rather than considering all objects in the knowledge base to satisfy the definite description, this rule takes advantage of the structural properties of partitioned representations to restrict the candidate projections to a small domain, namely a single space. Although the problem of definite descriptions is not so acute in partitioned representations. Nevertheless, I anticipate that partitioned representations do not solve this problem altogether. Accordingly, our rule might not be discriminatory enough, as it stands, and might require an additional precondition that refers to relative focus of attention among all objects satisfying the description within the space **S**.

To see how the rule functions as it stands, suppose **sp_2 | wizard_8 is wizard** is inferable. Then restructuring the intermediate structure,

sp_2 | The wizard has a broom

will first cause U to be set to **wizard_8**. This will cause the following to be posted.

sp_2 | wizard_8 has a broom

Notice that the rule for the is able to find a unique referent as long as there is only one statement matching **sp_2 | U is a wizard**, regardless of how many wizards are represented in the knowledge base in various spaces. The framework of partitioned representations is doing much of the work of eliminating candidate referents by defining a restricted domain of reference.

Indefinite Descriptions

The rule for indefinite descriptions *creates* an object to satisfy the description in a local space.

> **(Indef)**
> **Conditions:** S | X "($_{NP}$ a D)$_{NP}$" Y
>
> **Actions:** create an object, W
> S | W is "D"
> S | X W Y

(Indef) would restructure the statement

> **sp_2 | wizard_8 has a broom**

into something like

> **sp_2 | broom_3 is broom**
> **sp_2 | wizard_8 has broom_3**

(Indef) is equivalent to Kamp's (1980) rule for indefinite descriptions. Kamp describes how (Def) and (Indef) work together in discourse, (Indef) to create a new object representation, which he calls a *discourse referent*, which can then serve later as the anaphoric antecedent mentioned in (Def). For instance, processing

> *Pedro owns a donkey. He beats it.*

would create a single discourse representation which evolves as indicated in Figure 5.1 (which follows the style of Kamp's figures). In processing the first sentence *Pedro* and *a donkey* give rise to the discourse referents u and v respectively in (a). *Pedro* would probably actually refer to someone whose existence is already established, but *a donkey* would trigger something like (Indef) to produce the discourse referent v. In processing the second sentence *he* and *it* are replaced by the existing discourse referents u and v respectively in (b). This is suggested by (Def).

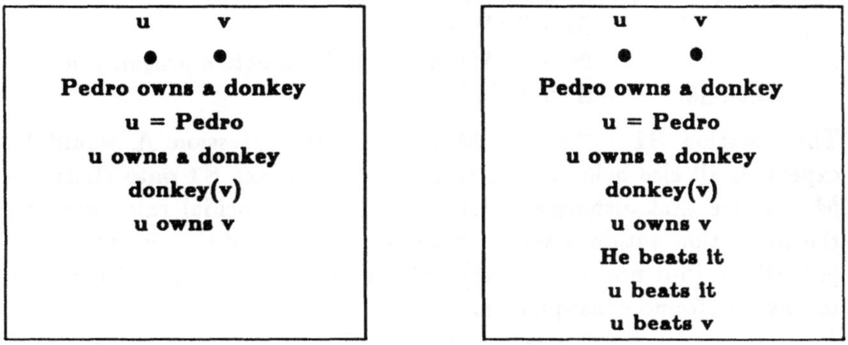

(a) (b)

Fig. 5.1. Evolution of the discourse representation for *Pedro owns a donkey. He beats it.*

Metonymy

Metonymy refers to the common semantic phenomenon of an expression normally standing for some concept A being used to refer to some distinct concept B when some salient relation between A and B is evident in the current discourse state. For instance, *Plato* can generally be used to refer to books by Plato and *the ham sandwich* can be used in a particular discourse about a restaurant to refer to Bif. We see this in the most likely interpretations for the following.

Plato is on the top shelf.
The ham sandwich is a big tipper.

There is a dearth of computational work on metonymy; it is a complex problem that ultimately will demand a solution whether or not a partitioned representations framework is utilized. Nunberg (1978) describes this process linguistically in terms of the concept of *pragmatic function,* a relation between objects that arises in a pragmatic setting under conditions that he attempts to describe. Nunberg posits the *identification principle* that if two objects, A and B, are related by a pragmatic function, call it F, as B = F(A), then a description of A may be used to identify B. We might formalize this in terms of a constructive rule as follows:

(IdentPrinc)
Conditions: S | X "A" Y
? S1 | "A" = M
? N = F(M), ***where* F** ***is an active pragm. funct.***
Actions: S | X N Y

The notation **S1 | "A" = M** means that expression **A** would be expected, all else being equal, to project into space **S1** onto structure **M**. Notice that although **(IdentPrinc)** is a parochial rule, affecting the projection within a single space **S**, this precondition is tagged for potentially (but not necessarily) distinct space **S1**. This will turn out to have profound consequences.

As an example of **(IdentPrinc)**, there is a pragmatic function **book_of** from authors to books by those authors. The following preconditions might affect the projection of the Plato sentence above into **sp_2** in a manner predicted by **(IdentPrinc)**:

sp_1 | "Plato" = Plato_1
books_2 = books_of(Plato).

such that we get the get the intermediate form

sp_2 | books_2 "is on the top shelf"

Notice that **Plato_1** and **books_2** are situated in different spaces, but that *Plato* would be expected to project onto **Plato_1**, all else being equal. This projection must fail if the sentence as whole is not projected into **sp_1**. Likewise, a pragmatic function **orderer_of** from foods ordered in a particular restaurant situation to the customers that ordered the food might become salient in a given pragmatic setting, satisfying the following preconditions:

sp_3 | "the ham sandwich" = ham_sandwich_6
Bif_2 = orderer_of(ham_sandwich_6).

This might induce the ham sandwich sentence above to be projected onto the following intermediate structure in accordance with **(IdentPrinc)**.

sp_3 | Bif_2 is a big tipper

Pragmatic functions are poorly understood. They are not entirely conceptual, but apparently belong to mechanisms of associative memory. They remain mysterious; I am convinced that they have no adequate description in purely symbolic terms. They may become active in one pragmatic setting, irrelevant in another. I do not attempt to describe these mechanisms in any more but suggestive terms, but point out that the ubiquity of metonymy is well recognized in the literature and that much research is devoted to uncovering these mechanisms. Notice that the precondition ? N = F(M) used in (IdentPrinc) is not a query for knowledge content, but a *metaquery* about structural conditions in the representation itself. This reflects the assumption that a structural feature of the representation not predicted by the theory of partitioned representations plays a discriminatory role in determining whether a metonymous interpretation exists.

Metonymy thus actually spills over the boundaries of spaces in that the pragmatic functions can relate objects in distinct spaces as easily as it can relate objects within a single space. This is a key claim in Fauconnier's (1985, 1986a, 1986b) theory of *mental spaces*, where objects in distinct spaces related by a pragmatic function are called *counterparts*. For instance, if Len paints a picture of Mary, then the real-world object Mary will have a counterpart in the image of Mary in Len's picture. Similarly, Mary might have a counterpart in Len's belief space, namely Len's conception of Mary. If Ingrid Bergman plays Golda Meir in a movie, then in one sense the character of Golda Meir in the play is the counterpart of Golda Meir in real life and in another she is the counterpart of Ingrid Bergman in real life. Similarly, a person in a particular temporal space typically has counterparts in other temporal spaces, namely the same person at different ages.

For instance, *Clint Eastwood* can be used to refer to the character played by Clint Eastwood in a particular movie, and *the president* can be used to refer to a child in one temporal space, who turns out to be the president in another temporal space. In this way we derive the most likely interpretations for

In Gone with the Wind, *Clark Gable falls in love with Vivien Leigh.*
In 1920 the president was a child.

Figure 5.2 (in Fauconnier's style of drawing mental spaces) illustrates the representation permitting the normal interpretation for this second sentence.

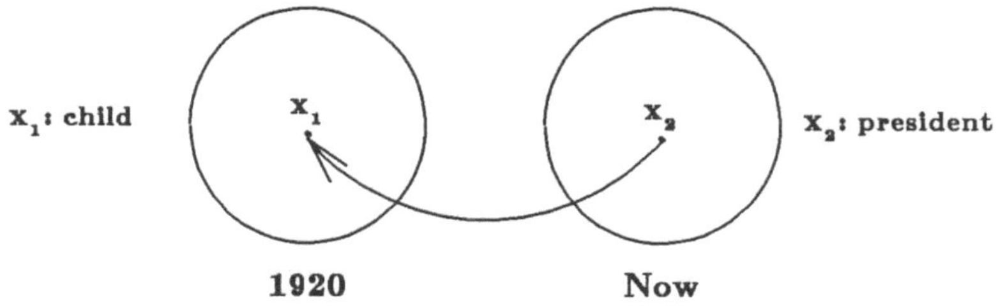

Fig. 5.2. A mental space representation underlying *In 1920 the President was a child.*

The identification principle may or may not be evoked in particular cases. Each of the last two sentences has an interpretation which uses a description that applies directly to the object referenced rather than to some counterpart. For each of these sentences this interpretation is unlikely, e.g., that we had an infant president in 1920. In Figure 5.2 this last interpretation would be realized with x_1: child and x_1: president both indicated for the **1920** space.

To see how **(IdentPrinc)** works, consider the *Gone with the Wind* sentence above. This involves the very common pragmatic function **played_by()** that maps a character in a movie or play onto the actor who plays that role for a particular movie. In each case two objects associated by the pragmatic function must be situated in distinct spaces. We know that Clark Gable played Rhett Butler in the movie *Gone with the Wind* This is represented with something like:

sp_0 | Clark_Gable plays Rhett_Butler
sp_0 | In Gone_with_the_Wind, ⟦sp_2⟧
sp_0 | • Clark_Gable
sp_2 | • Rhett_Butler

It is assumed that this representation gives rise to the satisfaction of the following preconditions of **(IdentPrinc)**.

sp_0 | "Clark Gable" = Clark_Gable
Rhett_Butler = played_by(Clark_Gable,
Gone_with_the_Wind)

Exactly analogous statements can be made about **Vivien_Leigh** and **Scarlett_O'Hara. (IdentPrinc)** collapses the projections of both of the following

In Gone with the Wind, *Clark Gable falls in love with Vivien Leigh.*

In Gone with the Wind, *Rhett Butler falls in love with Scarlett O'Hara.*

into the following:

sp_2 | Rhett_Butler falls in love with Scarlett_O'Hara.

The alternative projection

sp_2 | Clark_Gable falls in love with Scarlett_O'Hara.

fails, since **Clark_Gable** is not situated in **sp_2**.

Temporal Adverbs

Temporal adverbs occur in the following sentences.

In 1890, break dancing was unknown.
Bif went to the movie with Cliff on a rainy Sunday afternoon.

I will consider two alternative analyses of temporal adverbs. The first, which I will reject, involves distribution over two temporal spaces. Accordingly, the first sentence would project onto something like the following.

sp_0 | at time tm_5: ⟦sp_5⟧
sp_0 | tm_5 during 1890
sp_5 | break dancing is unknown.

Notice that this analysis, although expressively adequate, puts all the temporal relations in the parent space **sp_0** and no temporal information in **sp_5**. There are at least four major problems with this approach. First, there is no representation in **sp_5** itself of the year being 1890. The approach does not promote consolidation into this parochial domain. Within **sp_5** we would like to explore consequences of its being this particular year. Second, the approach generalizes poorly to the second sentence, which contains a non-temporal specification *rainy* within the same adverbial phrase as the temporal *Sunday afternoon.* A projection that splits the content of the prepositional phrase in one case but not the other over multiple spaces does not seem particularly proximate. Third, the approach does not explain the co-occurrence of temporal prepositional phrases with other temporal expressions. I consider these co-occurrence restrictions when I take up temporal aspect in Chapter 8. And fourth, the approach does not integrate well with the facts about contextualization. The analysis of temporal aspects to be proposed later is also motivated in terms of the interaction of aspectual constructions with contextualization. In Chapter 8 we will see that the first sentence above contextualizes into **sp_5**, not into **sp_0** as the proposed representation suggests.

An alternative approach is made possible because of the highly discriminatory role of partitioned representations. It is also suggested by the most proximate projections of *ambient* temporal or partially temporal sentences like

It was a dark and stormy night in June.

This projects naturally onto a representation like

sp_7 | it is dark
sp_7 | it is stormy
sp_7 | it is June

We propose that the sentence about break dancing projects onto representations like the following:

sp_5 | it is 1890
sp_5 | break dancing is unknown.

where **sp_0 | at time tm_5: [[sp_5]]** is already given. Likewise, the sentence about Biff and Cliff projects onto representations like the following:

sp_6 | it is rainy
sp_6 | it is a Sunday
sp_6 | it is an afternoon
sp_6 | Bif and Cliff go to movie_4

where **sp_0 | at time tm_6: [[sp_6]]** is already given. In Chapter 2 I called such projections *ambient representations.* They provide an alternative means for representing the same information, but shift the representational burden to more local spaces.

I claim that the ambient projections in these cases are proximate and uniform. However, in projecting content into **sp_5** the ambient projection does not attribute anything directly to the time **tm_5** of

sp_5, where sp_5 has the context sp_0 | at time tm_5: ⟦sp_5⟧. The question naturally arises, are we losing part of the semantic intent of the discourse sentence? The answer is no. Temporal relations can be reconstructed by inference in sp_0. Inferences in sp_0 can, of course, make use of the more global consequences of the contents of sp_5 by climbing the context sp_0 | at time tm_5: ⟦sp_5⟧, for instance to derive

sp_0 | at time tm_5: it is 1890

All we need is some means of performing an inference consistent with the following sanctioned inference introduced in Chapter 2.

(It is) S | at time T1: it is T2 iff S | T1 during T2.

As discussed in Chapters 2 and 3, *sanctioned inferences* are used abstractly to describe semantic relations among representations with no commitment to how they are actually realized in actual reasoning processes, but with the assumption that, if they are simple enough, normal reasoning will be consistent with these rules. These rules are used primarily, as (It is) is used here, to get clear about the semantics of certain constructions introduced into our representations by relating them to other constructions, like during, whose semantics is intuitively unproblematic. The semantics of temporal aspects will be defined using sanctioned inferences in Chapter 8. For instance, given

sp_0 | at time tm_5: ⟦sp_5⟧
sp_5 | it is 1890

we can conclude by (It is)

sp_0 | tm_5 during 1890

Of course context climbing plays a role in the inference too.

More generally, I suggest all temporal adverbials (as opposed to temporal aspects) have ambient projections. Specific constructive rules describing the ambient projections of the temporal adverbials *now* and *yesterday* are as follows.

(Now)
Conditions: S | "now" P

Actions: S | P
S | it is NOW

(Yest)
Conditions: S | "yesterday" P

Actions: S | P
S | it is YESTERDAY

In these rules, NOW refers to the interval of time in which the discourse occurs and YESTERDAY refers to the 24-hour interval of time ending at the midnight before NOW. Their precise projections are determined as a function of the speech time specified (deictically, as linguists say) in the pragmatic setting.

SOME COMMON CASES OF DISTRIBUTION

The understanding of certain surface structures involves constructing new spaces or distributing knowledge over existing spaces. *Space builders* are surface structures that project, at least in part, onto contexts.

For example, the sentence *The wizard thought that if Siegfried worked hard, he would be successful,* contains the space builders *thought* and *if* and is accordingly projected onto something like:

sp_2 | wizard_8 believes [[sp_3]]
sp_3 | Siegfried works hard □→ [[sp_4]]
sp_4 | Siegfried works hard
sp_4 | presumably: [sp_3]
sp_4 | Siegfried is successful

These constructive rules conspire to maximize the functional utility of spaces in accordance with the principles of coherence and consolidation. These rules, in other words, build the kinds of spaces described in Chapter 2 wherever the opportunity exists. In this section we will look at a few examples of constructive rules for space builders.

Possibility

A sentence with *might, possibly,* or *it is possible* projects onto an intermediate structure of the form S0 | It is possible that P. The following is an appropriate constructive rule for a structure with possible.

(Poss)

Conditions:	**S0 | "It is possible that" P**
Actions:	**create a space, S1**
	S0 | it is possible that ⟦S1⟧
	S1 | [S0]
	S1 | P

As an example of the application of **(Poss)**, if

It is possible that the coffee is hot

is contextualized into **sp_1**, this rule would result in a projection something like the following, where **sp_8** is a newly created space.

sp_1 | It is possible that ⟦sp_8⟧
sp_8 | [sp_1]
sp_8 | coffee_6 is hot

An important thing to note about the constructive rule for possible is that it creates a new space every time another statement of possibility is reconstructed. That is, it will not project the embedded sentence into an already existing possibility space. This means that if we now contextualize

It is possible that the coffee is cold.

into **sp_1**, this rule would result in a projection something like the following, where **sp_9** is a newly created space.

sp_1 | It is possible that ⟦sp_9⟧
sp_9 | [sp_1]
sp_9 | coffee_6 is cold

It is appropriate that we set up this second possibility space. If we were to internalize **sp_8 | coffee_6 is cold** this would mean that **coffee_6** could be both hot and cold at the same time. Because of the concern for *coherence* different spaces must be created.

Notice that aside from the distribution of the projection of this sentence over two spaces, I have attributed the creation of an inheritance context **sp_9 | [sp_1]** to the new space. This makes the content of **sp_9** an extension of the content of **sp_1**, thus contributing to consolidation, as discussed in Chapter 2.

I might point out that under certain circumstances we might actually want to express that something is possible *together with* something previously given to be possible. One way to do this appears to be by means of the space cue *at the same time*, as in

> *It is possible that the room was full of fumes. This is what normally happens when the pilot light goes out in a vintage furnace. What is more, it is possible at the same time that someone lit a cigarette.*

The construction of parallel spaces must be suppressed by some other constructive rule in this case.

Conditionals

A sentence with *if*, *given that* or *assuming* typically projects onto a statement of the form **S0 | P → Q**. Two rules are used for interpreting *if*:

(Condit1)
Conditions: S0 | "if" P "then" Q

Actions: create a space, S1
S0 | P → ⟦S1⟧
S1 | P
S1 | [S0]
S1 | Q

(Condit2)
Conditions: S0 | "if" P "then" Q
? S0 | P → ⟦S1⟧

Actions: S1 | Q

(Condit1) looks a lot like (Poss) in that it creates the inheritance context S1 | [S0]. The ? in (Condit2) indicates that the associated statement must be present in the knowledge base, but that it is not itself restructured. That is, when (Condit2) fires, S0 | P → Q will be replaced by S1 | Q, but the context S0 | P → ⟦S1⟧ will remain in its present form.

Two rules are used for conditionals in order to secure *consolidation*. Both rules restructure statements of the same form, but (Condit2) has a more specific condition. As is normal for *conflict resolution* strategies in production systems (Brownston, et al. 1985), it is assumed that the rule with the more specific condition will fire rather than that with the more general condition, if the conditions of two rules are simultaneously satisfied. As a result, (Condit1), unlike (Poss), will fire only once for a given space S0 and a given antecedent. For instance, suppose the following two sentences processed in sequence and that both are contextualized into sp_6.

> *If the Enterprise is under attack then Spock is an enemy agent. And assuming the Enterprise is under attack, the Enterprise is doomed*

For the first, (Condit1) must fire, since the precondition of (Condit2), marked with ?, will fail, and will construct something like

> **sp_6 | The Enterprise is under attack → [[sp_8]]**
> **sp_8 | The Enterprise is under attack**
> **sp_8 | [sp_6]**
> **sp_8 | Spock is an enemy agent**

Now, the ? condition of (Condit2) is satisfied when the second statement is processed.* (Condit2) will construct only

> **sp_8 | The Enterprise is doomed**

The processing of the second statement will reuse the space and the context initiated by the processing of the first. This maximizes *consolidation* without sacrificing *coherence*. This makes sense, since if the Enterprise is under attack then **Spock is an enemy agent** and the **Enterprise is doomed** should be true *together*. Kamp's (1980) rule for conditionals is essentially like (Condit1). The additional rule (Condit2) is necessary for the reasons cited, but actually leads to a more general treatment of the kinds of facts Kamp is concerned with, as we will see.

---

* I've used *assuming* rather than *if* to underscore that different constituents have parallel interpretations. A similar rule would exist for *assuming*.

Quantification

A sentence with *each* or *every* projects onto a representation with the structure

S0 | for any W, W is D → : ⟦S1⟧

The following rule, similar to one proposed by Kamp (1980) produces such representations.

(Each1)
Conditions: **S0 | X "($_{NP}$ each D)$_{NP}$" Y**

Actions: **create an object, W**
create a space, S1
S0 | for any W, W is "D" → : ⟦S1⟧
S1 | [S0]
S1 | • W
S1 | W is "D"
S1 | X W Y

Like **(Condit1)**, **(Each1)** should be supplemented by a rule, **(Each2)**, that ensures consolidation by avoiding duplicate quantification spaces. For instance, for

Each mailman has lost his mail bag to an angry dog and each mailman has also been bitten by the dog.

only a single quantification space should be created.

Although one would expect that the quantifiers *each* and *every* would project onto a representation semantically equivalent to that of the quantifier *all*, the former are space builders, while the latter is not. This is why *his* is readily interpretable in the first of the following sentences but not in the second.*

Each mailman has lost his mail bag to an angry dog.
* *All the mailmen have lost his mail bag to an angry dog.*

In brief, *his* refers to the unique object **W** located in **S1**. This analysis agrees with that of Fauconnier (1978).

---

* Recall that the * before an English example indicates that speakers of English find the sentence in some sense intuitively anomalous.

Counterfactuals

Like normal *if*, two rules are also used for interpreting the *subjunctive if*:

(Counter1)
Conditions: **S0 | "if P_{subj} then" Q**

Actions: **create a space, S1**
S0 | "P" □→ ⟦S1⟧
S1 | "P"
S1 | presumably: [S0]
S1 | Q

(Counter2)
Conditions: **S0 | "if P_{subj} then" Q**
? **S0 | "P" □→ ⟦S1⟧**

Actions: **S1 | Q**

The main difference is that **S1** inherits differently from **S0**. The statement **S1 | presumably: [S0]** indicates that **S1** inherits from **S0** by *default*, that is only wherever the information that would be inherited from **S0** does not conflict with information already given in **S1**.

For example, processing the sentence

If Michael Dukakis had won the election then Kitty would redecorate the White House in green.

would cause something like the following to be constructed by **(Counter1)**.

sp_4 | Michael Dukakis has won the election □→ ⟦sp_8⟧
sp_8 | presumably: [sp_4]
sp_8 | Michael Dukakis has won the election
sp_8 | Kitty redecorates the White House in green

The secondary context allows most things true in **sp_4** to carry over to **sp_8**, such as the fact that Kitty is Michael Dukakis' wife, that the winner of the presidential election by convention becomes President and lives in the White House, that the president's wife is the First Lady, and so on. However, certain facts fail to carry over because they conflict with information given in **sp_8**, such as the fact that

George Bush has won the election and that George Bush becomes president.

Propositional Attitudes

Two rules are similarly used for interpreting belief sentences.

(Believe1)
Conditions: **S0 | X "believes that" P**

Actions: **create a space, S1**
S0 | X believes that [[S1]]
S1 | P

(Believe2)
Conditions: **S0 | X "believes that" P**
? **S0 | X believes [[S1]]**

Actions: **S1 | P**

Recall from Chapter 2 that *hope* can be analyzed as a conditional embedded within a belief and that wishing can be analyzed as a counterfactual within a belief. This is accounted for as follows.

(Hope)
Conditions: **S0 | X "hopes that" P**

Actions: **S0 | X "believes that if " P "then" it is favorable**

(Wish)
Conditions: **S0 | X wishes that P**

Actions: **S0 | X "believes that if it were the case that" P "then" it is favorable**

These rules set up the conditions for (Condit1) and (Counter1) to fire. For instance,

George wishes that his dog were a cat.

gives rise, after contextualization and the application of (Wish) to something like

sp_1 | George believes that ⟦sp_4⟧
sp_4 | his dog is a cat $\Box\!\!\rightarrow$ ⟦sp_5⟧
sp_5 | his dog is a cat
sp_5 | presumably: [sp_4]
sp_5 | it is favorable

Temporal Aspects

Aspect refers intuitively to the temporal *perspective* from which an event is viewed (Comrie 1976). In English, the following use different aspects to view the same event, that of Bif building a barn.

Bif built the barn.
Bif began building the barn.
Bif finished building the barn.
Bif was building the barn.
Bif was going to build the barn.
Bif had built the barn.

In Chapter 8 I will argue that the English *perfect* aspect makes use of a constructive rule as follows.

Conditions: **S1 | P "has occurred"**

Actions: **create a space, S2**
S1 | ⟦S2⟧ has occurred
S2 | P

Keep in mind that spaces set up in this way are temporal spaces; the semantics of the perfect for instance tells us that **P** is true at some earlier time; in fact everything satisfied in **S2** is. Therefore, the semantics of the perfect would actually sanction the following more elaborate rule.

Conditions:	**S1 ∣ P "has occurred"**
?	**S0 ∣ at time T1: ⟦S1⟧**
Actions:	**create a space, S2**
	S1 ∣ ⟦S2⟧ has occurred
	create a time, T2
	S0 ∣ at time T2: ⟦S2⟧
	S0 ∣ T2 < T1
	S2 ∣ P

S1 and **S2** are thus both temporal spaces ordered within **S0**. We can think of the aspect as projecting onto a context that allows **S1** and **S2** to communicate directly. We are also justified in deriving the context **S2 ∣ it is going to happen that [S1]**, according to the semantics of the Prospective. (It is a matter of speculation at what point we stop deriving contexts in constructing the full representation of an aspectual sentence, including which of our alternative constructive rules for the perfect generally applies. Experimental evidence on the reaction times in answering a question like the following, with **S0** in focus

Did P happen at some time?

might shed light on this.)

In summary, we have demonstrated how a constructive semantics might be formulated for some important syntactic structures. The process of constructing an internal representation for these structures involves setting up new spaces along with primary and possibly secondary contexts, accessing existing spaces, and allocating the parts of the continuing construction process to multiple spaces. This is done in a way that supports efficient reasoning about the knowledge conveyed in the discourse.

INTERACTION OF DISTRIBUTION AND PAROCHIAL PROCESSES

Beyond their consequences for language understanding per se, we will see that the way that these parochial processes interact with the distribution of knowledge over spaces elucidates numerous linguistic problems that have otherwise been difficult to account for.

Let's look at some examples of the interaction of parochial processes with distribution.

Donkey Sentences

Geach's (1952) *donkey sentences* can be accurately accounted for as an interesting interaction between the rules (Indef) and (Def) and distribution over partitioned representations roughly as foreseen by Kamp (1980). It This interaction is observed in the following sentence.

If Pedro has a donkey then he beats the donkey.

In the projection of this sentence, the rule for → will apply causing the following to be posted.

sp_0 | Pedro has a donkey → ⟦sp_2⟧
sp_2 | "Pedro has a donkey"
sp_2 | [sp_0]
sp_2 | he beats the donkey

(Indef) will apply to the second statement to produce something like

sp_2 | • obj_3
sp_2 | obj_3 is donkey
sp_2 | Pedro has obj_3

(Def) will check the precondition **? sp_2 | Y is a donkey**, binding Y to **obj_3**, and so will post

sp_2 | Pedro beats obj_3.

This *the donkey* finds a referent in the space into which it is projected. Distribution has put the right object into the right space. It can be shown that the following, a kind of discourse not considered by Kamp, also result in finding a referent for *the donkey* in the appropriate space.

If Pedro is a farmer then he has a donkey. Pedro is a person of bad character. Therefore, if Pedro is a farmer then he beats the donkey.

The first of these sentences projects onto something like the following, using (Condit1) and (Indef).

sp_0 | Pedro is farmer → ⟦sp_3⟧
sp_3 | Pedro is farmer

sp_3 | [sp_0]
sp_3 | • obj_3
sp_3 | obj_3 is donkey
sp_3 | Pedro has obj_3

We can ignore the contribution of the second sentence for this discussion (it is included to make the discourse flow better; the discourse without it is somewhat stilted for reasons having to do with normal patterns of contextualization, discussed in Chapter 4). The third sentence will project onto an intermediate structure, after (Condit2) applies, like this:

sp_3 | he beats the donkey

Now, (Def) can apply to produce

sp_3 | Pedro beats obj_3

Again, the right object is found in the right space to allow a very proximate interpretation of *the donkey*. Another example underscores the importance of *inheritance*.

Pedro has a donkey. If he is mean then he beats the donkey.

Here, the first sentence will project onto something like the following, again applying (Indef).

sp_0 | • obj_3
sp_0 | obj_3 is donkey
sp_0 | Pedro has obj_3

The second sentence will project onto an intermediate structure, after (Condit1) applies, like this:

sp_0 | Pedro is mean → ⟦sp_4⟧
sp_4 | [sp_0]
sp_4 | "he beats the donkey"

Now, *the donkey* projects successfully onto **obj_3** since the inheritance context **sp_4 | [sp_0]** gives us a window from **sp_4** to **sp_0**. This means that we have effectively

sp_4 | • obj_3
sp_4 | obj_3 is donkey

This gives us

sp_4 | Pedro beats obj_3

Again, we have a successful and very proximate projection for *the donkey*.

These last examples should be contrasted with the following, which turns out to be anomalous.

* *It is possible that Pedro has a donkey. If Pedro is a farmer then he beats the donkey.*

In this case the first sentence projects onto something like the following, by (Poss).

sp_0 | it is possible that ⟦sp_5⟧
sp_5 | [sp_0]
sp_5 | • obj_3
sp_5 | obj_3 is donkey
sp_5 | Pedro has obj_3

The second sentence then projects into an intermediate form like

sp_0 | Pedro is farmer → ⟦sp_6⟧
sp_6 | [sp_0]
sp_6 | Pedro is farmer
sp_6 | "he beats the donkey"

Now (Def) cannot fire to project *the donkey* further. obj_3 is in the wrong space! Distribution has put the right object in the *wrong* place. Hence the anomaly.

Finally, let's look at a couple of discourses using *every*.

Every farmer who owns a donkey beats the donkey.

This sentence projects, after (Each) and then (Indef) apply, onto the following.

sp_0 | For any farmer, obj_4, obj_4 owns a donkey → ⟦sp_7⟧
sp_7 | [sp_0]
sp_7 | • obj_4
sp_7 | obj_4 is farmer who owns obj_5
sp_7 | • obj_5
sp_7 | obj_5 is donkey
sp_7 | "he beats the donkey"

Now, (Def) can apply to the last statement to derive the projection of *he* and of *the donkey* to produce:

sp_7 | obj_4 beats obj_5

Now, a little more complicated case.

I have a dog. Every neighbor of mine hates the dog.

The first sentence projects into something like this

sp_0 | • obj_3
sp_0 | obj_3 is dog
sp_0 | me has obj_3

The second sentence projects into the intermediate structure that follows, after **(Each)** applies.

sp_0 | For any neighbor of me, obj_50: ⟦sp_3⟧
sp_3 | [sp_0]
sp_3 | • obj_50
sp_3 | obj_50 is neighbor of me
sp_3 | obj_50 hates the dog

By **(Def)** *the dog* is projected onto **obj_3**, since the *inheritance context* **sp_3 | [sp_0]** gives us effectively,

sp_3 | • obj_3
sp_3 | obj_3 is dog

allowing us to apply **(Def)** to find the projection **obj_3** of *the dog*.

In summary, the way knowledge is distributed over spaces during the constructive process correctly accounts for the accessibility of anaphoric antecedents in complex sentences. As a result, the semantically correct internal representations of these structures can be derived by relatively simple parochial processes. This explains the kind of data that motivates much of discourse representation theory, but generalizes to a much broader range of examples than Kamp envisions. It is significant that even in complex cases the principles guiding distribution situate the right objects in the right spaces every time to allow the interpretation to succeed.

Referential Opacity and Attributiveness

If two expressions refer to the same object it is generally the case that one of the two expressions can be substituted for the other in a sentence without a change in truth conditions. Thus from the now outdated example,

Daniel Ortega is the President of Nicaragua.
Daniel Ortega is in Sweden.

we may infer

The President of Nicaragua is in Sweden.

This general pattern is often known as the rule of *substitution of equals*. However, substitution of equals generally fails in modal environments. For instance, under the assumption that Jocasta is Oedipus' mother the following do not have the same truth conditions, at least in one sense (the other sense is discussed below).

Oedipus believed he would marry Jocasta.
Oedipus believed he would marry his mother.

In fact the first is true while the second is false. Quine (1953) calls the failure of the substitution of equals *referential opacity* and suggests that the expression for the object of belief be treated as an unanalyzed whole, as if it had quotes around it.

In fact, in partitioned representations substitution of equals is very (possibly completely) general, but as a *parochial* rule. For instance, after contextualization and the application of (Believe1) or (Believe2), something like the following intermediate structure is constructed for *Oedipus believed he would marry his mother*

sp_3 | Oedipus believes that ⟦sp_4⟧
sp_4 | Oedipus will marry Oedipus's mother

Accordingly, we predict that the substitution of equals *fails* if the following is given,

sp_3 | Jocasta is Oedipus's mother

but will *succeed* if the following is given (see Figure 5.3).

sp_4 | Jocasta is Oedipus's mother

Thus, for substitution of equals we must be given not that Jocasta is Oedipus' mother, but that Oedipus *believes* that Jocasta is Oedipus' mother. This agrees with intuitions about these sentences.

Closely related to the account of referential opacity that falls out from partitioned representations is an account of the differences between the *attributive* and *referential* uses of noun phrases discussed by Donnellan (1966). This ambiguity is found in the following sentence.

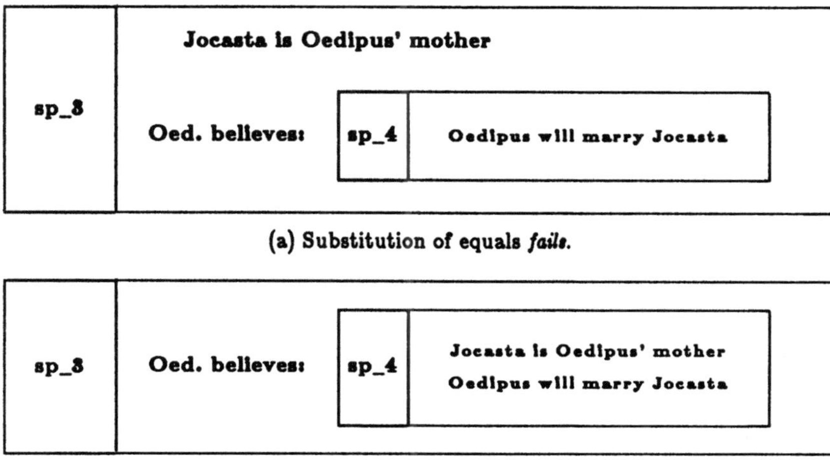

(a) Substitution of equals *fails*.

(b) Substitution of equals *succeeds*.

Fig. 5.3. Substitution of equals as a parochial rule.

George thinks the best dancer will go to Hong Kong.

Under the *referential* interpretation this sentence means that George thinks of some particular person, who happens to be the best dancer, that he will go to Hong Kong. Under the *attributive* interpretation George might not have any idea who the best dancer is but might think that whoever fills that *role* will go to Hong Kong.

In fact, the apparent ambiguity in such a sentence is an artifact of non-partitioned approaches, which seem to require the representation of two distinct concepts: *individuals* and *roles*. In a partitioned representation we make use of a belief space, call it **sp_6**, that is able to represent objects independently of reality and to support reasoning about objects. There is no difficulty in projecting the sentence unambiguously onto something like

sp_5 | George believes that [[sp_6]]
sp_6 | • person_8
sp_6 | person_8 = best dancer
sp_6 | person_8 will go to Hong Kong

The apparent ambiguity is then completely predicted: The referential use arises just in case something of the following form is given

sp_6 | Bif_8 = the best dancer

The referential use arises where the preconditions for parochial substitution of equals for a noun phrase describing a role occurs. The attributive use arises elsewhere. Thus, the *referential/attributive* distinction requires no special mechanisms. A more *proximate* projection from surface discourse sentence to internal representation is achieved and the perceived ambiguity explained in terms of the differing potential in the pragmatic setting for a particular parochial inference.

Johnson-Laird (1983) makes what I think is the same point in his mental models framework. His example involves the two readings of

Phil would like to meet the man who lives at 211b Baker Street.

one of which (the referential) entails

Phil would like to meet Sherlock Holmes.

and one of which (the attributive) does not. In mental model terms, the first sentence is in fact unambiguous. It becomes equivalent to the second exactly when it happens to be given in Phil's belief model that Sherlock Holmes is the man who lives at 211b Baker Street, since in that case Phil's belief model will be constructed in exactly the same way for either sentence. Fauconnier (1986b) discusses more complex examples.

De Dicto, De Re and Specificity

There is another dimension to the Oedipus sentences above. The sentence

Oedipus believed he would marry his mother.

might be interpreted as both true, roughly synonymous with *Oedipus believed he would marry Jocasta,* simply because *his mother* might not be intended as the description *Oedipus* would attribute to that person at all (called the *de dicto* reading), but rather as the speaker's own description (called the *de re* reading). In partitioned representations this sentence would, in the de re reading, project onto something like

sp_3 | Oedipus believes that ⟦sp_4⟧

sp_4 | Oedipus will marry Jocasta

where

sp_3 | Jocasta is Oedipus' mother

is given. We have seen how the de dicto reading is naturally predicted in partitioned representations since *his mother* projects into Oedipus's belief space sp_4. But where does the de re reading come from?

In models of partitioned representations different objects may exist in different spaces and relations between objects in distinct spaces may exist. This gives many more opportunities for *metonymous* processes to operate than in models that do not partition knowledge. Fauconnier (1985) shows how these processes give rise to the de re reading and how this account generalizes to a vast variety of related interpretations, many of which are not so well known. Recall that metonymy is driven by the *identity principle*, which we have formalized as follows.

(IdentPrinc)
Conditions: S | X "A" Y
? S1 | "A" = M
? N = F(M), *where* F *is an active pragm funct*
Actions: S | X N Y

The de re reading for *Oedipus believes he will marry his mother* arises from the following preconditions.

sp_3 | Jocasta_3 is Oedipus's mother
Jocasta_3 = same_as(Jocasta_4)

This occurs as follows (see Figure 5.4). After contextualization and the application of (Believe1) or (Believe2) we arrive at an intermediate structure something like:

sp_3 | Oedipus believes that [[sp_4]]
sp_4 | Oedipus will marry his mother

(IdentPrinc) applies to derive the following.

sp_4 | Oedipus will marry Jocasta_4

This gives us the *de re* reading in which Oedipus is not necessarily aware that the person he will marry is his mother.

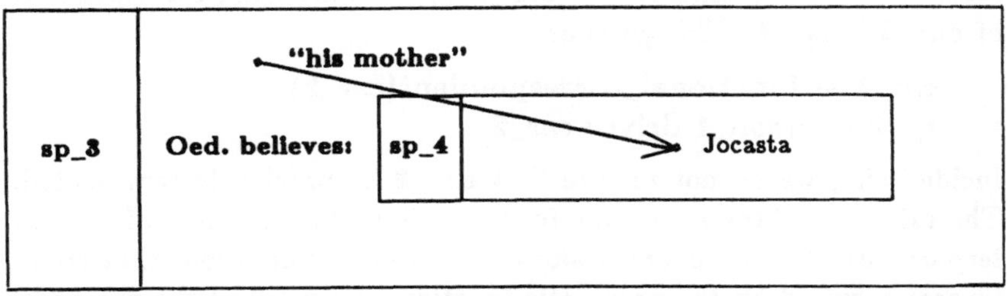

Fig. 5.4. A Pragmatic Function Underlies the De Re Reading for *Oedipus believes that he will marry his mother.*

This account generalizes to many non-belief sentences as Fauconnier (1985) shows in detail. Consider his following example:

If I were a millionaire, my VW would be a Rolls.

For this sentence, after contextualization and the application of either **(Counter1)** or **(Counter2)**, we arrive at intermediate structures something like this:

sp_1 | person_1 is millionaire ⊡→ [[sp_2]]
sp_2 | "my VW is Rolls"

Now, presumably something like the following preconditions are satisfied,

sp_1 | • car_2
sp_1 | car_2 is person_1's VW
sp_1 | person_1 drives car_2

That is, in **sp_1**, **person_1** (*I*) drives a Volkswagen, which we will call **car_2**. Notice that *my VW* would project onto **car_2** in **sp_1**, i.e.,

sp_1 | "my VW" = car_2

This satisfies one of the preconditions of **(IdentPrinc)**. Let **functional_correspondent** be the *pragmatic function* that maps objects in **sp_1** to objects in **sp_2** that play the same functional role. Thus, the functional correspondent of Harry's dog Bowser in **sp_1** is Harry's dog Fifi in **sp_2**. The functional correspondent of Harry's favorite restaurant, Sam's Eatery, in **sp_1** is Harry's favorite restaurant, Chez Pierre, in **sp_2**. The functional role of **car_2** in **sp_1** is that of being the car driven by **person_1**. Such pragmatic functions seem to be very common. Let **car_3** be the functional correspondent of **car_2** in **sp_2**. This gives us

car_3 = functional_correspondent(car_2)
sp_2 | person_1 drives car_2

Incidentally, we do not require that **car_3** be previously represented. The existence of the pragmatic function allows the situation of a counterpart **car_3** to be inferred along with information about that counterpart required by the pragmatic function. Now, all of the preconditions for the application of (**IdentPrinc**) are satisfied, giving us

sp_2 | car_3 is Rolls

(see Figure 5.5). Thus, the application of the identity principle captures the observed meaning of *if I were a millionaire, my VW would be a Rolls* the same way it captured the de re reading of *Oedipus believes he will marry his mother.*

Another example of the kind Fauconnier cites is

George believes that Peter runs faster than he does.

Assume that *he* is used here to refer to Peter, not to George. For this sentence, after contextualization and the application of either (Believe1) or (Believe2), we arrive at intermediate structures something like this:

sp_1 | George believes that ⟦sp_3⟧
sp_3 | "Peter runs faster than he does"

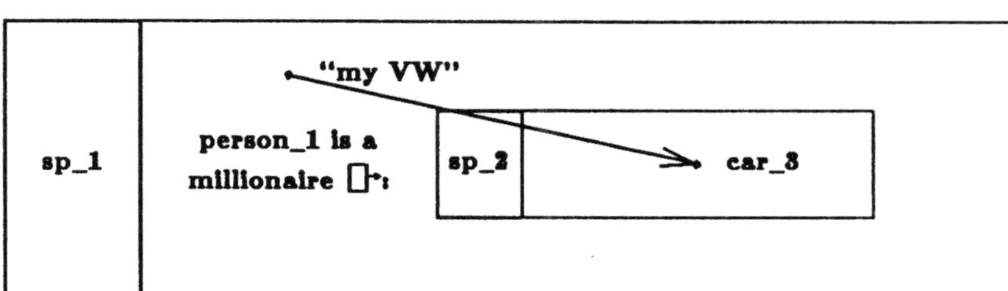

Fig. 5.5. A pragmatic function underlies the natural reading for *If I were a millionaire, my VW would be a Rolls.*

Now, presumably something like the following preconditions are satisfied,

sp_1 | • speed_8
sp_1 | Peter runs speed_8 fast
sp_3 | • speed_9
sp_3 | Peter runs speed_9 fast
sp_3 | • speed_8

That is, there is some speed, call it **speed_8** at which Peter runs in **sp_1** and there is some speed, call it **speed_9** at which Peter runs in **sp_3**. It is presumed that the same speeds exist in any space, in particular that **speed_8** exists in both **sp_1** and **sp_3**. Notice that *(than) he does* would project onto **speed_8** in **sp_1**, i.e.,

sp_1 | "than he does" = compared to speed_8

although it would project onto **speed_9** in **sp_3**. This satisfies one of the preconditions of (IdentPrinc). Let id be the *pragmatic function* that maps objects onto themselves. id is the identity function. This gives us

speed_8 = id(speed_8)

Now, all of the preconditions for the application of (IdentPrinc) are satisfied (see Figure 5.6), giving us

sp_3 | Peter runs faster than speed_8

or

sp_3 | speed_9 is faster than speed_8

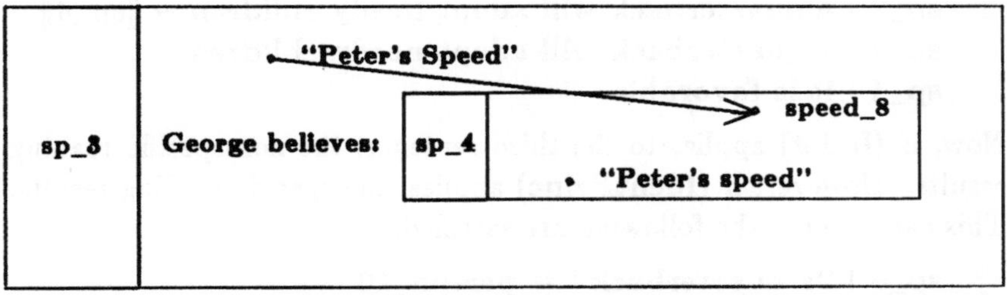

Fig. 5.6. A Pragmatic Function Underlies the Natural Reading for *George believes that Peter runs faster than he does.*

Thus, the application of the identity principle captures the observed meaning of *George believes that Peter runs faster than he does* the same way it captured the de re reading of *Oedipus believes he will marry his mother* or the natural reading of *if I were a millionaire, my VW would be a Rolls.*

This account of the perceived de dicto/de re ambiguity is closely related to the account of the perceived ambiguity between *specific* and *non-specific* readings found in the uses of indefinite noun phrases. For instance, two readings are often observed for sentences like the following:

> *John Paul hopes that a former quarterback will adopt needy children.*

On one reading, there is a *specific* quarterback in the real world that John Paul hopes will adopt needy children (whether or not John Paul knows that this person is a quarter back). On a second reading, John Paul imagines a situation in which a *non-specific* quarterback adopts needy children. The non-specific reading is like a de dicto reading; it is derived by projecting a noun phrase into a specific space and applying applicable rules parochially, but not **(IdentPrinc)**. The specific reading is like the de re reading; it is derived by projecting a noun phrase into a specific space and then applying **(IdentPrinc)** on the basis of a pragmatic function mapping from another space. In either case this sentence will project, after contextualization and the application of **(Hope)** and **(Condit1)**, onto an intermediate structure something like

sp_0 | John Paul believes: ⟦sp_2⟧
sp_2 | a quarterback will adopt needy children → ⟦sp_4⟧
sp_4 | a quarterback will adopt needy children
sp_4 | it is favorable

Now, if **(Indef)** applies to the third sentence, the non-specific reading results. However, if **(IdentPrinc)** applies, the specific reading results. This can occur if the following are satisfied:

sp_0 | "a quarterback" = person_10
person_14 = F(person_10)

Notice that **(Hope)** predicts that three spaces are involved in the interpretation of this sentence. The application of **(IdentPrinc)** here did not refer to John Paul's belief space, **sp_2**. But we should just as

easily get a third reading also using (IdentPrinc) if the following are satisfied.

sp_2 | "a quarterback" = person_10
person_12 = F(person_10)

Indeed this reading exists. It is the one in which John Paul has a particular person in mind who he believes is a former quarterback (whether of not he actually is a quarterback in the real world, or for that matter whether or not he actually exists in the real world), and John Paul hopes that that particular person will adopt needy children.

In summary, (IdentPrinc), when allowed to interact with the model of partitioned representations, leads immediately to an account of referential opacity and transparency, specificity of reference, and the interaction of quantifiers with modalities, much as Fauconnier describes. (IdentPrinc) itself, in particular with respect to the pragmatic functions it presupposes, is only poorly understood, but something like (IdentPrinc) is needed in any case, independently of the concerns of partitioned representations, to account for general cases of metonymy.

Traditionally, the perceived ambiguities in these sentences have been accounted for in terms of differing *semantic scopes* rather than in differences in the processing strategies made available in particular pragmatic settings. For instance, the John Paul sentence might be analyzed as being composed in either of the following two ways:

∃x (x is quarterback & J_P hopes x adopts needy children)
J_P hopes ∃x (x is quarterback & x adopts needy children)

There are at least four things wrong with this account that the partitioning account overcomes.

First, the account in terms of semantic scope leads to serious semantic issues that are not easily resolved. The semantics of propositional attitude expressions must refer to agents' mental representations or agents' conceptions of certain objects. In this example John Paul has a representation of someone who adopts needy children. John Paul's representations arise to a large extent from his interactions with the real world in many subtle ways. In particular, there

may be causal relations between his representations and real world objects of varying directness. Now, the *wide-scope* representation above purports to connect an object in one of John Paul's representations with an object in the real world simply by asserting that John Paul's representation is about some specific real world entity. Not only does this not do justice to the subtlety of the relation that might exist between John Paul's representation and some real world object, but it doesn't even allow us to talk about the relation. Partitioned representations, on the other hand, can situate distinct objects in distinct spaces and acknowledge any number of causal or other relations between objects in distinct spaces. The connectedness of objects in different spaces is studied as a cognitive phenomenon and, as we have seen in our discussions of pragmatic functions, can have any of a variety of sources. (Asher (1986) and Barnden (1989) discuss issues in identifying objects in separate spaces. Barden actually suggests that under certain circumstances the same object might be represented in more than one space, but that there are various degrees of identity below this, captured by pragmatic functions.)

Second, the scopal account often fails to get all of the possible readings. In the John Paul case it fails to get the intermediate reading in which John Paul has a particular person in mind who he believes is a former quarterback and hopes that that particular person will adopt needy children. This reading cannot be realized by scopal ambiguities implicit in the surface sentence, since there are only two clauses in the surface sentence to serve as potential scopes of a quantifier. Overcoming this objection would involve motivating some level of syntactic analysis at which the quantifier could occur in a third position.

Third, the account in terms of semantic scope fails to give any idea of under what circumstances one reading will arise as opposed to another reading. The account in terms of partitioning explicitly states the factors in the pragmatic setting that underlie one or another reading.

Finally, and most decisively, the account in terms of semantic scope confuses existence and specificity when in fact these two properties occur independently. This argument is made by Fauconnier with regard to the following sentence:

Hob thinks a witch has blighted Bob's mare, and Nob believes that she killed Cob's sow.

In the most natural reading of this sentence *a witch* is specific, but is not entailed to exist. Two alternative scopes are permitted for this sentence. The first,

∃x (x is witch & Hob believes (x has blighted Bob's mare) & Nob believes (x killed Cob's sow))

expresses the specific reading, because it allows both x's to be bound by the same quantifier. Unfortunately it entails the existence of the witch. The second,

Hob believes ∃x (x is witch & x has blighted Bob's mare) & Nob believes (x killed Cob's sow))

does not entail the existence of a witch. But it also does not allow reference to a common witch. In short, the scope account does not provide the correct set of discriminations. In the account in terms of partitioned representations, a witch is represented in Hob's belief space, and a witch is represented in Nob's belief space, and the two witches are counterparts, as in Figure 5.7. The reference again succeeds by the (IdentPrinc) in the normal fashion.

In summary, the account in terms of partitioned representations thus overcomes the weaknesses of traditional accounts, is much more general than traditional accounts and is independently motivated in a way that traditional accounts are not.

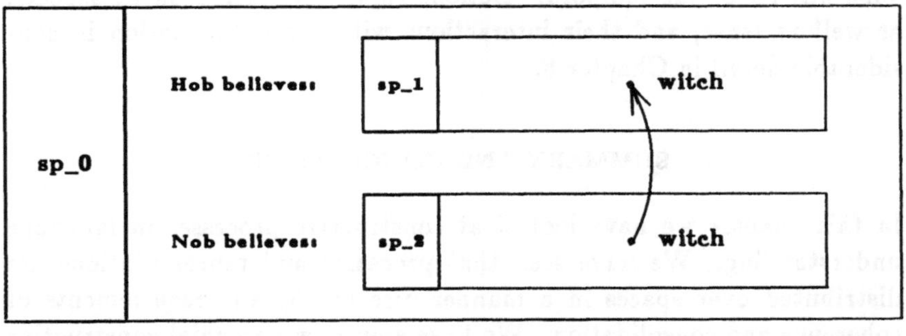

Fig. 5.7. A Pragmatic Function Underlies the Natural Reading for *Hob thinks a witch has blighted Bob's mare, and Nob believes that she killed Cob's sow.*

Temporal Expressions

We observe that the parochial ambient projections of temporal adverbs interact with the distributed projections of aspects in a way that results in semantically correct projections overall. Let's look at a sentence with *two* temporal adverbs and the past perfect.

In June, 1960, Marie had joined the Girl Scouts two years earlier.

Outside of a specific pragmatic setting this sentence will seem like a rather convoluted way to say that Marie joined the Girl Scouts in 1958. However it would be used if a temporal space, say **sp_1**, is already active and **sp_1** is a natural focus space. The principles underlying this are discussed in Chapter 8. For instance, if we are already focusing on June, 1960, this sentence would be appropriate to present evidence of Marie's accumulated scouting experience as of that time. This sentence projects onto something like

sp_1 | It is June, 1960
sp_1 | It has occurred that ⟦sp_2⟧
sp_2 | It is June, 1958
sp_2 | Marie joins the Girl Scouts

By **(It is)** we can easily reconstruct the statements

sp_0 | tm_11 during June, 1960
sp_0 | tm_12 during June, 1958
sp_0 | tm_12 < tm_11

This has all of the temporal relations right. We will look at aspects, as well as tense, and their interactions with contextualization in considerable detail in Chapter 8.

SUMMARY AND CONCLUSIONS

In this chapter we have looked at constructive processes in language understanding. We have seen that processes and representations are distributed over spaces in a manner directed by the requirements of coherence and consolidation. We have seen how parochial constructive processes work in the limited domains defined by individual spaces. Distribution puts the preconditions necessary for their success in the *right* spaces while keeping much information not relevant to their performance *out* of those spaces. This way in which intermediate structures and preconditions meet half-way makes understanding both proximate and discriminatory.

In the next chapter, we will consider the interaction of one particular kind of parochial process with distribution in detail. This is the *satisfaction of presupposition.* We will find that the theory of construction in partitioned representations provides an immediate solution to one of the most intriguing and puzzling problems in linguistic theory, the so-called *projection problem for presupposition.*

CHAPTER SIX

Satisfying Presuppositions in Discourse

Theoretical linguists have long grappled with what is known as the *projection problem for presupposition.* In this short chapter I demonstrate that what has long been considered a formidable problem requiring a complex solution is in fact a direct consequence of the use of partitioned representations in language understanding.

THE PROBLEM OF PRESUPPOSITION

Presuppositions are intuitively propositions that are intuitively taken as given or irrefutable in the utterances of sentences. For instance,

The King of France is bald

is said to *presuppose* that there is a King of France and to *assert* that that individual is bald. This means that this sentence would normally be used in a pragmatic setting in which the existence of the King of France is already represented as true (in the focus space). Some general references for presupposition are Strawson (1954), Sellars (1954), Oh and Dinneen (1979), Horton and Hirst (1988). Others will be mentioned in context.

Presuppositions are observed in association with certain lexical items and syntactic structures, which we can group together as *presuppositional constructions.* One of these is the definite description, such as *the King of France* found in the last example. Another is the *factive verb* construction like

Fred knows that his hat is on fire.

which presupposes that Fred's hat is on fire. Still other

presuppositional constructions are *clefts* and *pseudoclefts.*

It was Bif who bagged a bunny.

presupposes that someone bagged a bunny. Then, some aspectual verbs like *stop* are presuppositional. For instance,

Bif stopped drinking schnapps.

presupposes that Bif had been drinking schnapps. Some adverbs like *too* and *only* carry presuppositions.

Tom toasted a taco, too.

presupposes that someone else toasted a taco. The placement of sentence stress, and various other lexical items such as *bachelor* and *criticize* are presuppositional as well.

Mary's math teacher is a bachelor.

presupposes that Mary's math teacher is male.

The behavior of presuppositions in complex sentences has been one of the most intriguing sets of data investigated by linguists (Langendoen and Savin 1971; Karttunen 1973; Karttunen and Peters 1979; Schiebe 1975; Soames 1979; Wilson 1975; Gazdar 1979). Langendoen and Savin (1971) have defined the *projection problem* for presupposition as that of predicting the presuppositions of complex sentences as a function of their structures and of the simple presuppositional expressions that they embed. For instance, the simple sentence *Max stopped smoking* presupposes that Max used to smoke. Let's see what happens when this sentence is embedded as part of some larger complex sentences.

Each of the sentences

It is possible that Max stopped smoking.
If Max stopped smoking than he is smarter than I thought.

leaves the presupposition, that Max used to smoke, intact and unaltered.

On the other hand, each of the sentences

If Max has smoked then Max stopped smoking.
Max used to smoke and he stopped smoking.

fails to have the presupposition at all.

Each of the sentences

Fred believes that Max stopped smoking.

presupposes not that Max has smoked but that Fred *believes* that Max has smoked.*

The following presupposes not that Max has smoked, nor that Fred hopes that Max has smoked, but—like the last sentence—that Fred believes that Max has smoked.

Fred hopes that Max stopped smoking.

On the other hand,

Someone believes that Fred stopped smoking.

presupposes not that *someone* believes that Fred has smoked, but that *everybody* (or at least everybody in some group) believes that Fred has smoked. Finally,

If Max has ashtrays all over his house, then Max has stopped smoking.

presupposes that if Max has ashtrays all over his house, then Max has smoked.

The observations that can be made about the presuppositions of complex sentences go on and on. Karttunen and Peters (1979) have described such observations in particular detail.

---

* In early literature on presupposition this sentence would be taken to have the stronger presupposition that Max has smoked. However, the satisfaction of this proposition is neither necessary nor sufficient to avoid presupposition failure for this sentence. That it is not necessary is indicated in the following discourse where the first sentence guarantees satisfaction of the presupposition of the second.

Fred mistakenly believes that Max used to smoke. He also believes that Max stopped smoking.

That it is not sufficient is indicated in the following, where the first sentence fails to guarantee satisfaction of the presupposition of the second.

* *No one but me knows that Max used to smoke. Fred believes that Max stopped smoking.*

The point is that sometimes one must try out a few discourse settings to get an accurate idea of what must be satisfied. The claims I make about these data are in accord with Karttunen and Peters (1979).

PRESUPPOSITION AND PAROCHIAL PROCESSING

Presuppositions are most commonly identified with information that is *given* before a sentence is uttered. For instance, a common discourse pattern is exemplified in the following,

> *Fred's hat is on fire. Furthermore, Fred knows his hat is on fire.*
> *Someone bagged a bunny. And it was Bif who bagged a bunny.*

in which a previous assertion *satisfies* the presupposition by guaranteeing that the presupposition of a later sentence will be given by the time that that sentence is processed. Generally if the presupposition *fails*, that is, is not satisfied, a sentence will be infelicitous or difficult (or even impossible) to interpret. I will assume minimally that any common information shared by both the speaker and hearer in a pragmatic setting or any knowledge that can be easily inferred through normal common-sense processes by both can be regarded as given.

Actually, as I have argued elsewhere (Dinsmore 1979, 1981a, 1981c), presupposition is not a homogeneous phenomenon at all but, like headaches, arises from a variety of factors. Among other things, presuppositions result from the following:

- *Preconditions of processes involved in understanding.* In view of the discussion of Chapters 4 and 5, it is not surprising that definite descriptions should be presuppositional. Recall that in order to fire the rule for *the* requires that the precondition ? S | U is "D" succeed, which is to say that it requires that an object satisfy the description "D" in S. For this reason a definite description, like *the king of France*, will presuppose the existence of an object satisfying the description. If the presupposition is not satisfied, then the definite description cannot be interpreted in the normal way.

- *Normal temporal trajectories.* Normally events are described in the order that they occur. Doing something tends to be described before stopping that thing. A sentence like *George stopped eating his sandwich* is likely to occur in a speech setting in which it has already been stated that George had been eating a sandwich. This is what makes *stop* presuppositional.

- *Folk-theoretic perspectives.* Many words we use refer to conditions that are defined in a specific mode of interpretation or value system. They are therefore presuppose elements of that framework. For instance, the word *stingy* is meaningful only against background assumptions in which not spending much money is regarded as bad. The word *thrifty* is meaningful only against background assumptions in which not spending much money is regarded as good. The choice of word depends on the choice of folk theory. This idea is discussed by Lakoff (1987) and by Fillmore (1982, etc.).

- *Strategies for presenting new information.* Clark and Haviland (1977) and Van der Auwera (1980) have suggested that speakers tend to balance given and new information. If some of the information communicated in a given sentence is already given for the hearer, then the hearer can more readily assimilate the remaining information. In the case for a relatively complex sentence like *George knows that the squirrel stole Fred's sandwich*, it is unlikely that both the fact that the squirrel stole Fred's sandwich and the fact that George knows about it will be communicated as new information in a single sentence. The fact about the squirrel can be communicated without reference to the fact about George, but not vice versa. Therefore the fact about the squirrel is likely to have been communicated earlier.

- *Pure presuppositions.* Some constructions are probably established as presuppositional by convention, but these, I think, are the exception. Clefts and pseudoclefts, discussed earlier, are likely members of this group.

Two points emerge from these observations.

First, presuppositions usually arise indirectly. Therefore to say that a particular grammatical construction is presuppositional is only to say that the attributed presupposition *tends* to be satisfied in most speech situations. For some presuppositional constructions this tendency is likely to be very strong, for some very weak.

Second, if a presupposition associated with a presupposition is satisfied, it is satisfied *parochially*. This is because presuppositions arise from parochial processes, the dominant processes in the three-level theory. More specifically:

☞ If "P" presupposes Q, and "P" is projected into space S, i.e., as **S | "P"**, then the presupposition Q will be *satisfied* just in case **S | Q** is *given*.

For example, *Max stopped smoking*, presupposes that Max has smoked, so if this is contextualized as

sp_1 | "Max stopped smoking"

then the presupposition will be satisfied only if the following is given,

sp_1 | Max has smoked

since the presuppositional construction *stop* is projected into sp_1. This is illustrated in Figure 6.1. Likewise,

Fred believes that Max stopped smoking.

might be projected onto

sp_0 | Fred believes that [[sp_4]]
sp_4 | Max stopped smoking

In this case, as in the last,

sp_4 | Max has smoked

should be given in order to satisfy the presupposition, since the presuppositional construction *stop* is projected into sp_4.

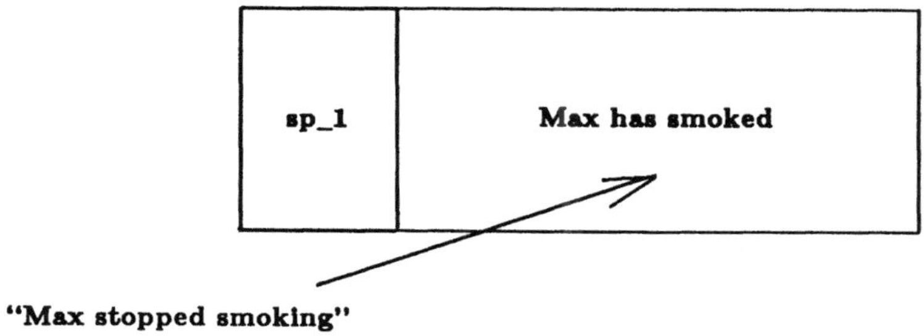

Fig. 6.1. The Parochial satisfaction of a presupposition.

WHAT HAPPENS IN COMPLEX SENTENCES?

This is where the parochial satisfaction of presupposition interacts with distribution. But first, let's see how others have answered this question.

Traditional Accounts

The traditional linguistic account of the projection problem (Langendoen and Savin 1971, Katz 1972; Katz and Langendoen 1976; Hausser 1976; Kartunnen and Peters 1979) proposes that grammatical rules apply recursively at each level of embedding in a way analogous to formal rules of semantic interpretation to derive the presuppositions of the current level as a function of the immediate structure of that level and the presuppositions of the next lower level. In Karttunen and Peters' system presuppositions of the next lower level may be maintained, altered, or lost completely at the current level. For instance, *believes* is associated with an explicit rule that takes the presuppositions of the complement and embeds them under the beliefs of the grammatical subject. *Possible* is associated with an explicit rule that takes the presuppositions of the complement and passes them on unaltered as the presupposition of the the next level of embedding. *Hopes* is associated with an explicit rule that takes the presuppositions of the complement and embeds them under the beliefs of the grammatical subject.

Such accounts of the projection problem are fundamentally inadequate for the following reasons (see Dinsmore (1981a, 1981b) for more details on these). First, they do not venture beyond the descriptive level, as Gazdar (1979) and Morgan (1973) point out. The generalizations about the conditions under which presuppositions are lost, retained or altered, belong purely to the description of linguistic structures. To posit formal rules which cancel, retain or alter presuppositions when the appropriate conditions given in the description are present adds nothing to the description, and in particular doesn't explain anything. Second, such accounts are forced to treat presupposition as a uniform grammatical category over which the projection rules are defined. This is inconsistent with the account of the last section that explains presuppositions as arising from other factors, such as preconditions of constructive rules. Third, this approach has failed even to attain descriptive adequacy. Every such account has required a large number of rules or specialized lexical features, yet still has allowed a lot of counterexamples. The elimination of even a small set of counterexamples in turn has required adding many more rules or lexical features to the grammar. On the other hand, virtually all of the facts about the presuppositions of complex sentences are precisely predicted from the current theory.

Presuppositions and Distribution

These complex and diverse kinds of intuitions about such sentences are due not to any special conditions on how presuppositions are satisfied (the rule stated above is completely general) as Karttunen and Peters and others propose, but rather on how knowledge is distributed over spaces in discourse understanding, along with the assumption that presuppositions are satisfied parochially.

To show this, we need to divide the problem of presuppositions into two separate questions:

(1) What embedded presuppositions are likely to be satisfied. Recall that presuppositions are not always satisfied, but tend to be.

(2) What must be given in the focus space for the sentence as a whole *if* the embedded presuppositions *are* satisfied parochially.

We find that what are identified as the presuppositions of complex sentences are just what must be given in the focus space in order to satisfy those embedded presuppositions that are likely to be satisfied. The second question is the more significant, so let's look at it first.

When Embedded Presuppositions are Satisfied

Lets look at a variety of complex presuppositional sentences, assuming in each case that the embedded presuppositions are satisfied. I will assume in each case that the given sentence is contextualized into the focus space sp_0. In each case, it turns out, where the complex sentence as a whole is observed to presuppose Q, a definitive argument exists that sp_0 | Q *must* be given if the presuppositions associated with the embedded presuppositional constructions are satisfied parochially. This argument is in every case fully supported by the principles of partitioned representations articulated in Chapter 2.

In these arguments we will see that the most significant recurring factor is whether the presuppositional construction is projected into a *new* space or not, that is, a space initialized in processing the sentence. If so, the presupposition must often be also given in some other space from which it is inherited into the new space, since the content of the new space will be minimal.

(1) *If Max stopped smoking then Max is truly amazing.*

Since sp_0 is the focus space, this might be projected onto:

sp_0 | "Max stopped smoking" → ⟦sp_5⟧
sp_5 | Max is truly amazing.

Since the presuppositional *stop* is projected into sp_0, the presupposition can be satisfied only if sp_0 | Max has smoked is given. Accordingly, we correctly predict that this sentence presupposes that Max has smoked.

(2) *Fred believes that Max stopped smoking.*

This is projected onto:

sp_0 | Fred believes that ⟦sp_2⟧
sp_2 | "Max stopped smoking"

Therefore sp_2 | Max has smoked must be given. Unlike the previous example, the presupposition need not be satisfied by inheritance. Since sp_2 is not necessarily a new space, knowledge might well already be given specifically in sp_2. If sp_2 | Max has smoked is given then sp_0 | Fred believes that Max has smoked is given (immediately inferable by context climbing) as well, since sp_2 is Fred's belief space relative to sp_0. Therefore, we predict that (2) presupposes that Fred believes that Max has smoked. Accordingly, in a discourse like

Fred believes that Max has smoked. And Fred believes that Max stopped smoking.

The first sentence projects "Max has smoked" into sp_2 where it satisfies the presupposition of *stop* in the second sentence.

I have shown why belief sentences should appear to embed the embedded presuppositions under belief. But earlier I pointed out that many researchers used to feel that the embedded presuppositions were passed through unchanged, for instance, that *Fred believes that Max has smoked* has the stronger presupposition that Max has smoked. In support of this position, observe that the presupposition *does* seem to be satisfied in discourses like the following:

Max used to smoke. Fred believes that Max stopped smoking.

The satisfaction of the presupposition in this case is easy to explain in terms of Ballim and Wilks' (forthcoming) theory of *ascription* in belief environments, discussed briefly in Chapter 2. Their *default strategy* for ascribing beliefs will generally copy beliefs from a parent space to an embedded belief space on demand if no contradictions thereby result in the belief space. This predicts that the projection of *Max used to smoke* will be copied into **sp_2** as required to satisfy the presupposition. The point is that the presupposition *must* be satisfied in **sp_2** in some way or another. There are a variety of ways in which the presupposition might be satisfied, all of them part of a broader theory of partitioned representations.

The next sentence contrasts with the last in a subtle but surprising way.

(3) *Someone believes that Max stopped smoking.*

This is projected onto something like:

sp_0 | obj_9 believes that ⟦sp_8⟧
sp_8 | "Max stopped smoking"

where **obj_9** is a *new* constant, and **sp_8** is a *new* space with a *new* primary context (even if we do not introduce a new constant, but rather use a primary context of the form **sp_0 | Someone believes that ⟦S⟧** we observe that S would not be a unique belief space; we would need to introduce a new space S in any case). So the following must be given:

sp_8 | Max has smoked

How is this satisfied? Since **sp_8** is a new space, **Max has smoked** must be inherited from some other space, i.e., from an *everybody* *believes* space **sp_3**, with

sp_0 | everybody believes that ⟦sp_3⟧
sp_3 | Max has smoked

Therefore, we correctly predict that the sentence (3) presupposes that everybody believes that Max has smoked. For instance, we observe that in the following discourse the presupposition of the second sentence is satisfied.

Everybody believes that Max has smoked. And someone believes that Max stopped smoking.

On the other hand, the first sentence does not satisfy the presupposition of *stop* in the following.

Someone believes that Max has smoked. And someone believes that Max stopped smoking.

In this case *Max has smoked* would be projected into one space and *stopped* into another, so the presupposition is not satisfied. Sentences of possibility are somewhat like this last example.

(4) *It is possible that Max stopped smoking.*

This would be projected onto something like:

sp_0 | it is possible that ⟦sp_1⟧
sp_1 | [sp_0]
sp_1 | "Max stopped smoking"

where **sp_1** is a *newly initialized* space. Since *stopped* is projected into **sp_1**, the following must be given:

sp_1 | Max has smoked

However, since **sp_1** is a new space, **Max has smoked** must be inherited from another space, namely **sp_0**. Therefore, the presupposition will be satisfied only if **sp_0 | Max has smoked** is given. Therefore, we correctly predict that the sentence (4) presupposes that Max has smoked. For instance, we observe that in the following discourse the presupposition of the second sentence is satisfied.

Max has smoked. And it is possible that Max stopped smoking.

On the other hand, the first sentence does not satisfy the

presupposition of *stop* in the following.

> *It is possible that Max has smoked. And it is possible that Max stopped smoking.*

In this case *Max has smoked* would be projected into one space and then *stopped* into another, so the presupposition is not satisfied.

(5) *Fred hopes that Max stopped kicking his dog.*

This is projected onto something like

sp_0 | Fred believes that ⟦sp_2⟧
sp_2 | "Max stopped kicking his dog" ▯→ ⟦sp_8⟧
sp_8 | favorable

Since the presuppositional construction *stopped* is projected into sp_2 the following must be given

sp_2 | Max has kicked his dog

How is this satisfied? In exactly the same way as the presupposition is satisfied in (2) above. Therefore, we correctly predict that the sentence (5) presupposes that Fred believes that Max has kicked his dog. For instance, we observe that in the following discourse the presupposition of the second sentence is satisfied.

> *Fred believes that Max has kicked his dog. Fred hopes that Max stopped kicking his dog.*

(6) *If someone at the conference solved the problem, then it was Julius who solved it.*

This is projected onto something like

sp_0 | someone at the conference solved the problem
→ ⟦sp_2⟧
sp_2 | someone at the conference solved the problem
sp_2 | "it was Julius who solved it"
sp_2 | [sp_0]

Since the presuppositional construction, a *pseudo-cleft, it was ...* is projected into sp_2 the following must be given

sp_2 | someone at the conference solved the problem

How is this satisfied? The answer is that no matter what is given in the current pragmatic setting it already is satisfied in the initialization of the space, as indicated in the projected representation above. Therefore, we correctly predict that the sentence (6) loses the presupposition.

(7) *If Nixon appoints J. Edgar Hoover to his Cabinet, he will regret having appointed a homosexual.*

This is projected onto something like

sp_0 | Nixon appoints J. Edgar Hoover to his Cabinet
→ [[sp_3]]
sp_3 | Nixon appoints J. Edgar Hoover to his Cabinet
sp_3 | [sp_0]
sp_3 | "he will regret having appointed a homosexual"

Since the presuppositional construction *regret* is projected into sp_3 the following must be given

sp_3 | Nixon appoints a homosexual

How is this satisfied? Since we are not necessarily dealing with a new space, it could be simply already given directly in sp_3. Therefore, we correctly predict that the sentence (7) presupposes that if Nixon appoints J. Edgar Hoover to his Cabinet, he will have appointed a homosexual. Notice this might, and probably would be, inferred by inheritance from sp_0. Notice that each of

sp_0 | Nixon has appointed a homosexual to his Cabinet.
sp_0 | J. Edgar Hoover is homosexual.

leads to the satisfaction of the presupposition in sp_3. For instance, we observe that in the following discourse the presupposition of the second sentence is satisfied in either of the following discourses.

Nixon has appointed a homosexual to his Cabinet. If Nixon appoints J. Edgar Hoover to his Cabinet, he will regret having appointed a homosexual.

J. Edgar Hoover is homosexual. If Nixon appoints J. Edgar Hoover to his Cabinet, he will regret having appointed a homosexual.

When Embedded Presuppositions are Not Satisfied

Presuppositional constructions per se tend to be satisfied parochially. Often conditions are present in a particular sentence, however, that contradict this tendency. When these conditions arise, the intuition generally is that the presupposition does not get satisfied. Such an example is the following.

Although Max never smoked, someone believes that he just stopped smoking.

Here, as noted above, if it is given that *everybody* believes that Max has smoked then the presupposition will be satisfied. But if everybody believes that, why is the speaker telling us it is not true? The presupposition is not satisfied, but that's O.K., since presuppositionality is just a tendency anyway. As a result, there seem to be no intuitions that the sentence as a whole has a presupposition about Max's smoking.

CONCLUSIONS

In summary, if the satisfaction of a presupposition is viewed as a part of parochial processes operating locally within a space, the complex, diverse and heretofore puzzling data about the presuppositions of complex presuppositions receive an immediate account as the interaction of this process with the way knowledge is distributed over spaces during language understanding. This account explains the linguistic data in terms of the independently motivated principles of partitioned representations, and what is more, it gives us the correct results virtually every time.

CHAPTER SEVEN

Space Frogs and Henry Ford

Let's turn our attention to the consequences of contextualization. This chapter shows how evidence from language makes it clear that the account of contextualization into spaces developed here must be correct. It then makes some points about the ways in which space cues end up contributing to semantics in discourse.

LINGUISTIC EVIDENCE FOR CONTEXTUALIZATION

The model of contextualization in partitioned representations, in effect, turns more traditional models of filling in implicit information inside out. Most traditional models of language understanding take the discourse sentence as central. The discourse sentence provides a core meaning which is then elaborated under the influence of various pragmatic factors. Such an account would begin with a sentence or intermediate structure of the form **P** and try to build this up to an intermediate structure of the form **X P Y**. For instance, it might begin with the discourse sentence

Their economy would be booming.

and construct an intermediate representation corresponding to

If the Japanese had won the war, their economy would be booming.

in a manner sensitive to the structure and content of the preceding discourse, thus capturing the full semantic intent of the original sentence. Let's call this more traditional approach to implicit content the *ellipses account* since it works by completing the sentence.

Instead of adding the context to the utterance, contextualization adds the utterance to the context. Contextualization projects a sentence as a whole into a space, called the *focus space*, in which to begin reconstructing the explicit content of the discourse structures. Figure 7.1 illustrates how contextualization projects the discourse sentence *The turtle bit Sherlock* into a space **sp_3**. This space **sp_3** will tell us if Sherlock *really* got bitten by a turtle, or if this occurred only within some *fictional* story, or whether this is something that Fred only *believes* to be the case. **sp_3** will also specify *when* the event occurred in the potential reality. For instance, the focus space **sp_3** might have a primary context like **sp_1 | At time tm_46: [[sp_3]]**, where **sp_1** will have a primary context like **sp_0 | In** *The Dog of the Burgervilles*, **[[sp_1]]**. Accordingly, the speaker will have no commitment to the literal real-world truth of the sentences expressed in the discourse. However, the semantic intent of every proposition expressed in this discourse will be captured in terms of context structure in which **sp_3** will be embedded. This will identify the content of the discourse as belonging to a particular time within a particular fiction. Accordingly, the full meaning of the discourse will be represented, and questions like *In the penultimate scene of 'the Dog of the Burgervilles', what bit Sherlock?* will be answerable even when **sp_3** is no longer in focus.

Two kinds considerations will show the decisive advantages of the partitioning account over the ellipses account. The first of these is the viability of the resulting internal representations, both in terms of efficiency and correctness. The second is the predictions each makes about possible discourse structures.

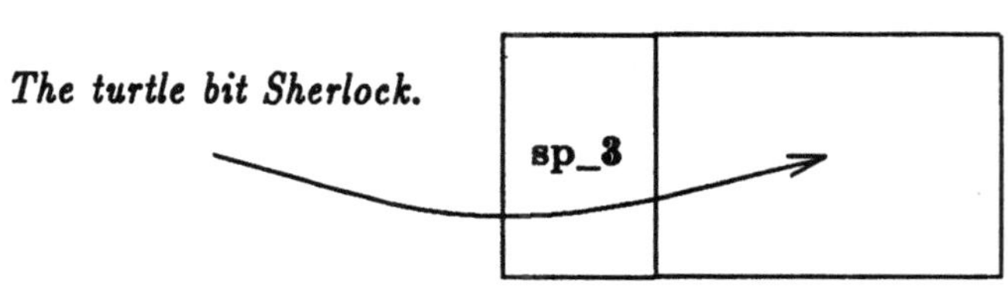

Fig. 7.1. Contextualization, finding the focus space.

Efficiency and Correctness

The ellipses account would produce internal representations that are from computational perspective highly inefficient as well as highly redundant. Consider, for instance, the following discourse:

> *In chess, each player tries to capture the opponent's king. If he moves a piece into a position that attacks the king, then he must say, "check." If his own king is attacked by a piece of his opponent's, then he must either make a move to avoid the attack, or resign the game. ...*

The representation of the chess discourse in the ellipses account would end up as something like

> **During any chess game game_4 each player player_5 is such that player_5 tries to capture the opponent's king. During any chess game game_4 each player player_5 is such that if player_5 moves a piece into a position that attacks the king, then player_5 must say "check." During any chess game game_4 each player player_5 is such that if player_5's own king is attacked by a piece of player_5's opponent's, then player_5 must either make a move to avoid the attack, or resign game_4.**

The ellipses account would augment each sentence with essentially the same structure. The resulting internal representations would also badly support any inferences we might want to derive about the game of chess, since there will be no representation of the generic game of chess in the form of a model of a potential reality.

The partitioning account, on the other hand, uses a single *quantification space* into whose primary context this redundancy collapses . After the first sentence of the second discourse the focus space might have a primary context something like **sp_0 | during any chess game obj_4** each player **obj_5** is such that **⟦sp_3⟧**. The focus space for the subsequent discourse is a quantification space, defined by the existential assumption of a generic chess player within a generic chess game. The following are essentially satisfied.

sp_3 | • obj_4
sp_3 | obj_4 is chess game

sp_3 | • obj_5
sp_3 | obj_5 is chess player

The subsequent discourse can refer to those objects using pronouns and definite descriptions, e.g. *he* and *his own* to refer to **obj_5** and *the game* to refer to **obj_4**, but from the (more objective) perspective of **sp_0** large ranges of objects are being discussed. Contextualization in this form successfully accounts for the observed semantic intent and the same time describes the generic chess game completely and coherently in one place.

Furthermore, the ellipses account would often lead to internal representations that mean something *different* from the intended meanings of the surface discourses. Consider the following discourse:

> *It is possible that the President is lying. He will have snuck out the back door of the White House and taken a cab to the red-light district. Of course, he will have worn sun-glasses so no one would recognize him.*

The ellipses account would project this discourse onto a representation something like

> **It is possible that president_1 is lying. It is possible that president_1 has snuck out the back door of the White House and taken a cab to the red-light district. It is possible that president_1 has worn sun-glasses so no one would recognize him.**

However, this representation *loses* the information that all of these things are possibly true *together*, i.e., that we are talking about one possibility, not several.

The partitioning account, on the other hand, fixes on a single possibility space for contextualization with the result that each sentences serves to augment that representation of a single reality. Understanding the first sentence constructs the possibility space, call it **sp_3**, with a context something like **sp_0 | it is possible that ⟦sp_3⟧**. Subsequently **sp_3** becomes the focus space and discourse sentences are simply projected into **sp_3** to recover the semantic intent of the sentences.

Focus Spaces and Possible Discourses

From contextualization we can make correct predictions about possible and impossible discourses that we cannot make in the ellipses account. To begin with, it turns out that *any* of the coherent spaces exemplified in Chapter 2 can serve as a focus space. I will illustrate a variety of possible focus spaces with examples of contextualization into a belief space, into a conditional space, into a counterfactual space, and into a temporal space. In the previous two pages we have already seen examples of contextualization into a quantification space (the chess discourse) and into a possibility space (the sneaky president discourse). Then I will demonstrate that there are no discourses that would correspond to contextualization into spaces that are not permitted for reasons of incoherence.

Our next example involves a focus space of belief:

> *Arthur believes it is the duty of everyone to fight what he thinks is an invasion of space frogs. Before this situation gets out of hand, every homeowner should defrog his own yard, taking care to check behind every shrub.*

In this and in each of the subsequent examples, as well as in the earlier chess and sneaky president examples, an initial shift in focus from the parent space will make the identity of the focus space for the subsequent sentences clear, that is, each discourse follows the *construct then contextualize* pattern discussed in Chapter 4. After the first sentence of the first discourse the focus space is **sp_7** with a primary context something like **sp_3 | Arthur believes that ⟦sp_7⟧**. The contents of all but the first sentence will be projected directly into that space. Thus, the reconstructed semantic intent is that Arthur *believes* that every homeowner should defrog his yard, and so on, rather than that every homeowner *really* should do this. The observed semantic intent is evidence that contextualization has occurred as we have described.

Roberts (1987) discusses the next sentence, which involves a conditional focus space:

> *If Joan forgets to fill the birdfeeder, she will feel very bad. The birds will get hungry.*

The first sentence introduces a conditional space, call it **sp_5**, with a context something like **sp_1 | Joan forgets to fill the birdfeeder → ⟦sp_5⟧**. Subsequently **sp_5** becomes the focus space and the next sentence is simply projected into **sp_5** to give **sp_5 | the birds get hungry**. This recovers the semantic intent of the sentence.

The next discourse involves contextualization into a counterfactual space.

> *If the Japanese had won the war, they would have established secure sources of raw materials. They would also have a big market for manufactured goods. Their economy would be booming.*

The first sentence introduces a counterfactual space, call it **sp_2**, with a context something like **sp_0 | japanese have won ww2 □→ ⟦sp_2⟧**. Subsequently **sp_2** becomes the focus space and discourse sentences are projected into **sp_2** to recover the observed semantic intent of the sentences.

Another example involves a temporal/situational focus space:

> *At 12 o'clock, Bif was munching lunch. He was dressed in a tasteful hawaiian shirt with flowers and palm trees. He also wore plaid shorts and was listening to the news. He was about to go out on one of the hottest of dates.*

The first sentence introduces a temporal space, call it **sp_4**, with a context something like **sp_0 | at time tm_6: ⟦sp_4⟧**. Subsequent discourse sentences are then simply projected into **sp_4** to capture the implicit semantic content of the sentences.

Still another example, discussed by Karttunen (1976), involves a generic situational space:

> *Harvey courts a girl at every convention. She always comes to the banquet with him. The girl is usually very pretty.*

Finally, Roberts (1987) attributes the following to Jerry Morgan, illustrating a dream space.

> *Last night I dreamed I got a Red Porsche for my birthday. I drove it all over the country and loved every minute of it. This morning I woke up and much to my surprise found it parked in my driveway.*

The focus space in this last discourse moves to a dream space then back to the original space.*

In summary, the discourses illustrated are ones that are in fact expected in the contextualization account based on the theory of partitioned representations. However, observe that they are not ruled out in the ellipses account either. *Score: contextualization-1, ellipses-1.*

On the other hand, contextualizations *rules out* some impossible discourses, which the ellipses account fails to rule out. For instance, the ellipses account would seem to lead to the unfortunate prediction that discourses like the following are possible, in analogy to Arthur's frog discourse. Here, the environment X...Y used after the initial sentence would be *It is not the case that ....*

> *It is not the case that there is an invasion of space frogs. It is the duty of every homeowner to defrog his own yard...*

But patently this discourse cannot mean that the negation of each sentence is true. Partitioned representations, on the other hand, prohibit such discourses: There can be no *not* spaces since they would violate the criterion of coherence, as discussed in Chapter 2.

We should point out with regard to this last argument what might at first sight look like a counterexample, but on closer inspection actually strengthens the argument. There are discourses like the following,

> *It is not the case that there is an invasion of space frogs. It would be the duty of every homeowner to defrog his own yard...*

in which an embedding environment of the form *it is not the case that ...* would in fact have to condition a shift in focus space in spite of our claim that this environment does not correspond to any primary context. However, observe that this environment does not correspond to the implicit semantic intent of the subsequent sentences either. The primary context of the focus space, sp_4 used in this discourse is something like

sp_3 | there is an invasion of space frogs □→ ⟦sp_4⟧

---

* The reference of *it* is handled readily by (IdentPrinc), as described in Chapter 5; it depends on recognizing a correspondence, or counterpart relation, between the object in the dream and a real-life object.

That is, we are in fact dealing with a *counterfactual* space to which the *unavailability* of the not space directs us. The intended meaning of the discourse makes this clear. Thus it and not the ellipses account makes the correct prediction.

Similarly, we do not find discourses in which each sentence is implicitly embedded under *Fred hopes that ...*, *If ... then Warren will be furious* and so on. Contextualization would rule these out, but the ellipses account would fail to rule these out. *Score: contextualization-2, ellipses-1.*

In summary, the partitioning account is *more functional* than the ellipses account because it realizes the underlying efficiency of the partitioned representations. The partitioning account is *more proximate* than the ellipses account because it involves building less structure. And finally, the partitioning account is *more discriminating* than the ellipses account in that it makes correct predictions about both impossible and incomplete discourses.

THE SEMANTIC CONTRIBUTIONS OF SPACE CUES

Space cues generally seem semantically thin. Consider the conditional *would*. As space cues, these expressions do not project onto semantically pregnant internal representations the way *jump* or *Fred's nose* do. Rather their contribution is less direct, in influencing the direction of contextualization. Nevertheless, in this task they do have a semantic influence. It will be interesting to look at that influence at this point.

The Semantic Contribution of Moods

The most consistently present type of space cue in English seems to be associated with the form of the main verb of a discourse sentence, e.g., **past**, **present**, or **conditional**, that is, with a *tense* or a *mood*. Both Fauconnier (1985) and Roberts (1987) independently identify the mood of a verb as a determinant in what I call contextualization. English apparently requires the conditional verb form (usually indicated by *would*) for any other sentence or embedded clause to be projected into a *counterfactual* space **S1**, one whose primary context is of the form **S0** | **P** $\Box\!\!\rightarrow$ [[**S1**]] and prohibits its use in any sentence or embedded clause. For instance, in the following discourse,

> *If cars had never been produced, people would still ride horses. Furthermore, shopping malls would not exist. At least there would be less smog.*

processing the first sentence will set up a space, call it **sp_2**, with a context something like

> **sp_1 | cars have never been produced $\Box\!\!\rightarrow$ ⟦sp_2⟧**

The clause *people would still ride horses* uses the conditional verb form since it is projected into **sp_2**, where **sp_2** is a counterfactual space. This space then becomes the focus space for the next two conditional sentences. Now, let's contrast the use of the conditional verb form with the use of a non-subjunctive form in sentences that are otherwise identical. If the discourse continues,

> *We would have a lot to blame Henry Ford for.*

sp_2 will likely remain in focus, since it is a counterfactual space as required. *We have a lot to blame Henry Ford for* will be projected into **sp_2**, in which Henry Ford is represented as having *failed* to develop cars. The semantic intent would therefore be

> **sp_1 | cars have never been produced $\Box\!\!\rightarrow$ we have a lot to blame Henry Ford for.**

This, the semantic intent we actually observe, will entail, indirectly, a positive assessment of cars.

On the other hand, if the discourse continues,

> *We have a lot to blame Henry Ford for.*

then a shift to some other space, probably back to the previous focus space **sp_1**, will be forced because no conditional is present. *We have a lot to blame Henry Ford for* will be projected into **sp_1**, in which Henry Ford is represented as having *succeeded* in developing cars. This will entail, indirectly, a negative assessment of cars. The two continuations actually lead to opposing implications, but these are accounted for in terms of the differing contextualizations called for by the differing space cues, not in terms of a difference in the contents constructed in each case.

English apparently uses the auxiliary verb *will* for any sentence or embedded clause to be projected into a speculation ("candidate reality") space, that is, into a possibility space, into a plausibility space, or into a conditional space. This is illustrated in the following discourse.

If Fred made it to Europe at all, then he will be in Liechtenstein right now. He will have spent most of his money and will be homesick. He is as irresponsible as ever.

Notice that the focus space has changed to a non-conditional for the last sentence. The meaning would be different if the last sentence were

He will be as irresponsible as ever.

Roberts (1987) contrasts the following discourses with and without the occurrence of *will* in the second sentence.

If John bought a book, he'll be home reading it by now. It'll be a murder mystery.

If John bought a book, he'll be home reading it by now. * *It is a murder mystery.*

The second sentence in the first discourse contextualizes into the conditional space created in processing the first sentence. This is consistent with the use of *will* and allows *it* to be interpreted (e.g., according to (Def), see Chapter 5), since the book is situated there. The second sentence of the second discourse cannot contextualize into that space, since it does not use *will* and therefore does not allow *it* to be interpreted, since the book is only situated in that conditional space.

The Semantic Contribution of Tenses

Likewise, tenses can be used to direct the contextualization process. As described in Chapters 2 and 5, a *temporal space* is any space S with a primary context of the form **S0 | at time T: [[S]]**. I will say, given such a context, that **T** is *the time of* **S**. Also, if a sentence *P* is projected into **S**, I will say that **T** is *the time of P*, as well.

A temporal space has the same role as any other space in the contextualization process. We can therefore explain a lot about tense and time sequencing in discourse in terms of more general principles. For instance, the following discourse exhibits the usual pattern of *inertia,* discussed above with regard to non-temporal spaces, which includes the tendency to use the same focus space for consecutive sentence until a space cue indicates a shift, as well as the tendency to return to a previous focus space.

> *Fred's car was parked at the corner. Fred himself was looking under the hood. Fred is a good mechanic. Unfortunately, he had forgotten his tools. It was already dark.*

As a result of contextualization into the same temporal focus space, a sequence of descriptions with fixed tense is, by inertia, typically interpreted implicitly as having contextualizing into a fixed temporal space such that the time of the space is some past time tm_2. This accounts for the observed semantic intent that the states of Fred's car being parked at the corner, of Fred's looking under the hood, of the tools' having been forgotten, and its being dark. Notice that when the tense changes, as in *Fred is a good mechanic,* the temporal space changes. The next sentence, *Unfortunately, he had forgotten his tools,* shifts back to the past tense and back to the earlier temporal space (The state of his *having* forgotten his tools is true at tm_2; the role of the perfect in such sentences will be explained more clearly in Chapter 8).

English apparently permits the past tense only in a sentence or embedded clause that is projected into a temporal space that has a time **T** before the *time of speech* **NOW**, i.e., $\mathbf{T} < \mathbf{NOW}$. Recall that **NOW** is used to refer to the time of speech, specified as part of the pragmatic setting. English apparently permits the so-called *present tense* in a sentence that projects into virtually any kind of space, including a non-temporal space, as in:

> *Chess is a game of skill.*

into a temporal space situated *at* the time of speech:

> *Fred is as mad as a hornet.*

into a temporal space situated *after* the time of speech:

> *Tomorrow it snows.*

or even, though less commonly, into a temporal space situated *before* the time of speech:

> *Then George starts to get mad and punches this guy out.*

This last case occurs most often in narrations.* Typically the choice between present tense and past tense will be made on the basis of temporal relations to NOW as in Figure 7.2.

Space Cue or Ambient Projector?

Having analyzed tenses as space cues, we want to develop an alternative, deeper, analysis whereby tenses are not space cues at all, not in the strict sense that the conditional verb form is a space cue. Rather a tense may project onto an internal representation with real semantic content but then interact with plausibility constraints on contextualization to produce effectively the same behavior of space cues. This alternative analysis is suggested by an account of other temporal expressions, for instance:

In 1890, break dancing was unknown.
I went to the movie with Clint on a rainy Sunday afternoon.

Either of these sentences might occur in Bif's story about going to a Clint Eastwood movie with Clint Eastwood discussed in Chapter 4.

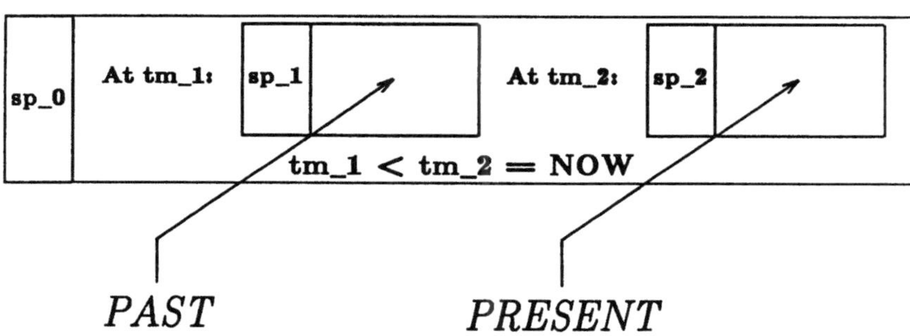

Fig. 7.2. The effect of tense on contextualization.

---

* I might speculate that the reason the use of the present in past temporal spaces is not more common is simply that past is available in such cases and serves to remove a potential ambiguity that the present cannot. Since a present temporal spaces is always somewhat active (to represent the speech situation) the focus space can easily shift to that present space. The past tense keeps the focus space fixed in some past temporal space when that is desired; the present tense will not.

The first will contextualize into the more recent movie theater space **sp_4**, the second will contextualize into the cowboy space **sp_5**. Notice that *in 1890* and *on a rainy Sunday afternoon* behave effectively as space cues insofar as they help determine the focus space. However, from Chapter 5 we know that these sentence project onto representations like the following:

sp_5 | it is 1890
sp_5 | Break dancing is unknown.
sp_4 | it is rainy
sp_4 | it is a Sunday
sp_4 | it is an afternoon
sp_4 | Bif and Cliff go to the movie

In analogy, the projection for a *past* sentence might be constructed as follows.

(Past)
Conditions: **S | past P**

Actions: **S | P**
S | it is PAST

where **PAST** is a time constant defined semantically to refer to the time interval that begins indefinitely early an ends immediately before **NOW**. Because of its dependence on **NOW**, the precise projection **PAST** is determined in the pragmatic setting.

From this projection of past, we can show that a blatant contradiction, the worst kind of implausibility, results in the *parent space* if we fail to project a past sentence into a space with a past time. This contradiction can be inferred according to the semantic rule (It is), which, it will be recalled, takes the following form:

(It is) S | at time T1: it is T2 iff S | T1 during T2.

For instance, suppose that sp_7 is a present space, i.e.,

sp_0 | at time NOW: [[sp_7]]

and we project the sentence *Fred ate a sandwich* into sp_7.

sp_7 | Fred eats a sandwich
sp_7 | it is PAST

Context climbing tells us that the following is implicitly satisfied.

sp_0 | at time NOW: it is PAST

And (It is) tells us that the following semantic contradiction is satisfied

sp_0 | NOW during PAST

Thus, the plausibility constraint on contextualization forces past to behave like a space cue, a consequence of the semantics of its projection.

In conclusion, we can analyze the past tense either as a focus cue or as something that actually projects onto a meaningful ambient element of the content of a space. Either analysis appears to have the same results.

SUMMARY

Contextualization is achieved by projecting the discourse sentence directly into a *focus space*, a space identified at least partly on the basis of *activation* of spaces, *communicative function*, and grammatical *space cues*.

Contextualization has a dual effect in language understanding. First, it helps to determine appropriate use and the structure of discourse. This is because it is critically conditioned by a variety of pragmatic factors, most particularly by the activations of spaces. Second, it helps to recover meaning. The projection of a sentence into a focus space supplies (for those who might be counting) *most* of the conceptual content of the discourse sentence.

This model of contextualization is superior to more traditional accounts in terms of proximity, discrimination, and functionality. This model also leads to explanations of some observed linguistic structures, especially patterns observed over extended discourse. Among the linguistic problems that contextualization also underlies is *temporal aspect*, which the next chapter looks at in detail.

CHAPTER EIGHT

Temporal Aspect

Aspect refers to what has intuitively been called the temporal perspective from which an event is viewed (Comrie 1976). In English, the following use different aspects to view the same event, that of Bif building a barn. The technical names of the aspectual forms are given in parentheses.

Bif built the barn.	(Perfective)
Bif began building the barn.	(Inceptive)
Bif finished building the barn.	(Terminative)
Bif was building the barn.	(Progressive)
Bif was going to build the barn.	(Prospective)
Bif had built the barn.	(Perfect)

This chapter demonstrates that the multitude of linguistic problems—syntactic, semantic, and pragmatic—associated with aspect are a direct consequence of the partitioning framework, along with very minimal and well-motivated assumptions about the specific semantics of the projections of aspect.

REFERENCE TIME: TEMPORAL PERSPECTIVE

Researchers in the semantics of tense and aspect have looked at sets of sentences like the following,

Fred won $1,000,000 in the lottery.
Fred has won $1,000,000 in the lottery.
Fred had won $1,000,000 in the lottery.

and in view of their apparent truth-conditional identity have generally proposed semantic analyses which attribute the same explicit semantic content to them, leaving open the question of what the differences in such sets are supposed to be.

The most common answer is that the distinctions between the aspects have something to do with the *perspective* from which an event is viewed. This idea is discussed by Jespersen (1924), Bull (1960), Joos (1964) and others, although the best known exposition of this idea is that of the logician Reichenbach (1947), who introduces the term *reference time* (R)–as distinguished from *event time* (E) and *speech time* (S)–to refer to this temporal perspective. In the current example E would be the time at which Fred wins the lottery. In the first sentence, R is the same as E, and both precede S, that is, $R = E < S$. For the second, $E < R = S$. For the third, $E < R < S$. More generally, R, E and S for different combinations of tense and aspect are related as in Figure 8.1.

Unfortunately, although Reichenbach's description makes some kind of intuitive sense, its substance has been hard to pinpoint, because Reichenbach never provided a clear definition of reference time: It has been unclear whether his description says something about *truth conditions* of sentences, or makes claims about the *pragmatic conditions* under which the aspects are actually used felicitously in discourse. However, there seems to be a consensus among semanticists who have been concerned with this topic, articulated for instance by Taylor (1977), that reference time is a purely pragmatic notion having nothing to do with semantic interpretation. The argument is that differences in reference time do not seem to correlate with differences in truth conditions.

The thesis of this chapter is that this conclusion is absolutely wrong. Aspectual distinctions are reflected in differing projections onto internal representations, that have, in their respective spaces, clearly different semantics. That is, different aspects are used within a given space to describe different potential situations or realities. On the other hand, in the three-level model the semantic contribution of contextualization under certain circumstances *offsets* the semantic contribution of distribution. This is the origin of the paradox.

In this chapter, I will define the semantics of the aspects explicitly and show why we *must* assume a semantic basis for aspectual distinctions. Then we will show how the semantics of the projections of aspects interacts with what we all ready know about the

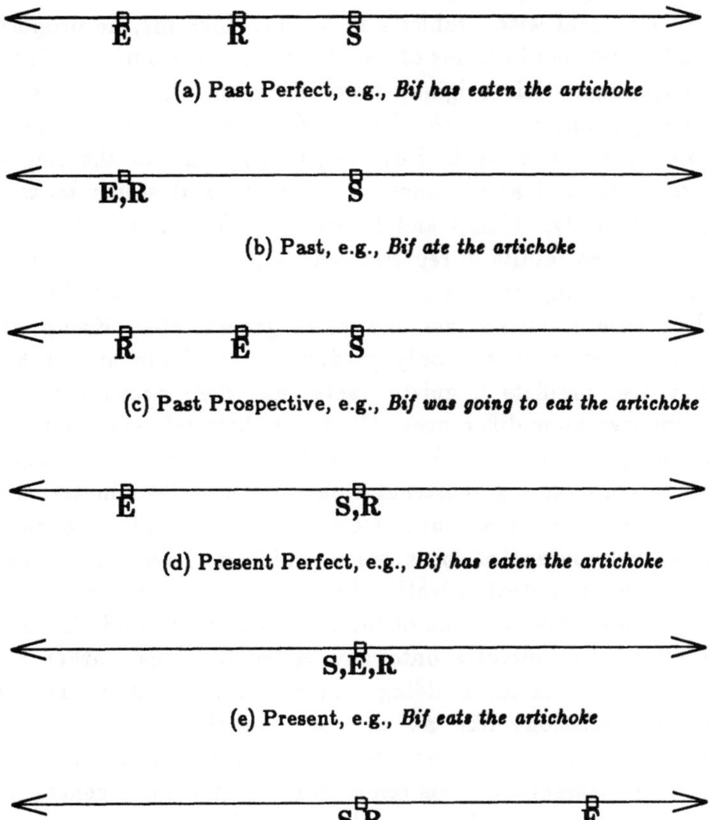

(a) Past Perfect, e.g., *Bif has eaten the artichoke*

(b) Past, e.g., *Bif ate the artichoke*

(c) Past Prospective, e.g., *Bif was going to eat the artichoke*

(d) Present Perfect, e.g., *Bif has eaten the artichoke*

(e) Present, e.g., *Bif eats the artichoke*

(f) Present Prospective, e.g., *Bif is going to eat the artichoke*

Fig. 8.1. Reichenbach's Tense System.

contextualization process to explain why aspectual distinctions are not always reflected in differing truth conditions, but are reflected in differing uses. Finally, we will undertake to analyze the aspectual construction that has been found most problematic in the English language, the present perfect, to see how the theory of partitioned representations holds out when we look at linguistic data in fine detail.

I should point out that the relationship of the account of aspect discussed here to that developed in discourse representation theory. Kamp's (1979) originally proposed the idea of discourse representations in order to deal with problems in aspect. Like me, he proposed that aspect be analyzed in terms of its particular contribution to internal representations. His original emphasis is on the French *passé simple* and *imparfait*, and much of what Kamp says probably carries over to English at some level. However, a large part of the English aspect system (as well as of many other languages) seems to work quite a bit differently. Kamp and Rohrer (1983) take a look at the English system that results in representations that are similar to what I will propose, but only up to a point. In a sense the account that will be described here is lower-level and more general than Kamp and Rohrer's and accordingly not only predicts what Kamp and Rohrer predict, but also predicts linguistic facts that their account misses. Let me summarize some differences. First, for them reference time is a primitive concept, a kind of pointer into the discourse representations referred to in constructing representations and described in terms of that role. In the present account reference time defined in terms of the more general concept of focus space, which we have seen plays a very general role in contextualization for all kinds of discourses. The reference time is simply the time of the focus space. Second, for them aspects don't project directly onto any representations, rather into very specific procedures for building representations that incorporate more primitive relations like **at** and $<$. In the present account aspects project in a more proximate way onto representations that can be given a clear semantics. This semantics captures some generalizations about co-occurrence of temporal adverbials with aspects. The very specific procedures that Kamp and Rohrer suggest in fact emerge from the interaction of these representations with completely general principles of contextualization. Finally, for them aspects do not contribute to more local representations; all new structures are build in effect in the parent space. In the present account, making use of the general concept of secondary context, the function of aspects is found in their ability to consolidate information into ambient representations in the more local spaces. Looking at the same event from a particular temporal perspective has a real functional basis in the present account.

SEMANTICS AND CONSTRUCTION

A major thesis of this work is that surface English aspects map onto corresponding structures in the internal representation in a very proximate and (perhaps surprisingly) uniform way, and that these structures in the internal representation represent temporal relations. I will represent the projection of each of the aspects, as follows.

Perfect	___ has occurred
Prospective	___ is to occur
Progressive	___ is occurring
Inceptive	___ begins to occur
Terminative	___ finishes occurring

Within a space, such a representation must potentially be true of a possible situation or possible reality, and must also support inferences about temporal relations. Thus, it is appropriate to talk about the *semantics of the projection* of an aspectual construction, but I will refer to this informally as the semantics of the construction for short.

Semantics

Recall that I use *sanctioned inferences* defined over internal representations to state generalizations about the semantics of internal representations in the way that logicians use meaning postulates. The semantics of temporal representations is assumed to be based primarily on temporal *intervals* rather than on time *points*. Intervals are contiguous segments of time having duration as well as position on a time line such that one interval can be before another, overlap with another or be contained within another. I will make use of the set of simple representations for relations among temporal intervals described by Allen (1983). These are described as follows:

(during) If T1 is contained within T2, then we write T1 during T2.

(begins) If T1 and T2 begin at the same point, but T2 ends after T1, we write T1 begins T2.

(finishes) If T2 begins before T1 but both end at the same point, we write T1 finishes T2.

(<) If T1 is entirely before T2 we write T1 < T2.

I assume that propositions are true at time intervals. We can express this with statements, for instance, of the form

sp_3 | at time tm_8: Fred_7 jumps onto horse_8.

Observe that even if we have

S | T1 during T2
S | at time T1: P
S | at time T2: Q

we do not necessarily have either of

S | at time T1: Q
S | at time T2: P

For instance, the time at which Fred opens a can of tuna is distinct from the time at which he pulls off the lid.

The semantics of each aspectual representation is in effect a mapping from a proposition true at one time interval onto a proposition true of some other time interval. If Fred builds the barn at T1 then the *state* of Fred's *having* built the barn is true at any time *after* T1, the process of Bif's *building* the barn is true at any time *during* T1, and so on. Graphically, given the occurrence of the event P at some time interval, as shown in Figure 8.2, a time at which each of the aspectual representations is true is shown on the time line in the figure.

In order to formalize this somewhat I will express this semantics in terms of the sanctioned inferences it entails:

(Perf) S | at time T: P has occurred iff for some time T1:
S | at time T1: P and S | T1 < T

(Pros) S | at time T: P is to occur iff for some time T1:
S | at time T1: P and S | T < T1

(Prog) S | at time T: P is occurring iff for some time T1:
S | at time T1: P and S | T during T1

(Ince) S | at time T: P starts to occur iff for some time T1:
S | at time T1: P and S | T begins T1

(Term) S | at time T: P finishes occurring iff for some time T1:

S | at time T1: P and S | T finishes T1

Observe how the rules for perfect and prospective begin to suggest Reichenbach's description of the reference times for these: **R** is to **E** as **T** is to **T1**. Dinsmore (1982) and Johnson (1981) both propose that the notion of reference time is naturally extended to the other aspects in an interval-based temporal representation. The relationship of **R** to **E** in these proposals also corresponds to those of **T** to **T1** in the rules above.

In all fairness, it should be pointed out that these rules are not quite adequate, though they are good approximations and illustrative of the approach advocated here. The weakness of the rules has to do with the modal character of the prospective, inceptive and progressive. None of these actually entails that the event described by P actually occurs or is completed (Dowty 1979).

The function of aspects is to provide correct ambient representations for the same event from the perspective of different temporal spaces. *Consolidation* is the key principle here. In brief, aspectual representations with the semantics suggested provides an alternative means of expressing temporal relations. Thus rather than representing that **P** happens before **Q** as

at time tm_1: P
at time tm_2: Q
tm_1 < tm_2

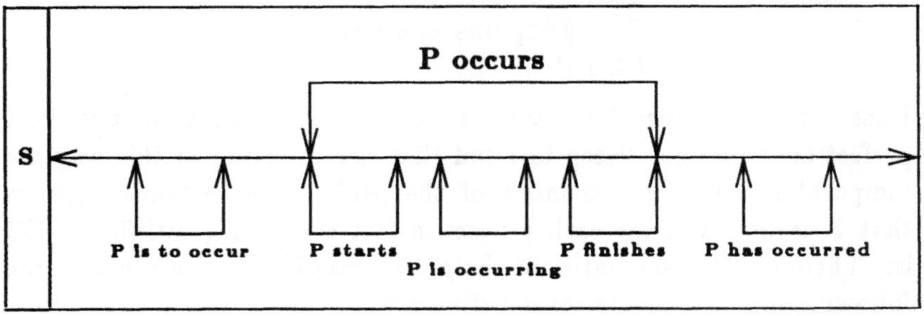

Fig. 8.2. Semantics for Aspects.

we can represent it effectively as

at time tm_2: Q
at time tm_2: P has occurred

In most computational systems of temporal reasoning and understanding something like the first representation is generally preferred because if involves lower levels of embedding of predicates. However, in partitioned representations the embedding of relations actually improves *consolidation* into more local spaces in most cases. The second representation is therefore often preferred. In Chapter 4 I discussed of the advantages of *ambient expressions* in this regard.

Constructive Rules

Turning to constructive rules for aspectual expressions, it is not surprising that aspects are space builders: we have contexts of the forms

sp_0 | it has been the case that ⟦sp_1⟧
sp_0 | it is happening that ⟦sp_2⟧

Spaces like **sp_1** and **sp_2** are coherent domains for reasoning. If it has been the case that I ate stuffed grape leaves in a Greek restaurant then it has been the case that I have been in a Greek restaurant, and so on. Accordingly, we should have a constructive rule for the perfect as follows.

Conditions:	**S1 | P "has occurred"**
Actions:	**create a space, S2**
	S1 | ⟦S2⟧ has occurred
	S2 | P

I use "**has occurred**" to stand uniformly for the somewhat variant perfect construction. Keep in mind that spaces set up in this way are temporal spaces; the semantics of the perfect, for instance, tells us that **P** is true at some earlier time; in fact everything satisfied in **S2** is. Therefore, the semantics of the perfect would actually sanction the following more elaborate constructive rule.

(Perfect)
Conditions: S1 | P "has occurred"
? S0 | at time T1: ⟦S1⟧
Actions: create a space, S2
S1 | [S2] has occurred
create a time, T2
S0 | at time T2: ⟦S2⟧
S0 | T2 < T1
S2 | P

S1 and S2 are thus both temporal spaces ordered within S0. From the perspective of mental representation the use of the perfect improves consolidation into more local spaces, and thus improves the effectiveness of parochial reasoning. In this case, the representation created allows one to reason about the effects of P entirely within S1. Without perf there could be no representation within S1 of the previous occurrence of P. We can think of the aspect as projecting onto a context that allows S1 and S2 to communicate directly. We are also justified in deriving the context S2 | it is going to happen that [S1], according to the semantics of the Prospective.

In analogy to (Perfect) we also have the following constructive rules. Notice that the only differences in these rules, aside from the aspectual operator involved, are the temporal relations between T1 and T2.

(Prospective)
Conditions: S1 | P "is to occur"
? S0 | at time T1: ⟦S1⟧
Actions: create a space, S2
S1 | [S2] is to occur
create a time, T2
S0 | at time T2: ⟦S2⟧
S0 | T2 > T1
S2 | P

(Progressive)	
Conditions:	**S1 | P "is occurring"**
?	**S0 | at time T1: ⟦S1⟧**
Actions:	**create a space, S2**
	S1 | [S2] is occurring
	create a time, T2
	S0 | at time T2: ⟦S2⟧
	S0 | T1 during T2
	S2 | P
(Inceptive)	
Conditions:	**S1 | P "starts to occur"**
?	**S0 | at time T1: ⟦S1⟧**
Actions:	**create a space, S2**
	S1 | [S2] starts to occur
	create a time, T2
	S0 | at time T2: ⟦S2⟧
	S0 | T1 begins T2
	S2 | P
(Terminative)	
Conditions:	**S1 | P "finishes occurring"**
?	**S0 | at time T1: ⟦S1⟧**
Actions:	**create a space, S2**
	S1 | [S2] finishes occurring
	create a time, T2
	S0 | at time T2: ⟦S2⟧
	S0 | T1 finishes T2
	S2 | P

Independent Evidence for Semantics

The semantics of an aspect, or the constructive rules and sanctioned inferences that follow from it, can be motivated independently of discourse use by how it interacts with the semantics of other temporal expressions compositionally.

Certain syntactic structures in English express, among other things, temporal relations between events. For instance, each of the following example sentences will entail the simultaneity of two events or states.

Smelling something good, they went to the kitchen.

entails that the smelling and the going occur at the same time.

George was known to be in Borneo.

entails that someone knew of George's presence in Borneo at the time that he was in Borneo.

When George got home, Mabel was asleep.

entails that at the same time as George's arrival, Mabel was in a state of unconsciousness. We can express this (while avoiding details of syntactic composition) as the following conditions:

(Gerund)
Conditions: S | "V+ing X, NP VP"

Actions: S | "NP V X"
S | "NP VP"

(Known)
Conditions: S | "NP be known to VP"

Actions: .....
S | "NP VP"
....

(When)
Conditions: S | "When P, Q"
? S | "P"

Actions: S | "Q"

Here NP refers to the same syntactic noun phrase, VP to same verb phrase and V to the same verb throughout each rule. The rule (Known) is incomplete, since the remaining details are not simple but are also not relevant to the problem at hand. The condition for *when* is not quite adequate, but it will serve as a good approximation for demonstration. Notice that the *when*-clause is presupposed.

The rules for aspects lead immediately to correct predictions about temporal relations in similar sentences that use aspectual operators like the following (Dinsmore 1982).

About to smell something good, they went to the kitchen.
George was known to be building a house.
When George got home, Mabel had left.

For instance, if we have

sp_1 | "About to smell something good,
they went to the kitchen"
sp_0 | at time tm_1: [[sp_1]]

then by (Gerund)

sp_1 | "they were about to smell something good"
sp_1 | "they went to the kitchen"

and so climbing the context and applying (Prosp) gives us

sp_0 | at time tm_1: they went to the kitchen
sp_0 | at time tm_2: they smell something good
sp_0 | tm_1 < tm_2

Which correctly reflects the semantic relations involved. The smelling must follow the going.

Similarly, we can account for the observation that the knowing in *George was known to be building a house* occurs sometime during the building, and that Mabel's departure in *When George got home, Mabel had left* precedes George's arrival.

Likewise, temporal adverbs, as in the following, specify the times of events.

Yesterday I was building a house.
Now I see George.

The first of these sentences entails that the building occurs within the period of yesterday. The second entails that the seeing occurs at the present time. The following constructive rules, discussed in Chapter 4, account for these interpretations.

(Now)
Conditions: **S | "now" P**

Actions: **S | P**
S | it is NOW

(Yest)
Conditions: **S | "yesterday" P**

Actions: **S | P**
S | it is YESTERDAY

Recall that **NOW** refers to the interval of time in which the discourse occurs and **YESTERDAY** refers to the 24-hour interval of time ending at the midnight before NOW. Their precise projections are determined (deictically) in the pragmatic setting. Recall that the semantics of a statement of the form **S | it is T** is reflected in the following sanctioned inference:

(It is) **S | at time T1: it is T2 iff S | T1 during T2.**

The rules for aspects lead immediately to correct predictions about similar sentences with aspectual operators.

Now I am building a house.
Yesterday I was going to see George.
Now I have seen George.

For instance, the middle sentence projects onto something like

sp_5 | it is YESTERDAY
sp_5 | it is PAST
sp_5 | it is going to occur that ⟦sp_6⟧
sp_6 | I see George

where,

sp_0 | at time tm_5: ⟦sp_5⟧

By **(It is)** we have

sp_0 | tm_5 during YESTERDAY

By **(Prosp)**

sp_0 | at time tm_6: ⟦sp_6⟧
sp_0 | tm_5 < tm_6

Therefore, the time **tm_6** at which the seeing occurs follows a time **tm_5** during **YESTERDAY**. **tm_6** could therefore be later during **YESTERDAY**, or during **TODAY**, or sometime after **TODAY**. This agrees with the observed entailments of the sentence.

Now I have seen George projects by (Now) and (Perfect) onto something like:

sp_7 | it is NOW
sp_7 | it has occurred that ⟦sp_8⟧
sp_8 | I see George

Where

sp_0 | at time sp_7: ⟦sp_7⟧

By (It is) we have

sp_0 | sp_7 during NOW

By (Perf)

sp_0 | at time tm_8: ⟦sp_8⟧
sp_0 | sp_7 > tm_8

Therefore, the time tm_8 at which the seeing occurs precedes NOW. This agrees with the observed entailments of the sentence.

Finally, we observe the case where two adverbials occur in an aspectual sentence.

In June, 1960, Marie had joined the Girl Scouts two years earlier.

This projects onto something like

sp_3 | It is June, 1960
sp_3 | It has occurred that ⟦sp_4⟧
sp_4 | It is roughly June, 1958
sp_4 | Marie joins the Girl Scouts

By (It is) we can easily reconstruct the statements

sp_0 | tm_4 < tm_3
sp_0 | tm_3 during June, 1960
sp_0 | tm_4 during June, 1958

This has all of the observed temporal relations right.

In summary, the rules for aspects seem to interact properly with the semantics of other operators and structures to lead to correct entailments of sentences containing these. This shows independently that this semantics attributed to aspects is correct. This in turn motivates the constructive rules. Now let's add the consequences of the general principles of contextualization to the account

REFERENCE TIME: CONTEXTUALIZATION

Let's look at how our description of the semantics of aspects interacts with the roles of reference time and tense in contextualization. In essence alternative aspectual forms allow the same basic knowledge to have an ambient representation in alternative temporal focus spaces. From the perspective of contextualization, we will see how this allows the speaker to maintain a normal contextualization pattern, one that, in accordance with what I called *inertia* in Chapter 4, avoids shifts in the focus space.

Suppose we have the configuration of spaces as shown in Figure 8.3, i.e.,

sp_0 | tm_1 < tm_2 < tm_3
sp_0 | tm_4 during tm_2
sp_0 | At time tm_1, ⟦sp_1⟧
sp_0 | At time tm_2, ⟦sp_2⟧
sp_0 | At time tm_3, ⟦sp_3⟧
sp_0 | At time tm_4, ⟦sp_4⟧

Notice that the semantics of aspects sanction the following, for any proposition **P** satisfied in **sp_2**.

sp_1 | it is to occur that P
sp_3 | it has occurred that P
sp_4 | it is occurring that P

Suppose further that the following is satisfied:

sp_2 | Bif builds a barn.

Consider how this knowledge could be communicated if alternatively **sp_1**, **sp_2**, or **sp_3** is in focus.

The space **sp_2** might be in focus if we have a continuing narration about the events that occurred at **tm_2**. For instance, the preceding sentence might have been

Last summer, Bif had been laid off temporarily, but his wife was working.

In this case the narration could continue

So, Bif built a barn.

since this is satisfied in **sp_2**.

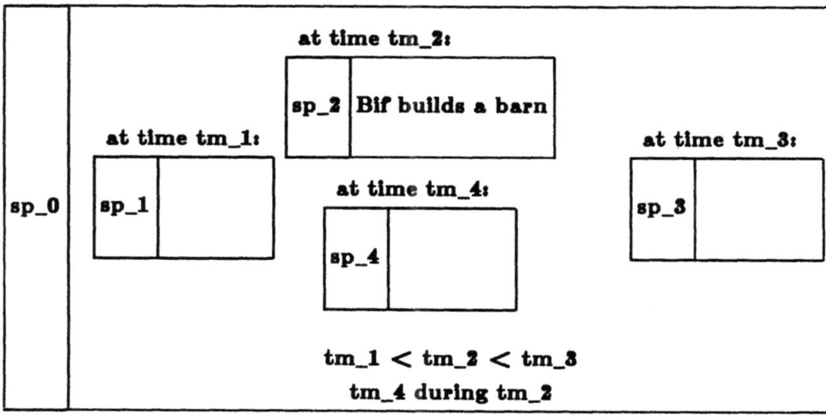

Fig. 8.3. A network of temporal spaces.

The space **sp_1**, on the other hand, might be in focus if we have a continuing narration about the events that occurred at **tm_1**, a time *before* the barn is built. For instance, the preceding sentence might have been,

Bif ordered a truck load of lumber.

Although **Bif builds a barn** is not satisfied in **sp_1**, **(Prosp)** tells us that

sp_1 | that Bif builds a barn is to occur

is, since the following are implicitly (by context climbing) satisfied,

sp_0 | at tm_2: Bif builds a barn
sp_0 | tm_1 < tm_2

and therefore the following is as well:

sp_0 | at tm_1: that Bif builds a barn is to occur

In this case the narration could therefore truthfully continue,

Bif was going to build a barn.

without a shift in the focus space.

Alternatively, **sp_3** might be in focus if we have a continuing discussion of the situation at **tm_3**, a time *after* the barn is built.

For instance, the preceding sentence might have been,

Bif knew that his cows would be safe.

In this case **(Perf)** tells us that

sp_3 | that Bif builds a barn has occurred

is satisfied, since the following are implicitly satisfied,

sp_0 | at tm_2: Bif builds a barn
sp_0 | tm_2 < tm_3

and therefore the following is as well:

sp_0 | at tm_3: that Bif builds a barn has occurred

Therefore, we could truthfully continue with

Bif had built a barn.

saying something satisfied in the focus space **sp_3**.

Finally, if **sp_4** is in focus, we might be talking about a situation that occurs at **tm_4**, a time *during* the building of the barn. For instance, we might say

It was a hot summer day. Bif hammered from dusk til dawn.

In this case **(Prosp)** tells us that

sp_4 | that Bif builds a barn is occurring

is satisfied, since the following are implicitly satisfied,

sp_0 | at tm_2: Bif builds a barn
sp_0 | tm_4 during tm_2

and therefore the following is as well:

sp_0 | at tm_4: that Bif builds a barn is occurring

Therefore, we could truthfully continue with

Bif was building a barn.

again without changing the focus space.

Observe that the processing of each of the resulting discourses has the following three properties. First, it faithfully reconstructs the semantic intent of the discourse. In particular, it gets all of the temporal relations among events right. Second, it follows the simplest contextualization pattern, that which maximizes inertia by maintaining a constant focus space. Third, all events are represented internally from the perspective of a single temporal space in which all information relevant to that space is consolidated to best promote reasoning about the situation that space represents.

This account additionally shows us what Reichenbach's R and E mean: We can *define* the *reference time* R as the time of the space into which the sentence as a whole is contextualized. We can define the *event time* E as the time of the space into which the description of the central event is projected. Reichenbach's S is, of course, simply what I have been calling NOW.

For instance, if

Bif had built a barn.

projects onto

sp_3 | it has happened that ⟦sp_2⟧
sp_2 | Bif builds a barn

where

sp_0 | at time tm_2: ⟦sp_2⟧
sp_0 | at time tm_3: ⟦sp_3⟧

then **tm_2** is the event time E and **tm_3** is the reference time R. With these definitions of R, E and S in hand, along with the constructive rules for aspects and the remarks about the influence of tense on contextualization of Chapters 5 and 7, we systematically and correctly predict the following relations among R, E, and S, for various combinations of tense and aspect.

Past Prospective	$R < E$	$R < S$
Past	$R = E$	$R < S$
Past Perfect	$R > E$	$R < S$
Present Prospective	$R < E$	$R = S$
Present	$R = E$	$R = S$
Present Perfect	$R > E$	$R = S$
Future Prospective	$R < E$	$R > S$
Future	$R = E$	$R > S$
Future Perfect	$R > E$	$R > S$

I hasten to point out that these predictions are not exactly consistent with Reichenbach's formulation, but are identical to that of Bull (1960), developed in response to some mistakes he points out in Reichenbach's formulation. I should also point out that the account developed here, beyond predicting something like Reichenbach's system, also extends the other aspects *inceptive*, *terminative* and *progressive*.

Looking from a functional perspective, we are now in a position to see two reasons why we have aspects in natural languages at all rather than making do with tenses, adverbials and temporal conjunctions like *while* and *before*. First, aspects provide more direct communication between temporal spaces since aspects project onto contexts that connect such spaces directly. This strengthens consolidation. For instance, if the occurrence of some event at one time is relevant to the situation at some other time, it is important to bring that occurrence to bear in parochial reasoning. An aspectual context does this. Second, the use of aspects allows us to refer to events that occur at various times while always having an active temporal space in focus for purposes of contextualization or even keep the same space fixed in focus over long stretches of discourse. Without aspects we would often be forced to shift the focus space extraneously in violation of the inertia of the focus space.

THE CASE OF THE PRESENT PERFECT

The English present perfect, in particular, has been the focus of much linguistic study. It displays some unusual linguistic structures and has spawned a number of complex analyses, some underlyingly semantic in nature, others pragmatic, some far-ranging but vague, some explicit but wrong, and many denying completely that the present perfect has anything to do with the present tense form or with the perfect aspect.

In this section I will show how the three-level account of tense and aspect cuts through the multitude of difficulties that have challenged linguists. As in many complex systems, we will see that the facts are the actually the result of an array of interacting influences. In particular, aside from the semantics of the present perfect and the process of contextualization, Gricean principles play a major role in the use of the present perfect. Additionally, we will discover a further very specialized pragmatic restriction on the use of the present perfect. This section illustrates the way partitioned representations interact with other subsystems, but also shows how partitioned representations often provide a perspective from which the other subsystems can be easily identified and understood.

Overview of Problems with Present Perfect

In general, the present perfect but not the past tense occurs with *adverbials of present time*, while the past but not the present perfect occurs with *adverbials of past time*.

At present (Now) I have eaten three of the mushrooms.
* *At present (Now) I ate three of the mushrooms.*
I was in an accident in 1970.
* *I have been in an accident in 1970.*

The present perfect is generally used in an *indefinite past*, and the past tense is used in a *definite past*, sense (Leech 1971, Allen 1966). For instance, discourses often begin with the present perfect, introducing a new past time, then shift to the past, referring to the previously introduced past time.

I've been to the Guggenheim. I liked it a lot.

The past tense but not the perfect aspect (present or past perfect) generally allows preceding *manner adverbials* (Jackendoff 1972).

Quickly George burst into the room.
* *Quickly George has (had) burst into the room.*

The present perfect, but not the past tense, usually implies *current relevance*, normally manifesting itself in specific suggestions about the present state of affairs (Comrie 1976). The use of the present perfect often suggests that the described past event or state carries over to the present, that the immediate result of the described past event carries over to the present, or at least that some other inferable consequence is true of the present.

I have been sick. (i.e., I am sick.)
The taxi has arrived. (i.e., it is here.)

Watch it! That ladder has fallen three times already. (i.e., it has the potential of falling again.)

Finally, the present perfect, but not the past tense, often carries a *presupposition of present existence* (Chomsky 1971). We get the following results, given that Hilary is still alive but Marco Polo is dead.

Hilary has climbed Everest.
* *Marco Polo has climbed Everest.*

But, interestingly, the second sentence is acceptable in the *passive* form.

Each of the traditional theories about how the past and the perfect work that I am aware of simply deals with some feature or small subset of features from this list in either semantic, syntactic or pragmatic terms, failing to integrate the rest of the features into the analysis. Allen (1966) and Webber (1988), for instance, emphasize the importance of definiteness, drawing an analogy to the determiners *the* and *a*. Huddleston (1969) focuses current relevance. Bach (1967), Huddleston (1969), and McCawley (1971) try to account for co-occurrence restrictions in syntactic terms. McCoard (1978) and Dowty (1980) try to do the same thing in semantic terms by attributing a specialized *extended now* interpretation specifically to the present perfect.

In this section I will argue that virtually all of the multitudinous and seemingly diverse facts about the English present perfect are in fact either the direct result of the three-level account of tense and aspect or the result of the interaction of this account with very general *Gricean* principles, in particular having to do with relevance.

The Partitioning Account of Present Perfect

Let's review the facts about the present perfect and assure ourselves that the present account is correct, that is, that *present* in the phrase *present perfect* refers to the present morpheme with the contextualization properties described, and *perfect* refers to the perfect morpheme, associated with the semantic and constructive rules attributed to it.

First, it has been observed that the present perfect cannot generally be preceded by manner adverbials like *quickly*. We observe that, according to the semantics attributed to the perfect, the perfect contributes to a *state* description, that is, that it describes a condition, not something that changes through time. Thus, although

George burst into the room.

describes a dynamic event,

George has (had) burst into the room.

describes as a whole a static condition that exists after the time of the bursting, that is, the condition of the bursting *having happened.* Certain adverbs, for instance *manner adverbs* like *quickly* or *timidly*, are known not to occur in state descriptions. For instance, the following is unacceptable,

* *Quickly George is a Unitarian.*

except in the non-stative sense of George *becoming* a Unitarian. The stativeness of the perfect in the semantics we have specified explains the unacceptability of

* *Quickly George has (had) burst into the room.*

Next, we observe that the use of temporal adverbials with the present perfect is entirely consistent with the present account.

Now I have missed class on a Thursday.

This projects onto something like the following (or at least allows the following to be inferred).

sp_2 | it is NOW
sp_2 | [[sp_1]] has occurred
sp_1 | it is a Thursday
sp_1 | I miss class
sp_0 | at time tm_1: [[sp_1]]
sp_0 | at time tm_2: [[sp_2]]
sp_0 | tm_1 < tm_2

We have seen that the time of a temporal focus space, in this case **sp_2**, for a present tense sentence tends to be **NOW**, that is the time of speech, or what Reichenbach calls **S**. This representation has all of the intuitively observed temporal relations right.

Now, let's see what contextualization has to say about a pair of sentences like the following, which are generally taken to be truth-conditionally equivalent and therefore problematic for semanticist accounts which try to associate sentences directly with truth conditions.

Fred won $1,000,000 in the lottery.
Fred has won $1,000,000 in the lottery.

Suppose **tm_1 < tm_2**, where **tm_2** is the time of speech **NOW**, and that we have the following contexts:

sp_0 | at time tm_1: ⟦sp_1⟧
sp_0 | at time tm_2: ⟦sp_2⟧

Suppose further that the following is satisfied:

sp_1 | Fred wins $1,000,000 in the lottery.

Consider how this event would be communicated if alternatively **sp_1** or **sp_2** is in focus.

First, **sp_1** might be in focus if we have a continuing narration about the events that occurred at the past time **tm_1**. For instance, the preceding sentence might have been

The moderator reached in and picked a number.

In this case the narration could continue, without changing the focus space, with the following:

Fred won $1,000,000 in the lottery.

The projection of this sentence is satisfied in **sp_1** and the past tense space cue is appropriate to the past time space **sp_1**.

Next, **sp_2** might be in focus if we have a continuing discussion of the situation at the time of speech. For instance, the preceding sentence might have been,

Hey! We don't need to give these old clothes to Fred.

In this case we could continue, without changing the focus space, with the following:

Fred has won $1,000,000 in the lottery.

Since we know **sp_0 | at time_1: Fred wins $1,000,000 in the lottery** and **sp_0 | time_1 < time_2**, we also know, by **(Perf)**, **sp_0 | at time_2: that Fred wins $1,000,000 in the lottery has occurred** or, more simply, **sp_2 | Fred wins $1,000,000 in the lottery has occurred**. Therefore the content of this last discourse sentence is satisfied in **sp_2**. Moreover the present tense space cue is appropriate to contextualization into the present time space **sp_2**.

Notice that both sentences serve to convey the past occurrence of Fred's winning $1,000,000 and in this sense the sentences do result in truth-conditionally equivalent internal representations. Yet looking at the truth-conditional equivalence alone misleads the semantic analysis: it in fact arises because the parochial projections of the sentences are *not* semantically equivalent. Truth conditions are associated with the semantics of the parochial representation *along with* the semantics of the contexts into which sentences are contextualized. The focus space is different in each case so the semantic contribution of the context is different in each case. The differing semantic contributions of the parochial representations effectively cancel out the semantic contributions of the contexts. Thus, we fully account not only for the *use* of the sentences in terms of contextualization in different focus spaces or, equivalently, looking at the same event from different temporal perspectives, but we account for the truth conditions as well.

The three-level account of the present perfect also leads to some more subtle predictions.

Why Present Perfect Acts like Indefinite Past

The present perfect has been described as introducing an *indefinite past* time, meaning roughly "at *some* time in the past" while the past has been described as referring back to a *definite past* time, meaning roughly "at *that* time in the past" (Webber 1988, Allen 1966, Leech 1971). Thus a typical pattern is found in the following.

I have seen "Lawrence of Arabia." I thought it was great.
But I was only 10, and not particularly critical.

The first reference to the past situation, at which I see "Lawrence of Arabia," uses the present perfect, whereas subsequent references use the past tense.

Under the partitioning account it is clear that this pattern is simply an instance of the far more general *construct then contextualize* pattern, first described in Chapter 4. The construct then contextualize patter is that found, for instance, in the following discourse.

If Little Freddy would clean his room everybody would be much happier. I, for one, would be very pleased.

The processing of the first sentence of this last discourse constructs a new space sp_8 with the context something like

sp_3 | Freddy_7 cleans room of Freddy_7 □→ [[sp_8]]

The new space becomes active and a primary candidate for focus space in subsequent discourse. Thus, we avoid using an inactive focus space or having to create a new focus space in contextualization.

Similarly, in the "Lawrence of Arabia" discourse the processing of the first sentence constructs by (Perfect) a new space, say sp_9, embedded in the focus space, say sp_1, with a context and associated representations something like

> sp_1 | [[sp_9]] has occurred
> sp_0 | at time_9: [[sp_9]]
> sp_0 | time_9 < time_1

The new space sp_9 becomes active and a primary candidate for focus space in subsequent discourse in accordance with the construct then contextualize strategy. The remaining sentences in the discourse are then contextualized directly into sp_9 as suggested by the change in tense.

This account assumes that the existing space sp_1, whose time is probably NOW, is in focus at the beginning of the discourse. Actually, this is a natural assumption even if there is no preceding discourse. The space representing the current speech situation is presumably always somewhat active, if not as a result of discourse understanding, then as the current recipient of extra-linguistic sensory input. This is why features of the current speech situation are generally available for deixis (finding referents for *here* and so on) and ostension (pointing to referents for *that* and so on). Thus a natural strategy for beginning a discourse about some past situation without contextualizing into a yet to be created space is to use the present perfect to contextualize initially into the space that represents the current speech situation.

Why Present Perfect Conveys Current Relevance

The present perfect is also said to convey a sense of current relevance lacking in the past tense (Huddleston 1969; McCawley 1971). This is also related to the difference in temporal focus space.

We have seen, in Chapter 4, that Gricean principles (Grice 1975) operate parochially within the focus space. For instance, they play a strong role in locating the focus space in contextualization: a space in which conversational maxims would be violated by the projection of the discourse sentence is a poor candidate for focus space. If such sentences do not lead to specific consequences within the focus space, they cannot be relevant to the focus space and therefore must violate a fundamental conversational maxim.

Current relevance manifests itself almost invariably in specific suggestions about the current state of affairs. For example,

We have lived in London since 1945.

suggests that we now live in London, and

The police have arrested my wife.

that my wife is now in jail. Although such suggestions have often been considered part of the semantics of a present perfect with multiple readings (McCawley 1971), I want to argue that these suggestions are in fact what Grice (1975) calls *conversational implicatures* that arise naturally as part of drawing relevant inferences within the focus space, in this case within a focus space whose time is the present.

First, these relevancy suggestions fluctuate wildly with pragmatic setting, like conversational implicatures and unlike semantic entailments. If, for instance, an elderly hearer in a particular discourse is interested in finding out what changes have occurred in London since WWII *We have lived in London since 1945* will probably not convey the suggestion attributed to it above at all, but rather something about the speaker's current ability to accurately describe post-war London because (s)he lived there at some time since 1945. Likewise discourse situations can be found in which *The police have arrested my wife* carries instead the suggestion that my wife is criminally inclined.

Second, well-known tests for semantic ambiguity fail for the present perfect. Inoue (1979) points out that allegedly distinct relevancy senses can be mixed in sentences like the following,

John has lived in Chicago from time to time since 1973, and Bill continuously since 1970.

The semantics of the present perfect must therefore be vague, not ambiguous, among the more specific readings it can assume to ensure current relevance.

Third, the relevancy suggestions associated with present perfect are analogous to those found in association with *other* structures and explainable in terms of relevance to the discourse topic. The use of a *passive* sentence, for instance, is strongly correlated with thematic subject and accordingly with suggestions about additional features of the subject. For instance,

The glass was drunk out of.

suggests that the glass was (or even is) dirty, and

This chair was sat on by John.

that the chair suffered some kind of damage or change.

Fourth and finally, the general, albeit poorly specified, principles which underlie other instances of conversational implicature also seem to go far in explaining specific suggestions associated with uses of the present perfect. Consider the fact, for instance, that

We have lived in London.

does not invite the same suggestion as *We have lived in London since 1945,* namely that we now live in London. Here is a Gricean explanation for this observation: Suppose we *do* currently live in London. Then *We have lived in London* would violate what is known as Grice's *maxim of manner,* since the shorter an more informative *We live in London* (which entails *We have lived in London*) would better serve to say something about the focus space. *We have lived in London* therefore specifically carries the implicature that we *don't* currently live in London. *We have lived in London since 1945* does not carry such an implicature because there is no shorter and more informative simple present alternative.

In summary, the general and specific features of current relevance associated with the present perfect are explainable as no more than consequences of general Gricean principles assumed to operate *parochially* in the focus space. Much of Inoue's (1979) analysis of the generation of implicatures in the use of present perfect carries over to the present account. She starts with the thesis that the present perfect indicates current relevance (which, as we have seen, is in fact predicted in the three-level account from other more general factors) and then traces out consequences of this thesis. Some of these consequences follow from the thematic status of sentential *subjects* which also put demands on relevance. The interaction of thematicity with current relevance explains why

**Marco Polo has climbed Everest.*

is peculiar, under the assumption that Marco Polo is dead, while

Everest has been climbed by Marco Polo.

is not. I refer the reader to her insightful work for additional examples and argumentation.

What is Really Unusual about Present Perfect

We see that the basic linguistic facts about use and interpretation of the present perfect follow from the role of tense in contextualization and the form of the semantic and constructive rules associated with aspect. The explanations of some of these facts require reference to general principles which are not part of the three-level model per se, such as Gricean principles. But the validity of these external principles are motivated independently, in fact well established, in any case. Nonetheless, we can still compile a residual set of facts that are not direct consequences of the three-level account. For instance, why are sentences like the following peculiar?

* *I have seen "Lawrence of Arabia" in 1970.*
* *William Penn has founded Philadelphia.*
* *How have you broken your arm?*

Although the very general three-level account makes *more* correct predictions than any alternative of which I am aware, there is nothing in the three-level account that predicts that sentences such as these should be anomalous. Do such sentences undermine the three-level account?

The answer is *no*; something else is going on that requires a separate supplementary account. It is interesting to note, for instance, that the three-level account of the English present perfect carries over in its entirety to the *Danish* present perfect; for *all* of the English data discussed above in support of this account, corresponding data for Danish can be cited. On the other hand, *none* of the anomalous observations about the English present perfect carries over to Danish. Dinsmore (1981b) discusses these data. As Edward Sapir once stated, "all grammars leak." I interpret this to mean that there are virtually always isolated restrictions and special cases defined by the language that frustrate neat general solutions to linguistic problems. Nevertheless, one cannot trust a theory that leaves too many special cases to be accounted for. In fact, all of the residual facts about the present perfect that I am aware of fall under a simple restriction, first observed by me (Dinsmore 1981b, also 1991a), on the felicitous use of the present perfect that effectively determines whether present perfect or past tense should be used in pragmatic settings where the use of either would otherwise be appropriate to convey the occurrence of a past event. Because this restriction is really independent of partitioned representations, I will not discuss it further here. But I only point out that only after those parts of the problem of aspect that follow from the partitioned representations framework had been factored out was this simple restriction recognizable.

CONCLUSION

A result of the current investigation is a more comprehensive account of the aspects, one which bridges the gap between their semantics—what temporal relations they represent—and their pragmatics—how they are appropriately used in discourse. From the perspective of language understanding, this theory is functional and proximate. It is functional in that it projects aspectual expressions onto partitioned representations that are well suited for temporal reasoning. It is proximate since it allows the completely general principles of contextualization and distribution do most of the work. The projections of the aspectual expressions tend to be similar in structure to the surface sentences at least in the sense that every part of such an expression corresponds to a clearly recognizable part of the projection. There is relatively little restructuring of the kinds found in most systems of language understanding that deal with temporal expressions. From the perspective of linguistic structure this account is very explanatory of some long-standing problems: problems in truth conditions, syntactic distributional restrictions, and appropriate discourse usage. We find that this account also costs almost nothing. It relies on independently motivated and very general principles of contextualization along with a very simple and systematic semantics for the projections of aspectual expressions.

CHAPTER NINE
General Conclusions

In these chapters I have explored the consequences of the theory that representations are resolutely consolidated into appropriate coherent spaces. I have looked at the computational and semantic properties of this arrangement, the model of language processing that it entails and a variety of evidence for the correctness of the theory. It is time to reflect on what has been accomplished and where we go from here.

AN ASSESSMENT OF PARTITIONED REPRESENTATIONS

How successful is the theory of partitioned representations as a theory of mental representation and language processing? In the introductory chapter I argued that cognitive theories should be motivated from each of a variety of methodological perspectives. Let me summarize the evidence accrued for partitioned representations.

Experimental Evidence

Experimental support for a theory of mental representation requires that the system be consistent with empirical data like human reaction times in performing different reasoning tasks. Experimental support for the theory of partitioned representations would be found primarily in correspondences between quantifiable processing steps and the mechanisms by which processing is achieved in the partitioning framework. Aside from some direct support for the use of counterfactual spaces, much indirect support comes from evidence suggesting humans use a concrete representational scheme based on models of reality over which simulations of real-world processes can be run. Johnson-Laird, for instance, cites experimental evidence in support of the use of analogical or nearly analogical representations as opposed to such things as logical rules in reasoning. If we require, as we must on functional grounds, that the representation scheme be powerful enough to express *complex information*—propositional attitudes, conditionality, other modalities, time dependent information and so on—we must have some scheme for breaking complex knowledge apart into its concrete parts for which the analogical or concrete representations and reasoning processes make sense. For instance, reasoning about possibility would require creating a coherent model of the possible situation, marking it in some way as a possibility, but allowing analogical or concrete reasoning processes to take over within the model. This is exactly what partitioned representations provide for and is also, I presume, the conclusion Johnson-Laird reached in introducing multiple mental models.

Functionality

Expressiveness. Partitioned representations handle the most complex representation problems, providing natural representations for conditionals, possibilities, counterfactuals, quantified information, beliefs and other propositional attitudes, fictions, fictional genres, temporal information, alternative perspectives or folk theories, places, situations, and so on. The naturalness of partitioned representations is found in their ability to represent objects and the relations they enter into parochially in concrete terms. As a result there is no need to populate an internal representation with such things as *rigid designators* and *intensional objects* as modal and intensional logics are often forced to do. For instance, to capture the alternative attributive and referential readings of sentences like

Fred believes that the mayor of Carmel is a spy.

we simply recognize a parochial representation of Clint Eastwood, e.g., as **obj_2**, in Fred's belief space **sp_2**, as well as a representation of the mayor of Carmel, e.g., as **obj_3**,

sp_2 | • obj_2
sp_2 | • obj_3

then allow the sentence to mean exactly what it says,

sp_2 | obj_3 is spy

and finally attribute the distinction to the presence or absence of the content*

sp_2 | obj_3 = obj_2

At the same time, we will see in Chapter 10 that partitioned representations can be given a *semantics* at least as rigorous as that of the predicate calculus.

Efficiency. The efficiency of partitioned representations relies, as we have seen, on the *consolidation* of information into *coherent* spaces in which parochial reasoning processes, whatever their nature, can take over. *Secondary contexts* and *ambient representations* aid this consolidation. The efficiency of this arrangement results from two factors. First, the information relevant to parochial reasoning is strongly delimited. Rather than considering the entire knowledge base in drawing inferences, only the contents of specific spaces are considered. This helps control combinatorial problems. Second, inferences themselves are made simpler, and accordingly require fewer computational steps or may, in fact, be allowed to simply emerge from an analogical parochial medium.

In hindsight, we see these same advantages actually exploited in working artificial intelligence systems, such as planning systems, systems that represent agent beliefs, and general knowledge representation systems. They have also been exploited in the proof techniques of natural deduction, as well as in Johnson-Laird's mental models. All of these systems achieve efficiency by consolidating information into coherent parochial domains in which reasoning becomes more manageable.

Rationality. The principle of *coherence* ensures the rationality of reasoning in partitioned representations. In fact, adherence to a slightly stricter criterion of coherence than assumed so far, but adopted in the logical model of Chapter 10, ensures that inference in the scheme is provably *sound*, that is, not capable of leading to incorrect inferences on the basis of correct premises.

---

* Note that further readings arise as cases of *metonymy*, as described in chapter 5.

Linguistic Evidence

Mental representations play an integral role in language understanding, surface discourse structures are projected onto internal mental representations in a manner that ideally preserves the full semantic intent of the discourse. The *three-level theory* of language understanding describes how discourse structures project onto partitioned internal representations. In *contextualization* decisions are made about in which among the many spaces to begin building a representation. In *distribution* structures and processes are projected into multiple spaces, primarily in response to *space builders* occurring in the discourse structure. In *parochial processing* representations are built within spaces in a manner highly dependent on existing contents.

In Chapter 3 I underscored three factors in addition to functionality that determine how well a theory of mental representations supports a theory of language processing: (1) proximity, (2) discrimination and (3) explanation of constraints. Let's look at these factors one more time.

Proximity. Proximity entails that the distance between discourse sentences and internal representations be reasonably small, i.e., that the process of projecting surface structures onto internal representations is as simple as possible. Partitioned representations support proximity through their provisions for parochial representations and through their ability to quickly locate and access appropriate spaces into which to project linguistic expressions both in contextualization and in distribution. In effect the representations unfold dynamically to meet the surface structures half-way in realizing the full semantic intent of the discourse. Parochial processes, which carry most of the computational workload, become very proximate since they are allocated directly to small domains. Processes like those that find referents for definite descriptions or those involved in satisfying presuppositions become much easier to describe as parochial processes.

Discrimination. Discrimination is important because conceptual distinctions found in the internal representation are rarely sufficient to totally disambiguate surface structures or to determine unique projections. *What* is already represented often is not a sufficient basis for making these choices. *How* things are represented must also be taken into account. Partitioned representations provide discrimination most importantly by radically reducing the domains in which most cognitive and linguistic processes operate. We see, for instance, that in searching for a non-metonymous referent for a definite description in a well-structured discourse, distribution and contextualization ensure *in every case* that the intended object satisfying the description is situated there. Likewise whenever a presuppositional construction is used its associated presupposition will be satisfied precisely in the space into which the construction is projected.

Linguistic Constraints. The theory of partitioned and the three-level theory of language understanding leads to correct predictions about a multitude of linguistic problems. In fact, I am aware of no other independent cognitive theory that explains immediately such a wide variety of problematic observations. Geach's *donkey sentences* have an account in terms of the way distribution ensures that new object representations are put in the right place to be picked out as projections of definite descriptions and pronouns. *Referential opacity* as well as the *referential-attributive* ambiguity have natural accounts in terms of the object derived within individual spaces. The contrast between *transparent de dicto* readings and *de re* readings have, as Fauconnier has shown us, an account in terms of *metonymous* relations between objects with independent parochial representations in individual spaces. This account generalizes in a natural way to a wide variety of cases less studied in the literature, such as the use of comparatives in modal environments. The the most general account of *projection problem for presupposition* is in terms of the way presuppositional constructions are projected into spaces in distribution in which the associated simple presuppositions are satisfied parochially. The temporal perspectives generally attributed to different *aspectual* forms are predicted in the three-level theory. Taken together with the same general strategies also used in contextualization into non-temporal spaces, this account further predicts many of the more subtle problems never properly integrated into a comprehensive theory of tense and aspect, such as the *definite* vs. *indefinite past* distinction observed in the English past and present perfect and the implication of *current relevance* observed in the use of the English present perfect. Much of the large-scale *implicit semantic* structure of a discourse, the *anaphoric accessibility* of objects introduced in a discourse, restrictions on possible discourses, and so on, also have an account in terms of partitioned representations.

PROSPECTUS

Research in partitioned representations is only beginning. It still presents many future challenges and promises many further exciting results. There are a number of areas on which interdisciplinary research should focus in the years ahead.

Further Evidence

I have cited relatively little direct *experimental* evidence in support of partitioned representations. This is largely a function of certain gaps in my own background. Future effort is called for to bring this deficiency into line with the more advanced state of research in partitioned representations from the perspectives of functionality and linguistic evidence. Much relevant experimental evidence might already be sitting out there in the literature, awaiting discovery by future partitioned representationalists. Additional research on the specific mechanisms discussed here might discover such things as correlations between the postulated use of context climbing, including interspatial inheritance, or pure parochial reasoning on the one hand, and response times elicited in the performance of various cognitive tasks on the other. Research might also be directed toward the relative rate at which processing occurs in a variety of conceptual domains. One would expect, if the theory of partitioned representations is correct, to find close correlations among reasoning about the real world, reasoning about a fictional world, reasoning about a particular person's set of beliefs, reasoning about generic or quantified information and so on.

I have cited a large amount of *linguistic* evidence in favor of partitioned representations. Future research will no doubt unearth handfuls of additional linguistic phenomena that have an account at least partially in terms of partitioned representations. There are hundreds of outstanding problems out there for which partitioned representations might offer insights.

Further Refinements

I have discussed a number of mechanisms and levels of processing involved in the use of partitioned representations, such as primary and secondary contexts, parochial reasoning, contextualization and so on. Much more remains to be learned about many of these mechanisms and processes, more mechanisms that exploit the partitioned architecture remain to be discovered, and further progress in the understanding of processes that interact with partitioned representations in significant ways will no doubt occur.

One general and fruitful area of research will undoubtedly be *specialized inference techniques* that depend on partitioned representations. How, for instance, might the sentence

Harry would make a poor accountant.

lead so naturally to the inference, regressively in the *parent* of the counterfactual space, that Harry is unorganized?

Much more work should focus on the specialized problems of certain domains and the specific properties of certain types of spaces. For instance, we should look much more closely at the structure of *fiction* and the role of *genre* in reasoning about fictional events. We should also look more closely at *pretending*, and the role of *counterfactuals* in reasoning and communication. We would also like to know how well partitioned representations fare in solving numerous problems recognized in temporal or causal reasoning. These are outstanding problems to which the resources and unique perspective of partitioned representations might be well directed.

Future research is called for both to test and further to elaborate the three-level theory of language understanding. Much might be gained from developing more complete computational models than those I will describe in Chapter 12 and testing them on naturally occurring discourse. We would likely find that our understanding of pragmatic and grammatical factors influencing contextualization will become more refined. The study of the interaction of contextualization, distribution and parochial processing might proceed hand-in-hand with the study of more general interactive models of language understanding and reasoning.

One important area of future research will be the development of a model of mysterious parochial processes like *metonymy*, in particular a computational account of the *identity principle*. Although this principle enjoys intuitive plausibility, there is no explicit model that predicts where instances of metonymy will arise. This problem is doubtlessly connected to the whole realm of associative memory, and might help keep connectionists off the streets.

Finally, much work, barely begun in the *Spaceprobe* project, to be described in Chapter 12, remains to be done in the application of ideas developed in the theory of partitioned representations to practical computer systems. A *knowledge representation* system based on partitioned representations would encompass all the generality of schema- and frame-based systems, *belief spaces* and *context-layered data bases*, as well as facilities well suited for reasoning about *counterfactuals*, *time* and so on, all in one coherent system with a very small set of structural primitives. Such systems would be useful in the development of computer understanding systems and in many other applications in artificial intelligence such as *expert systems*.

THE IMPORTANCE OF PARTITIONED REPRESENTATIONS

Partitioned representations are important as a theory of human cognition, as a practical architecture for the design of intelligent computer systems and as an example of important methodological principles. As a theory it goes to the heart of many problems in language understanding, general reasoning and linguistic structure. Many of the problems it solves have stood for decades in spite of extensive research. As an instance of a methodology, it clearly demonstrates the fruitfulness and persuasiveness of applying the methods of multiple disciplines in cross-justifying a single theory. The methods clearly converge.

Perhaps just as significantly, the theory of partitioned representations allows us to *reframe* many fundamental problems not only in the processes of cognition but in ontology as well, problems that have never been solved, because we have never known exactly what questions to ask. We have seen that many previously vaguely understood cognitive processes take on a new personality when commuted to restricted and concrete parochial domains. In Chapter 1 I discussed the thesis that many concepts are not identifiable in the real world in any objective sense, but are imposed on the real world by the way objects are perceived and represented. For instance, color concepts share a closer correspondence with patterns in the neural responses of the human perceptual apparatus than with wavelengths. The lesson here is: to understand *what* is represented, understand first *how* it is represented. Partitioned representations allow us to better understand concepts like pretending and fiction, concepts that correspond to virtually *nothing* in the real world in an objective sense independently of interpretation, as well as counterfactuals. In partitioned representations these concepts are imposed on events and objects in the real world through our ability to consolidate information into spaces representing non-real but coherent possible realities.

APPENDICES
FORMAL MODELS

CHAPTER TEN

A Logic of Partitioned Representations

In this and in the next two chapters we investigate the logical and computational properties of partitioned representations. That you have entered the appendices reflects the fact that you are about to embark upon optional reading, a difficult task for those not versed in the ways of logic and AI. It is not too late to turn back. Yet, should you continue, your journey will be fruitful.

My hope is that transposing the criterial features of partitioned representations into a more formal and better understood model allows us to better understand the *functionality* of partitioned representations. This enterprise is an instance of the methodology of constructing logical and computational models discussed in Chapter 1. In particular we would like to specify more precisely the *semantics* of spaces and contexts, understand why certain propositions should be essentially satisfied in certain spaces, why certain types of spaces should be unique while others are not, why spaces should have the secondary contexts they do, and why there should be only certain kinds of spaces. What we will find in this chapter is corroboration for the assumptions that we made in Chapter 2 intuitively about the structures of spaces.

In addition to modeling elements of cognition at an abstract level, the development of a computational logic of partitioned representations can be undertaken for its own sake, both as a means of generalizing the techniques of natural deduction and as a means of recognizing many new applications in artificial intelligence. As we saw in Chapter 2, partitioned representations generalize a number of existing systems of artificial intelligence

The logic of partitioned representations, *PR*, is presented here in the form of a well defined *syntax*, a *semantics*, and a set of *rules of inference*. In addition a proof is presented that this logic is *sound*. In order to greatly simplify the presentation, we will follow the strategy of defining PR as an extension of a fairly standard *modal logic* or *higher-order predicate calculus*. Let's call this axiomatic language *PC*, for predicate calculus. We won't be concerned with precisely specifying the language PC; all reader's are no doubt familiar with such languages. But we assume that PC has a well-defined syntax, a set of axioms and rules of inference, and a well-defined model-theoretic semantics. Since we are not bothering to specify PC, we are in fact specifying a class of partitioning logics.

Kamp (1980) develops a logic of *discourse representations* for which he provides a syntax and a semantics but no rules of inference. As noted in earlier chapters this framework is similar in certain respects to partitioned representations. However, his formalism is substantially different.

THE SYNTAX OF PR

To define PR we add the following constructions to the syntax of PC:

(1) a set of *spaces*: **base, sp_0, sp_1, sp_2, sp_3, ...,**

(2) the syntactic category *statement* which always has the form **S | P**, where **S** is a space and **P** is a sentence (**S** here is also called the *tag* of the statement.), and

(3) a modification of the recursive definition of *sentence* (or *well formed formula*) that PC is assumed to have: If **S** is a space then [S] and ⟦S⟧ are sentences in PR. (Such sentences will be called *space terms*, a sentence of the form ⟦S⟧ will be called a *primary* space term, and a sentence of the form [S] a *secondary* space term.)

The following might therefore be statements in PR:

sp_4 | ∀x (cloud(x) → ∃Y(silver(Y) &lining(Y) & has(X, Y))
sp_1 | phone(Fred) = 123-4567
sp_6 | [sp_2]
base | believes(George, ⟦sp_1⟧)

Any statement whose sentence part contains at least one space term is called a *context*, while any other statement is called a *standard statement.*

The syntax of PR is designed with simplicity and modularity in mind. This results in a rather non-standard feature: we cannot attribute semantic interpretations directly to statements, but only to certain *sets* of statements. The reason is that the interpretation of a statement depends on the primary context associated with the space tag of the statement, but the primary context is not presented as a part of the statement. The alternative would be to build complex structures, as in Kamp's (1980) linear notation for discourse representation structures, which can be given a semantic interpretation as a whole. For instance, *If Pedro owns Eyore then Pedro beats him* would be represented as something like the following discourse representation structure,

K: <U:{R1, R2}
  C: {Pedro(R1), Eyore(R2), K' → K'',
    K': <C:{own(R1, R2)}>
    K'': <C:{beat(R1, R2)}> } >

or as the following set of PR statements.

base | owns(Pedro, Eyore) → ⟦sp_4⟧
sp_4 | owns(Pedro, Eyore)
sp_4 | beat(Pedro, obj_3)

Notice that no single statement in the PR representation can be given adequate truth conditions, but the set taken as a whole can.

The advantages of the modularity of PR are not only in the simplicity and readability it affords. The nature of inference in PR, most of which occurs locally within spaces (in the form of what I called *parochial reasoning* in Chapter 2) gives spaces some degree of autonomy, not anticipated by Kamp, which makes the ability to focus on individual spaces particularly useful. The rules of inference would be much more cumbersome in a representation like discourse representation structures. Nevertheless, I regard these two forms of representation as simply notational variants.

RULES OF INFERENCE FOR PR

I distinguish two kinds of rules of inference in PR, *standard rules*, adapted from PC to apply parochially within spaces, and *partitioning rules*, which create, access and allow communication between spaces. These rules are *space initialization, context climbing, space augmentation*, and *space identity*. We have met context climbing already.

A couple of simple notational conventions will be useful in formalizing the rules of PR. Where **P** is a sentence,

P{X/A}

will refer metalinguistically to the result of replacing any occurrences of **X** in **P** with **A**. For instance,

believes(George, ⟦sp_1⟧) {⟦sp_1⟧ / phone(Fred,123-4567)}

refers to the PR sentence

believes(George, phone(Fred, 123-4567))

Observe how this might be used to express context climbing. Likewise

P{X}

will refer to a sentence that contains **X**. Also, it will be useful to talk in the metalanguage about syntactic patterns that match sentences in the object language. Such a pattern, or *syntactic environment* will contain a ___ where some embedded sentence has been left out. Thus, we can say that in the sentence

believes(George, phone(Fred) = 123-4567),

phone(Fred) = 123-4567 occurs in the environment **believes(George, ___).**

Standard Rules of Inference

For any rule of inference or axiom in PC we have an equivalent rule or axiom in PR which may be produced by tagging each sentence in the PC rule or axiom by a common space variable, and making one other small modification. This thereby localizes normal inferencing to specific spaces. Rules and axioms in PR that enjoy this correspondence to rules and axioms in PC will be called *standard* rules and axioms. For instance, *modus ponens* can be formalized like this in PR,

S | P → Q (Modus Ponens)
S | P

S | Q'
where **Q'** *is like* **Q** *except that any term of the form* **⟦T⟧** *becomes* **[T]**.

In PR *modus ponens* is thus a rule that works parochially *within* any given space S. The *where* clause in this rule is common to most PR rules of inference. It is called the *primary-to-secondary convention* and ensures that no rule (except space initialization, described below) creates a new primary context. This convention is important because the rule of space augmentation, described below, can only apply to primary contexts.

Likewise, we can adapt *universal instantiation, modus tollens* or any of the reader's favorite rules to PR by tagging each line with a common space variable. Accordingly, given the following as premises,

sp_3 | ∀X (rich(X) → happy(X))
sp_3 | rich(Siegfried)

we should be able to infer

sp_3 | happy(Siegfried)

and so on.

Rather than directly stating a possibly large set of standard inference rules in PR, I will formally state two *correspondences* between PR. **(Stand1)** and **(Stand2)** tell us exactly what standard rules of inference can be assumed for PR. These more general correspondences are more interesting in any case. **(Stand1)** characterizes what I call *parochial reasoning* elsewhere in this book.

(Stand1) *If PC allows a derivation of this form:*

P1
P2
...

Q

Then PR allows a derivation of this form for any space **S**:

S | P1
S | P2
...

S |Q

It turns out that standard rules *generally* apply to contexts as well as standard statements. This is how secondary contexts are derived. For instance, from the following

spy(Bif) → ⟦sp_13⟧
∀X(Bulgarian(X) → spy(X))

we can derive the following.

sp_8 | Bulgarian(Bif) → [sp_13]

(Stand2) captures this generalization. The two almost identical consequents of this rule make explicit that standard rules will apply to both primary and secondary contexts.

(Stand2) *If PR allows a derivation of the following form for* any *standard sentence* R,

S | P1
S | P2 {R}
...

S | Q {R}

Then PR allows a derivation of this form for any space S1*:*

S | P1
S | P2 {R / ⟦S1⟧}
...

S |Q {R / [S1]}/fl

and PR allows a derivation of this form for any space S1*:*

S | P1
S | P2 {R / [S1]}
...

S |Q {R / [S1]}

For instance, (Stand2) tells us that from the following

spy(Bif) → [[sp_13]]
∀X(Bulgarian(X) → spy(X))

we can derive the following,

sp_8 | Bulgarian(Bif) → [sp_13]

since from the following

spy(Bif) → P
∀X(Bulgarian(X) → spy(X))

we can *always* derive the following, *no matter* what standard sentence P is.

sp_8 | Bulgarian(Bif) → P

Let me point out two features of (Stand2) that are important to observe in formulating specific rules of inference in PR. First, (Stand2) requires that all primary space terms become secondary space terms in the derived statements. This is again the *primary-to-secondary convention.* In actual formulations of specific PR standard rules, the primary-to-secondary convention can be implemented by appending the *where* clause we have seen above to require all primary space terms to be translated to secondary space terms.

The second feature of (Stand2) is subtle and easily overlooked, but important. I will call it the *immutability requirement.* It is that R is *immutable* in the antecedent PC derivation in the sense that it occurs unchanged in the derived sentence. For instance, (Stand2) fails to allow derivations like the following. From

∀X(Bulgarian(X) → [[sp_21]])

we cannot derive the following by universal instantiation,

sp_8 | Bulgarian(Bif) → [sp_21]

This is because it is not the case that for *every* sentence R from

$\forall$**X(Bulgarian(X) → R**

we can derive the following by universal instantiation,

sp_8 | Bulgarian(Bif) → R

Let **R** be **spy(X)**, for instance. In other words ⟦**sp_21**⟧ is not in an immutable position in this context.

Space Initialization

The rule of space initialization creates a new space along with its primary context. It is applicable whenever a statement contains an *entailment-preserving* environment, from which the primary context can be derived. The property of entailment preservation alone is what ensures what I have elsewhere called *coherence* in PR. An entailment-preserving environment is understood as follows.

(Ent-Pres)

P{___} *is entailment-preserving iff for any sentences* **Q** *and* **R**, *if* **Q** ⊩ **R** *in PC, then* **P{___/Q}** ⊩ **P{___/R}**.

The metasymbol ⊩ expresses *logical entailment* (necessitation). For instance, **R** → ___ is entailment-preserving, since if **P** ⊩ **Q** then **R** → **P** ⊩ **R** → **Q**. On the other hand, ___ → **R** is not entailment-preserving, because if **P** ⊩ **Q** then it is not necessarily the case that **P** → **R** ⊩ **Q** → **R**. Other demonstrably entailment-preserving environments are p **V** ___, **possible(___)**, **necessary(___)**, and ($\forall$**X)___**.

Notice that the statement **P{___}** *is entailment-preserving* is made in the metalanguage. In a higher-order predicate calculus we might in an alternative formalization identify complex predicates as entailment-preserving in the object language.

Notice that even though we have been using **believes** as a primary example of a predicate occurring in contexts in Part One of this book, an environment like **believes(George, ___)** should not strictly be an entailment-preserving environment if **believes** is given a semantics that reflects colloquial usage of *believes*. If it were, then George would have to always recognize all logical consequences of his beliefs. Nevertheless, there is doubtless heuristic motivation in assuming that such a thing is entailment-preserving for most applications as Creary (1979) points out and as we discussed in Chapter 2. For this reason, a computational belief representation would probably want to treat belief environments for convenience as if they were entailment-preserving.

Space initialization is formalized as follows.

P{___} is entailment-preserving **(Space Initialization)**
S | P {___/Q}

S | P' {___/[[S1]]}
S1 | Q'

where **S1** *is a previously unused space symbol, and where* **P'** *and* **Q'** *are like* **P** *and* **Q** *except that any term of the form* [[T]] *becomes* [T].

Notice that *two* statements are derived by this rule, one of which is the primary context of the new space, and one of which projects content into the new space. Notice also that the primary-to-secondary convention is observed in space initialization.

For instance, from

possible(___) is entailment-preserving
sp_1 | possible(spy(Fred))

we may derive

sp_1 | possible([[sp_2]])
sp_2 | spy(Fred)

From

fluffy(Puff) → ___ is entailment-preserving
sp_5 | fluffy(Puff) → cat(Puff)

we may derive

sp_5 | fluffy(Puff) → [[sp_7]]
sp_7 | cat(Puff)

Intuitively, the reason we require **P{___}** to be entailment-preserving is that this context should be appropriate to any other sentence in **S1** as it is to **Q** and any consequence of **Q** can potentially be derived locally in **S1** by standard rules. This property ensures what we called *coherence* in Chapter 2.

The statements **sp_1 | possible(⟦sp_2⟧)** and **sp_5 | p → ⟦sp_7⟧** are called *primary* contexts, since they contain primary space terms, i.e., ones with double brackets. Space initialization is the only rule that creates new spaces and the only rule that creates primary contexts. Almost all other contexts are created by the application of rules to existing contexts. Because of the primary-to-secondary convention only secondary contexts can be derived by these rules. Suppose, continuing the example we have started, that we have **sp_5 | large(Puff) → fluffy(Puff)**. Since we have **sp_5 | fluffy(Puff) → ⟦sp_7⟧** we can derive **sp_5 | large(Puff) → [sp_7]**. This last statement is a secondary context; because of the primary-to-secondary convention it loses the double brackets.

Context Climbing

The rule of *context climbing* does essentially the opposite of what space initialization does, and can be used to realize the global consequences of parochial reasoning.

```
S  | P{[S1]}              S  | P{⟦S1⟧}   (Context Climbing)
S1 | Q                    S1 | Q
--------------            ----------------
S  | P'{[S1] / Q'}        S  | P {⟦S1⟧ / Q'}
```

where **P'** *and* **Q'** *are like* **P** and **Q** *except that any term of the form* **⟦T⟧** *becomes* **[T]**.

These two separate but almost identical rules make it clear that context climbing works for both primary and secondary contexts. For instance, given

sp_1 | possible (⟦sp_2⟧)
sp_2 | spy(Bif)

we may infer

sp_1 | possible(spy(Bif)).

Or, given

sp_1 | [base]
base | lean(Clyde) & hungry(Clyde)

we may infer

sp_1 | lean(Clyde) & hungry(Clyde)

Space Augmentation

Space augmentation allows us to inject additional information into a space beyond what was originally put into the space by space initialization or by local inference. It is a primary means of achieving what I have elsewhere called *consolidation* in PR. It takes this form.

S | P {⟦S1⟧} (Space Augmentation)
S | P {⟦S1⟧ / ([S1] & Q)}

S1 | Q

Notice that the rule of space augmentation refers specifically to a *primary context.* This is actually the *only* reason we need to make a formal distinction between primary and secondary contexts, as upheld by the primary-to-secondary convention. However, without this distinction PR would no longer be sound.

For instance, given

sp_1 | possible(⟦sp_1⟧)
sp_1 | recapitulates(phylogeny, ontogeny)

we may infer

sp_1 | possible([sp_1] & recapitulates(phylogeny, ontogeny))

by standard means (using a reasonable axiom about possibility, since in modal logics **possible(P) & Q ⊩ possible(P & Q)**). Then by space augmentation, we have

sp_1 | recapitulates(phylogeny, ontogeny)

Given

sp_1| Bulgarian(Fred) → ⟦sp_2⟧
sp_1| Bulgarian(Fred) → spy(Fred)

(The first of these may have been derived, for instance, by space initialization from **sp_1| Bulgarian(Fred) → foreigner(Fred)**) we may infer by standard means

sp_1| Bulgarian(Fred) → ([sp_2] & spy(Fred))

since **possible(P) & Q ⊩ possible(P & Q)**). Then by space

augmentation, we have

sp_2 | spy(Fred)

Intuitively, space augmentation works in this case because in order to set up **sp_2** we *could* have derived **sp_1 | Bulgarian(Fred) → (foreigner(Fred) & spy(Fred))** first, then **sp_1| Bulgarian(Fred) → [[sp_2]]** and **sp_2 | foreigner(Fred) & spy(Fred)** by space initialization.

Space augmentation is particularly useful for *distributive* environments like **slim(Jim) → ___**, where distributive is understood as follows:

(Distr) P{___} *is distributive iff for any sentences* Q and R, P{___/Q} & P{___/R} ⊩ P{___/Q & R}.

An additional example of a distributive predicate is **necessary**, since **necessary(P) & necessary(Q)** logically entails **necessary(P & Q)**. **possible**, on the other hand, is not distributive, since **possible(P) & possible(Q)** does not necessarily entail **possible(P & Q)**. For distributive environments we can *derive* the following rule of inference from space augmentation.

P{___} is distributive (Distributive Space Augmentation)
S | P { ___ / Q }
S | P (___ / [[S1]] }

S1 | Q'

where **Q'** *is like* **Q** *except that any term of the form* **[[T]]** *becomes* **[T]**.

For instance, from

sp_1| necessary([[sp_2]])
sp_1| necessary(2 > 1)

we can immediately derive

sp_2 | 2 > 1

By *universal instantiation* we could derive

sp_8 | believes(wizard_8, [sp_9])

from **sp_8 | ∀X believes(X, [[sp_9]])**. From this last statement, if we have the context

sp_8 | believes(wizard_8, ⟦sp_10⟧)

we can derive

sp_10 | [sp_9]

by distributed space augmentation. Now **sp_10, wizard_8**'s belief space, inherits directly from **sp_9**, the space of *common* beliefs, by a single application of context climbing.

Space Identity

The space identity axiom allows any sentence to be mapped onto itself relative to some space by context climbing.

------- (Space Identity)
S | [S]

Notice that this rule has no preconditions. Space identity at first seems otiose. If we use it to introduce the statement

sp_1 | [sp_1]

and we are given

sp_1 | ∃X(banana(X) & eats(Bif,X))

then by context climbing we can derive

sp_1 | ∃X(banana(X) & eats(Bif,X))

which we knew to begin with. Its usefulness is realized when in conjunction with other rules it underlies the derivation of new secondary contexts. The following examples demonstrate this.

First, suppose we have

sp_1 | Bulgarian(Fred) → ⟦sp_2⟧

By space identity, we have

sp_1 | [sp_1]

Through normal axioms and rules of inference, since since **P → Q & P → R ⊩ P → (Q & R)).** we have

sp_1 | Bulgarian(Fred) → ([sp_1] & [sp_2])

By space augmentation we have

sp_2 | [sp_1]

This context specifies that **sp_2** inherits the entire contents of **sp_1**.

Second, suppose we have

sp_0 | before([sp_1],⟦sp_2⟧)
before(P,Q) → before(P,has_occurred(P) & Q)

(This means *If* **P** *is before* **Q** *then* **P** *is before* (**P** *has been the case &* **Q** *is the case*)). **has_occurred** is the aspectual operator corresponding to the English perfect, discussed in Chapter 8. From this we can infer

sp_0 | before([sp_1],has_occurred([sp_1]) & [sp_2])

by standard means, and

sp_2 | has_occurred([sp_1])

by space augmentation.

Third, let **P** □→ **Q** mean *if P were* the case then Q *would* be true. Then we could introduce the axiom

R → (P □→ presumably(R))

(*If* **R** *is the case then* **R** *would presumably be true if* **P** *were the case*). Here **presumably(R)** can be considered equivalent to **possible(R) → R**, or something like that, the idea being to treat **presumably(R)** like **R** unless this leads to a contradiction. This is consistent with work in *nonmonotonic logics* (e.g., McDermott and Doyle 1980). Now, if we have

sp_11 | Dukakis has won □→ ⟦sp_12⟧

we can derive

sp_11 | Dukakis has won □→ (presumably([sp_11]) & [sp_12])

by space identity, the axiom just given, and distributive space augmentation. From this follows

sp_12 | presumably([sp_11])

Contexts of the form **S1 | [S2]** and **S1 | presumably([S2])** are particularly interesting cases. The first says that **S1** is an extension of **S2** in the sense that anything satisfied in **S2** is also satisfied in **S1**. The second says that **S1** is a modification of **S2** in the sense that anything satisfied in **S2** can be assumed satisfied in **S1** unless some contradiction ensues in **S1**. These correspond to what we called *inheritance contexts* in Part One.

THE SEMANTICS OF PR

The last section cleverly avoided having to completely specify a syntax for the knowledge representation language PR by describing the relation of PR to an unspecified form of the predicate calculus PC. This chapter extends this practice by assuming that PC has a well-defined semantics and then adapting that semantics to PR.

We assume that some appropriate model-theoretic semantics for PC has been defined. Let **I** be the interpretation function that assigns an interpretation to every sentence of PC. If **P** is a sentence of PC then **I(P)** might, for instance, be a set of possible worlds (Kripke 1963). A semantics is easy to formalize for PR on the basis of **I**. Let **J** be a partial semantic evaluation function for *statements* of PR. We specify:

For any sentence **P** of PC, **J(base | P) = I(P)**.

For any statement **S | Q** *of PR, if* **S** $\neq$ **base** *or* **Q** contains a space term, then **J(S | Q)** *is undefined.*

For instance, **base | big(Clyde)** in PR means the same as **big(Clyde)** in PC. Interpretations cannot be assigned to other statements, like **sp_3 | green(Kermit)** or **base | possible([[sp_3]])**, individually since space terms and space tags have no interpretations in themselves but are syntactic objects that serve to connect separate statements together. On the other hand, these other statements have a *tacit* interpretation since a set of such statements can give immediate rise to the derivation of standard **base** statements through context climbing. Compare this to the occurrence of a sentence **Q** within the scope of an assumption **P** in a conditional proof in PC. **Q** has no meaning of its own in the sense of saying something about the real world, yet has the tacit interpretation corresponding to **P** → **Q**. We might, therefore, propose a semantic interpretation for certain *sets* of statements. For instance, the set of statements

sp_3 | green(Kermit)
base | possible([[sp_3]])

should have an interpretation, one equivalent to that of

possible(green(Kermit)) in PC. A set of statements that can be given a semantic interpretation is an *interpretable tree*, defined as follows

(I-Tree) *A set of statements,* T *is an* interpretable tree *iff each of the following hold:*

(a) For every statement in T *of the form*

Sn | Pn

there is a sequence of statements in T *of the form*

base | P1{[[S1]]}, S1 | P2{[[S2]]}, ..., Sn-1 | Pn{[[Sn]]}

(b) For every context in T *of the form*

S0 | P{[[S1]]}

there is a statements in T *of the form*

S1 | Q

(c) No primary space term occurs twice in T.

In other words, the spaces mentioned in T *form a tree such that the root of the tree is* **base**, for every branch from a space **S0** to **S1** there is exactly one context of the form **S0 | P{[[S1]]}**, and for every leaf node **S** of the tree there are standard statements of the form **S | P**.

The interpretation of an interpretable tree T, **J(T)** *can be defined as follows: Define* $\mathbf{E_T}$**(S)** (the expansion of a space S with respect to an interpretable tree T*) as follows:*

$\mathbf{E_T}$**(S) = S | P1 & ... & Pm &**
C1{[[S1]]/$\mathbf{E_T}$(S1) & ... & Cn{[[Sn]]/$\mathbf{E_T}$(Sn)
where **S | P1**, ..., **S | Pm** are all of the standard statements tagged for **S** in T, *and* **S | C1{[[S1]]}**, ..., **S | Cn{[[Sn]]}** *are all of the primary contexts tagged for* **S** in T.

Applying recursively, $\mathbf{E_T}$ effectively tells us all of the standard contents that can be derived for a space by applying context climbing. Now, we specify

For any interpretable tree T *in PR,* **J(T) = I(P)**, *where* **P = $\mathbf{E_T}$(base)**.

However, this is not necessary for proving that PR is sound.

SOUNDNESS

The rules of PR are claimed to be *sound with respect to base.* This means that, starting a set of standard statements tagged with **base** as premises, it is impossible to derive a statement tagged with **base** that is not semantically entailed by those premises, using the standard rules of inference along with space initialization, space augmentation, context climbing, and space identity. Since we are interested in the non-standard rules, I will just assume that the standard rules are sound in this sense. I will also assume without loss of generality that they are *complete.* The soundness theorem to be proved here can be paraphrased as follows:

(Sound) *Any standard statement of the form* **base | Q** *derived in PR from a set* **P** *of standard premises tagged with* **base** *is semantically entailed by* **P**.

Some Notation and Terminology

A *derivation* is a sequence of statements [S1, S2, ... Sn], each of which either is a *premise* or is derived from one or more preceding statements by some rule of inference in PR. A *premise* is a standard statement tagged with **base**. A *step* is a sequence of one or two statements in a derivation derived by some common rule of inference (recall that *space initialization* introduces *two* statements in one step with the application of one rule).

It will prove useful for our purposes to distinguish three kinds of steps:

(1) A *normal step* introduces a standard statement (i.e., one with no space terms) as a premise, by a standard axiom or rule of inference, or by context climbing.

(2) A *context-creating step* introduces a context by any means *except* by space augmentation.

(3) An *augmenting step* introduces any statement by *space augmentation.* (Since distributed space augmentation is a derived rule, we can ignore it here.)

For decomposing derivations into subsequences we will adopt the notation

M+N

to refer to the result of appending the sequences **M** and **N**. Let's say that a derivation **D+N**, where **D** and **N** are sequences of statements, is a *normal extension* of **D** iff every step used in introducing a statement in **N** is a normal step and no premises occur in **N**. Let's say that a derivation **D** is *solid* iff there is no normal extension of **D** that includes a statement of the form **base | P** such that **base | P** is not a logical entailment of the premises occurring in **D**.

Solid Derivations

The following lemma will be proved.

(Lemma1)

All derivations that have no augmenting step are solid.

The proof is by induction of the number of context-creating steps in the derivations. Specifically, a context-creating step derives:

(1) a secondary context using some *standard rule*, or

(2) a secondary context using *context climbing*, or

(3) a sequence of two statements of the form [S1 | P {[[S2]]}, S2 | Q] using *space initialization*, or

(4) a statement of the form S | [S] using the *space identity* axiom.

First of all, notice that any derivation with no context-creating steps is solid. This is because it will involve only premises, and standard rules applying in **base**. Such a derivation maps into a standard derivation in PC by removing the space tag **base** throughout.

Next, assume that any derivation with i context-creating steps is solid. Let **D** be a derivation of i + 1 context-creating steps. It will be shown that **D** is solid. The idea will be to demonstrate that the last context-creating step can be replaced. This will complete the proof of (Lemma1).

Let **D** have the form **C+S+N**, where **S** is the result of the i + 1th context-creating step. Notice that **C** contains i context-creating steps and is therefore solid and **N** contains only normal steps. Therefore if **C+S** is solid then **C+S+N** is solid. It will be shown that

C+S must be solid for each of the four kinds of context-creating steps that could have derived S.

Case 1. **S contains a secondary context S1 | P {[S2]}** derived by some ***standard rule*** of inference from a context **S1 | P'{[S2]}** (or **S1 | P' {⟦S2⟧}**).

Assume, contrary to what we want to prove, that C + S is not solid, that is, that some extension C+S+N' of C+S includes a statement base | R such that the premises do not semantically entail R. **This derivation must depend on deriving S1 | P {[S2]/Q} for some Q by context climbing, since this is the only normal rule that could use the result S. However, S1 | P {[S2]/Q} would have been derivable from C by normal means without first deriving S. Since we derived S1 | P {[S2]} from S1 | P' {[S2]} we could have first derived S1 | P' {[S2]/Q} by context climbing, then S1 | P {[S2]/Q} by similar means. The *immutability requirement*, described above, guarantees that there is such a derivation. Therefore base | R could have been derived in a normal extension of C, which contradicts our assumption that any derivation of i context-creating steps is solid. Therefore C+S must be solid.**

Case 2. **S is a secondary context S0 | P1 {[S1]/P2{[S2]}}** derived by ***context climbing*** from a context **S0 | P1{[S1]}** and a context **S1 | P2{[S2]}** (or **S1 | P2{⟦S2⟧}**).

Recall that the rule of Context Climbing is the following:

S | P{[S1]}	**S | P{⟦S1⟧}**	(*Context Climbing*)
S1 | Q	**S1 | Q**	
--------------	----------------	
S | P'{[S1] / Q'}	**S | P {⟦S1⟧ / Q'}**	

where **P'** *and* **Q'** *are like* **P** and **Q** *except that any term of the form* **⟦T⟧** *becomes* **[T]**.

Assume, contrary to what we want to prove, that **C + S** is not solid, that is, that an extension **C+S+N'** of **C+S** includes a statement **base | R** such that the premises does not semantically entail R. This derivation must depend on deriving **S0 | P1{[S1]/P2{[S2]/Q}}** for some **Q** by context climbing, since this is the only normal rule that could be applied to the result **S**. However, **S0 | P1{[S1]/P2{[S2]/Q}}** would have been derivable from **C** by normal means. First we derive **S1 | P2{[S2]/Q}** by context climbing, and then **S0 | P1{[S1]/P2{[S2]/Q}}** by a second application of context climbing. Therefore **base | R** could have been derived in a normal extension of **C** contrary to assumption. Therefore, **C+S** must be solid.

Case 3. **S** is the sequence [**S | P {[[S1]]}, S1 | Q**] derived by *space initialization.*

Recall that the rule of space initialization is the following:

P{___} is entailment-preserving (**Space Initialization**)
S | P {___/Q}

S | P {___/[[S1]]}
S1 | Q
where **S1** *is a previously unused space symbol.*

Assume, contrary to what we want to prove, that **C + S** is not solid, that is, that an extension of **C+S+N'** of **C+S** includes a statement **base | R** such that the premises does not semantically entail **R**. This derivation must depend on deriving **S1 | Q'**, where **Q** semantically entails **Q'**, followed by **S | P {[[S1]]/Q'}** by context climbing, since this is the only normal rule that could be applied to **S**. However, **S | P {[[S1]]/Q'}** would have been derivable in a normal extension of **C** since **Q'** is a logical consequence of **Q**, **P {[[S1]]/___}** is entailment-preserving, and **S | {[[S1]]/Q}** must be included in **C**.

Case 4. **S** is the statement **S | [S]** derived by the space *identity axiom.*

------- (**Space Identity**)
S | [S]

This case is trivial.

Derivations with Space Augmentation

We are close to proving the soundness theorem for derivations that do not use space augmentation. The following lemma will carry that proof over to derivations with space augmentation:

(Lemma2)

For any derivation using space augmentation of a standard statement of the form base | P, there is a derivation of base | P that does not use space augmentation.

The proof is accomplished by providing a procedure that translates a derivation of space augmentation into an equivalent derivation without space augmentation. Recall that the rule of space augmentation looks like this.

S | P {[[S1]]} **(Space Augmentation)**
S | P {[[S1]] / ([S1] & Q)}

S1 | Q

Suppose we have a derivation **C+S+N** where **S** is an augmenting step of the form [**S1 | Q**]. We will show how to replace this step with a sequence of non-augmenting steps. Within **C** statements of the following forms must occur (otherwise space augmentation could not have applied).

S | P { [[S1]] }
S | P { [[S1]] / ([S1] & Q) }

Since **S | P {[[S1]] / ____}** must be entailment-preserving, the following can be derived by space initialization, where **S2** is a new space.

S | P { [[S1]]/[[S2]] }
S2 | [S1] & Q

from which follow

S2 | Q
S2 | [S1]

by standard means. Observe that **S2** is exactly like **S1** in every relevant way. In particular, they have identical primary contexts and therefore for any secondary context in the derivation using the space term **[S1]** we can derive an equivalent secondary context using the space term **[S2]**. Also, the inheritance context **S2 | [S1]** ensures that for any statement in the derivation of the form **S1 | R** we can derive an equivalent statement of the form **S2 | R** by one application of context climbing.

We translate the derivation **C+S+N** into the derivation **C+S'+N'**. We specify **S'** as follows.

(1) **S'** includes the sequence

S | P { ⟦S1⟧/⟦S2⟧ }
S2 | [S1] & Q
S2 | Q
S2 | [S1]

which we showed how to derive above.

(2) For every statement of the form **S1 | R** occurring in C, S' includes the statement **S2 | R**, derived by context climbing as described above.

(3) For every statement of the form **S | T{[S1]}** occurring in C, S' includes all statements necessary to derive **S | T{[S1]/[S2]}** as discussed above.

N' is like **N** except every occurrence of **S1** in **N** is replaced by **S2** in **N'**. We are assured that every step in **N'** is legal.

The Soundness Theorem

The soundness theorem follows immediately from (**Lemma1**) and (**Lemma2**).

(**Sound**) *Any standard statement of the form* **base | Q** derived in PR from a set **P** of standard premises tagged with **base** is semantically entailed by **P**.

CONCLUSIONS

Aside from any value PR might have as a formal logic in itself, the development of PR tells us much about the functionality of partitioned representations.

First, PR specifies explicitly in a formal framework the conditions under which spaces *can* be set up with a guarantee of coherence, as well as the conditions under which secondary contexts, including inheritance contexts, can be derived and under which additional information can be injected into spaces in support of consolidation. It shows us how these conditions depend on the semantics of primary contexts. Comparison of the examples in this chapter with those of Chapter 2 will demonstrate the striking correspondence of the formal results and our intuitive assumptions about the structures of spaces. Where these assumptions fail to correspond to the formal results, for instance in the case of belief spaces, a heuristic basis can be found for assuming a correspondence.

Second, PR allows us to understand the *functionality* of partitioned representations. The soundness proof demonstrates that partitioned representations work because they support correct inferences. The rules of inference show us where consolidation and coherence are possible and where they are not. Consolidation is supported where space augmentation and the derivation of secondary contexts is possible. Coherence is guaranteed by entailment preservation.

The next chapter shows how the logic of partitioned representations generalizes several traditional AI knowledge representation frameworks, as well as all of the subproof methods in natural deduction. Chapter 12 then will describe a computational system of knowledge representation based on the logic developed in this chapter. It applies the rules of inference introduces here appropriately to achieve much greater efficiency and generality in reasoning in complex domains than previously available.

CHAPTER ELEVEN

Generalized Natural Deduction

This chapter demonstrates how the general theory of partitioned representations can be applied to some specific knowledge representation problems. It will be seen how the theory generalizes some existing AI knowledge representation systems, as well as some systems of logic. In particular, we will look at *natural deduction*, representing *time* and *action*, and *frames*.

GENERALIZED NATURAL DEDUCTION

In Chapter 2 I brought out the similarity between reasoning in partitioned representations and using methods of subproofs in natural deduction. I am are now in a position to show more rigorously how proofs in PC using naturally deductive subproofs map directly into proofs in PR using partitioning rules. In each case, the introduction of an assumption corresponds to initializing a space, reiteration generally corresponds to inheritance through a secondary context, the deduction within the subproof corresponds to a parochial deduction using standard rules within that space, and the discharge of the assumption corresponds to an application of context climbing.

Conditional Proof

A conditional proof in PC is any proof of the following form.

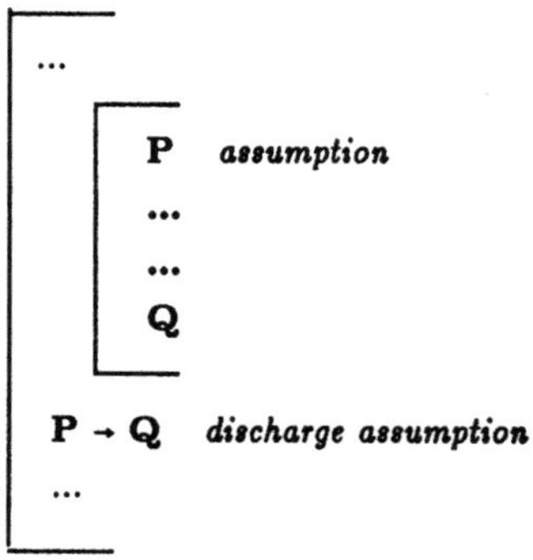

In the equivalent proof in PR the outer box corresponds to some space, call it **base**, and the inner box to some space, call it **sp_1**, with the primary context **base | P → ⟦sp_1⟧**. The equivalent PR proof structure might be pictured as follows:

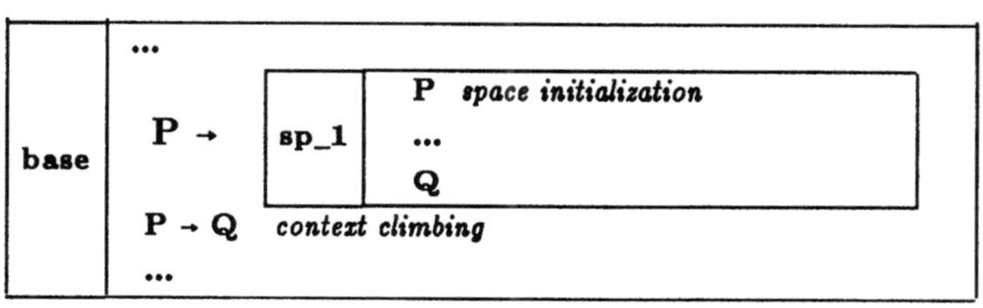

Something that is not clear in this figure is that **sp_1** inherits from **base**. In the natural deduction proof this is equivalent to saying that the scope of the premises includes the scope of the assumption. In the PR proof we require an inheritance context

sp_1 | [base]

The complete equivalent PR proof looks like this:

base | ...

base | P → P *standard axiom*
base | P → ⟦sp_1⟧ *space initialization*

sp_1 | P "

base | [base] *space identity*
base | P → [base] *standard rule*

sp_1 | [base] *distributive space augmentation*
sp_1 | ...
sp_1 | Q *parochial deduction*

base | P →Q *context climbing*
base | ...

Where reiteration is used in the natural deduction proofs, inheritance steps occur in PR by context climbing on sp_1 | [base].

Notice that setting up and making use of this inheritance context makes the PR proof longer than the equivalent PC proof. This is the cost of generality. Several steps in PR proofs may collapse into a single step in natural deduction in PC. On the other hand, PR permits more subtle distinctions. For instance, some PR proofs will not use such inheritance contexts, and therefore we must have some means of making this distinction explicit.

Universal Instantiation + Generalization

A proof using universal instantiation followed by universal generalization in PC may take the following form.

```
┌───
│ ...
│ ∀XP{X}
│    ┌───
│    │ P{X}   universal instantiation
│    │ ...
│    │ ...
│    │ Q{X}
│    └───
│ ∀XQ{X}   universal generalization
│ ...
└───
```

In the equivalent proof in PR the outer box corresponds to **base** and the inner box to some space, call it **sp_2**, with the primary context **base | ∀ ⟦sp_2⟧**. The equivalent PR proof structure might be pictured as follows:

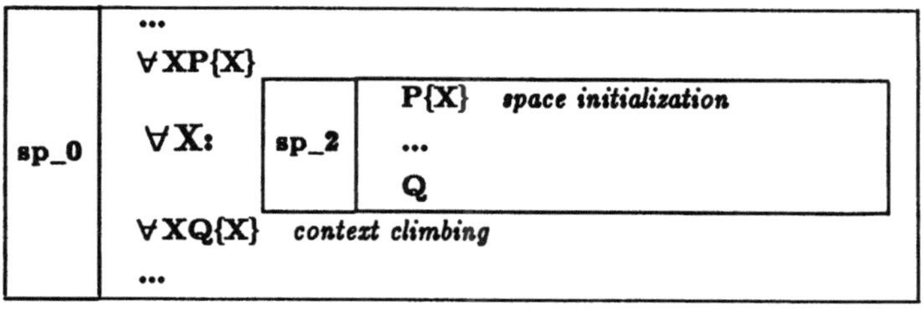

Like **sp_1**, **sp_2** inherits from **base**. In the natural deduction proof this is equivalent to reiteration. In the PR proof we require an inheritance context

sp_2 | [**base**]

The complete equivalent PR proof looks like this:

base | ...
base | ∀XP{X}

base | ∀X ⟦sp_2⟧ *space initialization*

sp_2 | P{X} "

base | [**base**] *space identity*
base | ∀X [**base**] *standard rule*

sp_2 | [**base**] *distributive space augmentation*
sp_2 | ...
sp_2 | Q{X} *parochial deduction*

base | ∀XQ{X} *context climbing*
base | ...

Within the steps tagged for **sp_2** some inheritance steps using **sp_2** | [**base**] may occur to make use of premises in **base** or sentences derived in **base**.

Proof by Cases

A proof by cases in PC assumes the following form.

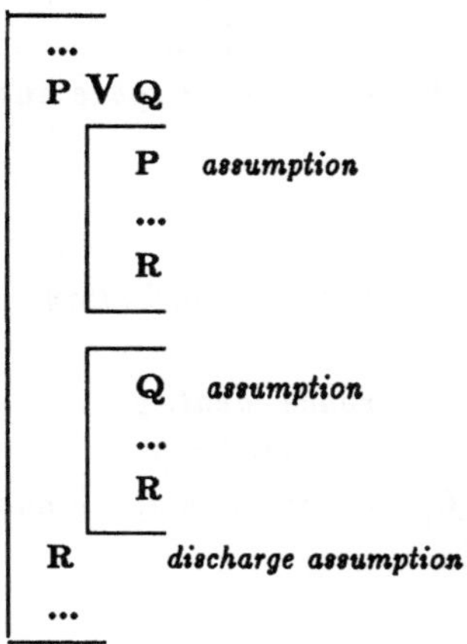

In the equivalent proof in PR the outer box corresponds to **sp_0** and the inner boxes to some space, call them **sp_3** and **sp_4**, with the context **sp_0 | ⟦sp_3⟧ V [sp_4]**. The equivalent PR proof structure might be pictured as follows:

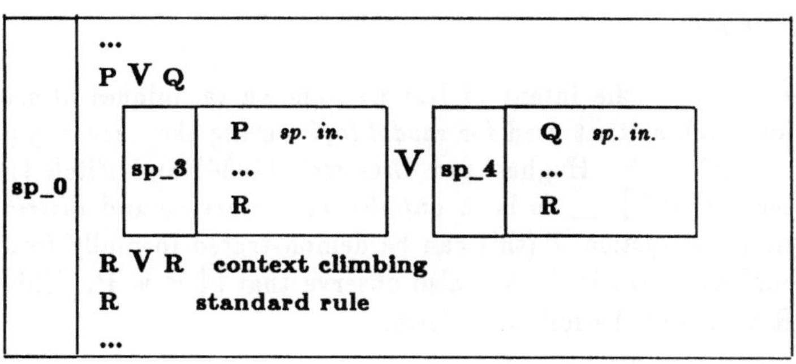

In the PR proof we require the inheritance contexts

sp_3 | [sp_0]
sp_4 | [sp_0]

The complete equivalent PR proof looks like this:

sp_0 | ...
sp_0 | P V Q

sp_0 | P V ⟦sp_4⟧ *space initialization*
sp_4 | Q "

sp_0 | [sp_0] *space identity*
sp_0 | P V [sp_0] *standard rule*
sp_4 | [sp_0] *distributive space augmentation*
sp_4 | ...
sp_4 | R

sp_0 | ⟦sp_3⟧ V [sp_4] *space initialization*
sp_3 | P "
sp_0 | [sp_0] *space identity*
sp_0 | [sp_0] V [sp_4] *standard rule*
sp_3 | [sp_0] *distributive space augmentation*
sp_3 | ...
sp_3 | R

sp_0 | R V [sp_4] *context climbing*
sp_0 | R V R *context climbing*
sp_0 | R *standard rule*
sp_0 | ...

Modal Proofs

PR also captures the intent of less well-known techniques of natural deduction, such as that used for *modal logics* using the *necessity* predicate □ described by Hughes and Cresswell (1968) and Fitch (1952). We observe that □ ___ is both *entailment preserving* and *distributive* in the minimal system T (this can be demonstrated formally from the traditional axiomization). We also observe that **□ P ⊩ P**. This permits PR proofs of the following form.

base | ...
base | (□ R)
base | ...

base | □ P
base | □ ⟦sp_5⟧ *space initialization*

sp_5 | P "

base | [sp_5] *necessity elimination*

sp_5 | ...
sp_5 | (R) *distributive space augmentation*
sp_5 | ...
sp_5 | Q *parochial deduction*

base | □ Q *context climbing*
base | ...

It is interesting that **sp_5** does not inherit from **base; sp_5 | [base]** cannot be derived because the inference of **□ P** from **P** does not succeed (in contrast, for instance, with the inference of **P → Q** from **Q**). On the other hand, if we have **base | □ Q**, we have **sp_5 | Q**. This corresponds to what Fitch (1952) calls *strict reiteration*, but for us this is simply distributive space augmentation. It is also interesting that **base** inherits from **sp_5** using the derived context **base | [S4]**.

PR is more general that natural deduction; there are some PR proofs that have no traditional natural deduction equivalent. Thus proofs about fictions, beliefs, counterfactuals, times, and so on are treated the same way as traditional natural proofs. For instance, we observe that **at(T, ___)** is entailment preserving and distributive, where **at(T, P)** means that **P** is true at time **T**. Accordingly, we have proofs like this:

base | ...

base | at(T, P)
base | at(T, [[S6]]) *space initialization*
S6 | P "

S6 | ...
S6 | Q *parochial deduction*

base | at(T, Q) *context climbing*
base | ...

TIME AND ACTION

Partitioned representations also generalize the idea of *context-layered data bases* (McDermott and Sussman 1972, McDermott 1983) used, for instance, in early planning systems like STRIPS (Fikes and Nilsson 1971). We first looked at context-layered data bases in Chapter 2. The core conceptual structure is similar to the *situation calculus*, the original logic-based treatment of action and change that context layered data bases were intended to supplant for reasons of efficiency. We find that in PR the knowledge expressed in the original formulas of the predicate calculus can be effectively partitioned into small data bases such that as in context layered data bases reasoning is performed with little explicit reference to situations.

Let **true(S, P)** mean that P *would be true* in situation S. A *situation* is a temporally and perhaps spatially bound situation or *possible* situation in which certain conditions are satisfied. For instance, for a particular situation in the *blocks world*, call it **sit_0**, we might have (in PC)

true(sit_0, on(block2, block1))
true(sit_0, on(block3, block2))
true(sit_0, on(block4, block3))
true(sit_0, clear(block4))
true(sit_0, holding(block5))

and so on. Observe that

true(S,___) is entailment-preserving.
true(S,___) is distributive.

For instance, we should be able to make the following inferences,

(on(A, B) & on(B, C)) ⊩ above(B, C)
----
true(S, on(A, B) & on(B, C)) ⊩ true(S, above(B, C))

true(S, on(A, B)) & true(S, on(B, C))
----
true(S, on(A, B) & on(B, C))

Therefore, from **base | true(s,P)** we should be able to derive

base | true(s,⟦sp_1⟧)
sp_1 | P

by *space initialization.*

An *action* is something that may be executed in one situation to produce a new situation. In the blocks world primitive actions are

unstack (pick up a block from on top of another block), **stack** (put a block down on top of another block), **pick_up** (pick up a block from on the table) and **put_down** (put a block onto the table). If action **A** is executed in situation **S1** and results in situation **S2** then we say

S0 | res(A, S1, S2)

The ability to execute **A** in **S1** depends on the satisfaction of certain preconditions. For instance, to put a block down we must be holding that block. If **A** is executed then certain results obtain. For instance,

S0 | true(S1, holding(B))
S0 | res(put_down(B), S1, S2)

S0 | true(S2, on_table(B))

We can summarize the satisfaction of the preconditions for a particular action by means of the predicate **can_do**. For instance, we can state

S0 | true(S1, holding(B))

S0 | true(S1, can_do(put_down(B)))

or more simply, since we set up situational spaces,

S | holding(B)

S | can_do(put_down(B))

This formalization does not seem to lend itself to consolidation of information into spaces, nor to relying significantly on parochial reasoning to produce inferences. The reason is that we must always return to the parent space **S0** in which the **res** relation is given to infer the relationship between the contents of the two situational spaces **S1** and **S2**. There is a way of *embedding* these relations between situations in the contents of the situational spaces themselves and thereby eliminate the need to make reference to situations altogether when reasoning about situations and results of actions. Let **result(A,Q)** mean that in the situation that results from executing action **A**, proposition **Q** will be true. This does not mean that **A** necessarily *causes* **Q**. For instance, we can no say,

```
S0 | true(S1, holding(B))
------------------------------
S0 | true(S1, result(put_down(B), on_table(B)))
```

We define **result** explicitly by means of the following axiom.

```
true(S, result(A, Q)) <-> ∃S1 (res(A, S0, S1) & true(S1, Q))
```

We can use **result** to formalize some rules of inference for possible actions in situations as follows.

```
S | can_do(unstack(B, C))
-------------------------
S | result(stack(B, C), holding(B) & ~hand_empty & clear(C))

S | can_do(stack(B, C))
-------------------------
S | result(stack(B, C), hand_empty & ~clear(C) & on(B,C))

S | can_do(put_down(B))
-------------------------
S | result(put_down(B), hand_empty & on_table(B))

S | hand_empty & on(B, C) & clear(B)
-------------------------
S | can_do(unstack(B, C))

S | holding(B) & clear(C)
-------------------------
S | can_do(stack(B, C))

S | holding(B)
-------------------------
S | can_do(put_down(B))

S | P
-------------------------
S | result(A, presumably(P))
```

Now, observe that

result(A, ___) is entailment-preserving.
result(A, ___) is distributive.

Therefore, by *space initialization* we can make the following inference:

S1 | result(A, Q)

S1 | result(A, ⟦S2⟧)
S2 | Q

and by *distributed space augmentation* we can make the following inference:

S1 | result(A, Q)
S1 | result(A, ⟦S2⟧)

S2 | Q

It is a fact about the real world that as we progress through a series of actions from one situation to the next changes occur very slowly. In fact they tend to be limited to the direct effects of the actions; most conditions remain constant over long periods of time. This can be accounted for by allowing the following rule:

S | (result(A, Q) & R)   (Beneralized Frame Axiom)

----

result(A ,Q & presumably(R))

This rule, along with *space identity* and *distributed space augmentation* allows inferences of the following form:

S1 | result(A, ⟦S2⟧)

S2 | presumably([S1])

These properties of result can be captured in a Spaceprobe restructure rule of the following form (see Chapter 12).

```
restructure_rule( S0 ! result(A, P),
    [ sp_distr(S0 ! result(A, P),
            lambda(X):result(A, X), C, S1 ! P),
      digest_statement(S1 ! P),
      sp_ident(S0, S0 ! T),
      intern_statement( S1 ! default(T)) ]).
```

Proceeding in this way we derive a tree of spaces with sp_1 as the root, and each non-root space **S** linked to its father **S0** by the contexts **S0 | result(A,⟦S⟧)** and **S | presumably([S0])**, for some action A. This system is largely equivalent to the context-layered data bases in CONNIVER, in which each context inherits by default from a father context from which it is derived by some action. A difference is that knowledge partitioning provides an explicit representation of what each space is used for in terms of a context **S0 | result(A,[[S1]])**.

Eliminating **res** in favor of **result** by defining a relation at a higher level of embedding that can be used to make semantically equivalent statements produces what I called an *ambient representation* in Chapter 2. This technique is very useful in realizing consolidation in partitioned representations. Producing ambient representations looks like it introduces complexity from the perspective of PC, but in fact reduces the complexity from the perspective of PR. Shoving a relation down into an increased level of embedding in PC corresponds to consolidating information into a more parochial domain in PR. We will see in Chapter 10 that English temporal *aspects* in fact correspond to such embeddings of temporal relations.

FRAMES

Frames are forms of representation widely studied in artificial intelligence and found in many computational applications from expert systems to natural language understanding. A frame (Minsky 1975) is a representation that consolidates all of the knowledge about an object or a *type* of object in one structural unit. Typically its internal structure consists of a set of *slots*, or feature categories, with associated *fillers*, or feature values. Figure 6.1 shows a structure with three frames. The bottom-most represents the individual object Fido, indicating his name as "*Fido*", his pastime as chasing cars and his owner as Bif. The top two frames, **Mammal** and **Dog** are *generic frames* representing the prototypical member of some type of object. These frames indicate, among other things, that the individual of type dog has a diet that makes it a carnivore and has a nose temperature that is cold, and that the individual of type mammal has a body temperature that is warm and a surface that is made of hair.

Aside from consolidating knowledge into natural units, frames support a particular mode of inference in which slot values of generic frames are readily *inherited* by appropriate frames. For instance, since Fido is a dog, knowledge in the generic **Dog** frame is made available when reasoning about Fido or answering questions about Fido. Since

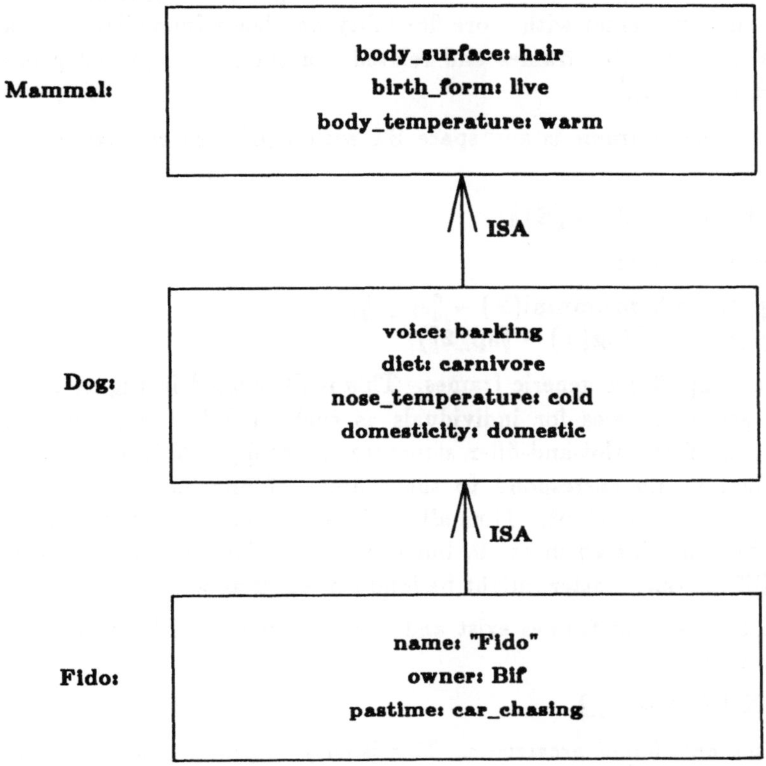

Fig. 11.1. Traditional Frames.

any dog is a Mammal, knowledge in the generic mammal frame is made available when reasoning or answering questions about dogs in general, or about specific dogs like Fido. Generic frames are in this sense specialized forms of *schema.* Inheritance is made possible by establishing an *ISA link* from a frame (individual or generic) to a generic frame. Figure 6.1 shows an ISA link from **Fido** to **Dog** and another ISA link from **Dog** to **Mammal**, since Fido *is a* dog and a dog *is a* mammal. Likewise, we might expect an ISA link from **Rover** to **Dog** and from **Uran-Utan** to **Mammal**, and so on.

In PR frames can be defined very simply as spaces which contain universal quantifiers in their primary contexts. ISA links can be derived as a certain kind of secondary context. Not only does this further demonstrate the generality of the knowledge partitioning framework, but it endows frames with more flexibility and leads immediately to a proper semantics for frames and related concepts, a recognized problem (Hayes 1979).

A *generic frame* is any space **S1** with a primary context of the form

S0 | ∀X(P{X} → ⟦S1⟧)

For instance, given

sp_0 | ∀X(mammal(X) → ⟦sp_1⟧)
sp_0 | ∀Y(dog(Y) → ⟦sp_2⟧)

sp_1 and **sp_2** are generic frames. This is illustrated in Figure 11.2. There are no frames for individuals as such in PR, nor do frames make use of the slot-and-filler structure internally. A frame for an individual would correspond to the content of any space sharing a common object constant. Thus all of the information specific to Fido might be consolidated in **sp_0**, but the information specific to Rover, or to Bif for that matter, might be found in **sp_0** as well.

To show that frames exist and can be derived in PR, we should point out that

∀X(P{X} → ___)

is in fact *entailment preserving*. This is easy to prove logically. This environment is *distributive* as well. For instance from

sp_0 | ∀Y(dog(Y) → domestic(Y))
sp_0 | ∀Y(dog(Y) → nose_temperature(Y, cold))

we can derive the following by *space initialization* and *distributed space augmentation*.

sp_0 | ∀Y(dog(Y) → ⟦sp_2⟧)
sp_2 | domestic(Y))
sp_2 | nose_temperature(Y, cold))

In this way we consolidate the description of the generic dog in one place.

An important property of generic frames is that they inherit from their parents, but only if we introduce an adequate restriction on the naming of free variables. Notice that in PC we can make the

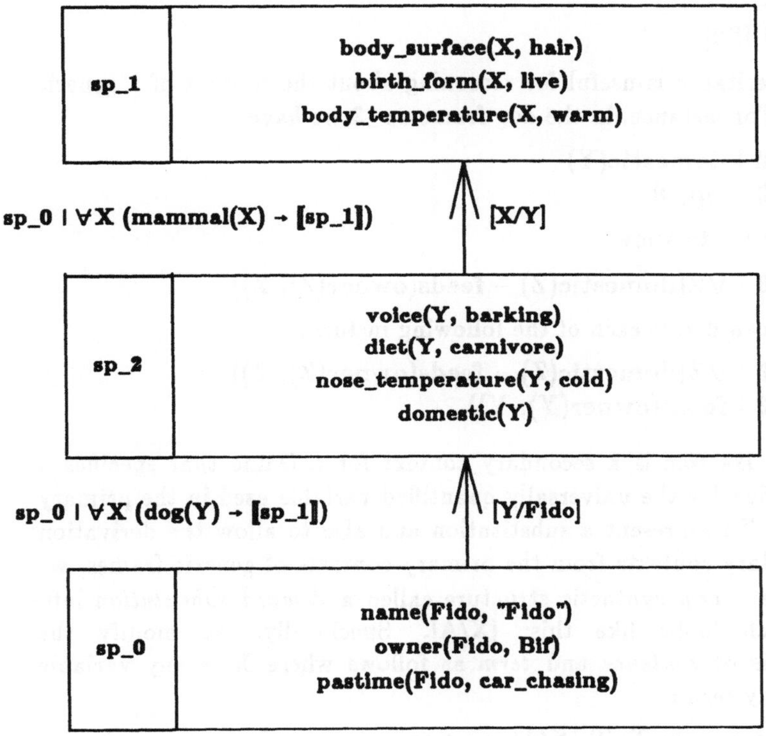

Fig. 11.2. Frames as Spaces.

following derivation

$$\begin{array}{l} R \\ \forall X(P\{X\} \to Q) \\ \hline \forall X(P\{X\} \to (Q \,\&\, R)) \end{array}$$

as long as X *does not occur as a free variable in* R. If a suitable convention for naming variables is adopted this derivation will succeed unconditionally. As a result, by *space identity* and *distributed space augmentation* the following will succeed as well.

S0 | ∀X(P{X} → ⟦S1⟧)

S1 | [S0]

This inheritance is useful for reasoning about the content of a generic frame. For instance, in the dog frame **sp_2** we have

sp_2 | domestic(Y)
sp_2 | [sp_0]

If we happen to know

sp_0 | ∀Z(domestic(Z) → feeds(owner(Z), Z))

then we can derive each of the following in turn.

sp_2 | ∀Z(domestic(Z) → feeds(owner(Z), Z))
sp_2 | feeds(owner(Y), Y))

An *ISA link* is a secondary context for a frame that specifies a substitution for the universally quantified variable used in the primary context. To represent a substitution and also to allow the derivation of secondary contexts from the primary contexts of generic frames, we introduce a new syntactic structure called a *delayed substitution* into PR which looks like this: [X/A]. Specifically, we modify the definitions of *sentence* and *term* as follows where **X** is any variable and **A** any term:

For any term **T**, **T** [X/A] is a term.
For any sentence **P**, **P** [X/A] is a sentence.

In general, **P**[X/A] is semantically equivalent to **P{X/A}**, i.e., to the result of substituting **A** for **X** in **P** (keep in mind that {...} is used in the *metalanguage*, whereas [...] is intended for the *object language*). For instance **barks(X)**[X/Fido] is exactly equivalent to **barks(Fido)**. This equivalence is captured in the following *substitution equivalences*.

(P Op Q)[X/A] = (P[X/A] Op Q[X/A])
where **Op** *is an operator (*→, &, etc.)
P(T1, T2, ... Tn)[X/A] = P[X/A](T1[X/A], T2[X/A], ..., Tn[X/A
where **P** *is a predicate or functor and* **T1, T2, ...** *are terms*
(∀Y P) [X/A] = ∀Y (P [X/A])
where **X ≠ Y**
(∃Y P) [X/A] = ∃Y (P [X/A])
where **X ≠ Y**

(∀X P) [X/A] = ∀X P)
(∃X P) [X/A] = ∃X P)
X[X/A] = A
B[X/A] = B
where is a symbol and A ≠ B

In effect, these equivalences sanction the substitution of X by A throughout an expression except in two protected positions. Substitutions cannot go into a quantification using the variable name X, and substitutions cannot go into a **space term**. For instance, the following

∀V(spy(V) → stabs(V, W) & ∃W shoots(V, W)) [W/Bif]

is equivalent to

∀V(spy(V) → stabs(V, Bif) & ∃W shoots(V, W))

The following

(spy(W) → ⟦sp_8⟧) [W/Bif]

is equivalent to

(spy(Bif) → ⟦sp_8⟧[W/Bif])

Notice that it is always possible to eliminate all occurrences of [X/A] using the substitution equivalences, *except when this has a space term in its scope*, as in this last case.

The rule of *universal instantiation*, seemingly our best opportunity for deriving variable substitutions from frame contexts, cannot apply to contexts in its standard formalization, because it disobeys the *immutability requirement*, i.e., it potentially make substitutions into space terms. However, relying on [S/A] to delay substitution, we can produce a weaker but more general rule of universal instantiation like this:

S | ∀X P (Universal Instantiation)

S | P' [X/A]
where P' *is like* P *except that any term of the form* ⟦T⟧ *becomes* [T].

Universal instantiation does not perform any substitutions, but simply specifies a substitution. Substitutions can be derived using the equivalences above, but cannot go into a space term. For instance, given

sp_0 | ∀Y(dog(Y) → ⟦sp_2⟧)

We can derive

sp_0 | dog(Fido) → [sp_2][Y/Fido]

by *universal instantiation* and by performing a couple of substitutions using the substitution equivalences. Then, given

sp_0 | dog(Fido)

we can derive the following by *modus ponens.*

sp_0 | [sp_2][Y/Fido]

This last secondary context is the bottom *ISA context* indicated in Figure 11.2

Now, watch the following derivation,

sp_2 | nose_temperature(Y, cold) *given*
sp_0 | [sp_2][Y/Fido] *just derived*
sp_0 | nose_temperature(Y, cold)[Y/Fido] *context climbing*
sp_0 | nose_temperature(Fido, cold) *subst. of equivalences*

In this way Fido inherits from the Dog frame.

More generally, an ISA context is defined as any context of the form

S0 | [S1] [X/A]

An ISA context specifies direct inheritance from one space to another subject to the uniform substitution of one term for another throughout. The following rule for generally introducing ISA contexts can be derived from universal instantiation, modus ponens the substitution equivalences. It will prove useful in what follows.

S | (∀ X) (P → Q) (ISA Introduction)
S | P {X/A}

S | Q [X/A]

For instance, the second ISA context indicated in Figure 11.2 can be derived from sp_2 | mammal(Y) as follows:

sp_0 | ∀X (mammal(X) → ⟦sp_1⟧ *given*
sp_2 | [sp_0] *given*

sp_2 | mammal(Y) *given*
sp_2 | ∀X (mammal(X) → ⟦sp_1⟧ *inheritance*
sp_2 | [sp_1] [X/Y] *ISA Introduction*

In summary, by introducing the simple concept of *delayed substitutions* we find that generic frames and ISA links are fully derivable in PR. Moreover, the semantics of ISA links is completely clear since they are not introduced as primitive constructs. In the literature it has been unclear whether ISA means "element of" "subset of", sometimes one and sometimes the other, or something else. It is interesting to note that all occurrences of the ISA link have the same analysis: each specifies a uniform substitution as we pass from one space to another.

SUMMARY AND CONCLUSIONS

In this chapter we have seen how a number of traditional knowledge representation and inference schemes that seem unrelated (at least no one to my knowledge has recognized the similarity) can in fact all be treated as specific instances of partitioned representations. This not only demonstrates the generality, flexibility and usefulness of partitioned representations, but also allows us immediately to recognize the logical properties of these schemes without additional analysis. Among these logical properties are the semantics of the constructs introduced in these schemes, and the soundness (or limits on soundness) of these schemes.

CHAPTER TWELVE

A Computational Model

The *computational knowledge representation system* described here is based on the logic of partitioned representations. It is designed to support reasoning in computational applications in artificial intelligence, such as language understanding, in addition to general theorem proving. It handles incoming knowledge by distributing that knowledge appropriately over multiple spaces and handles queries by allocating subqueries to the appropriate spaces.

This chapter describes our experiences with the successful implementation of the logic-based computational knowledge representation system *Spaceprobe* (Dinsmore 1986, 1991b; Likhitaworn 1986; Ng 1989) and its applications. We will review the way in which the computational advantages of partitioned representations have been successfully realized in Spaceprobe. We will see how Spaceprobe ensures that the partitioning rules of PR are applied at appropriate points to maximize coherence and consolidation. These rules apply both in a data-directed manner as new complex knowledge becomes available, and in a goal-directed manner as queries for complex knowledge are processed. We will also see how Spaceprobe utilizes special indexing mechanisms in order to climb inheritance contexts quickly and automatically in a goal directed manner.

THE DESIGN OF SPACEPROBE

Spaceprobe can be described at three different levels of abstraction, the *application level*, the *customization level*, and the *implementation level*.

Application Level

At the *application level* Spaceprobe is a system that can be used to store and retrieve statements deductively as part of a larger program. Spaceprobe provides a very clean high-level interface to larger applications, supporting two basic operations, the *input* of new knowledge and the *retrieval* of existing knowledge, that is, asserting and asking.

The basic unit of knowledge in Spaceprobe is the *statement*. The syntax of statements is a little different than that used elsewhere in this book, because of restrictions imposed by the implementation language, Prolog. In particular, primary space terms use double curly brackets like this: **{{sp_3}}** and secondary space terms use single curly brackets, like this : **{base}**. **!** is used to glue a tag onto a sentence to form a statement, like this: **sp_3 ! spy(bif) ==> {{sp_4}}**. **==>** is material implication, **/==>** is counterfactual implication.

To input new knowledge a call is made of the form,

?- **digest_statement(S ! P).**

The meaning of the statement **S ! P** is then remembered by Spaceprobe. For instance, the call

?- **digest_statement(sp_8 ! believes(bif, spy(harry))).**

might be used to add the content that Bif believes that Harry is a spy to **sp_8.**

To retrieve knowledge deductively a call of the following form is made,

?- **infer_statement(S ! P).**

where **S ! P** is a statement *pattern*. A statement pattern is like a statement but may contain *variables* that are assigned values or *bindings* by the call to **infer_statement**. The occurrence of a variable in a call to **infer_statement** is like the occurrence of the word *what* or *who* in an English question. **infer_statement** answers the questions by providing bindings. For instance, after making the call to **digest_statement** given as an example above, the following call,

?- **infer_statement(sp_8 ! believes(bif, spy(X))).**

meaning *who does Bif believe is a spy?* would cause the variable **X** to be bound to **harry***.

The names **digest_statement** and **infer_statement** suggest that more is happening than simple storage and retrieval. When **digest_statement(S ! P)** is called, *restructuring* of **P** typically occurs. When **infer_statement(S ! P)** is called, deductive inference is typically required to find a result. These processes are not apparent at the application level. However, the programmer can control the application behavior of Spaceprobe at the customization level.

Customization Level

At the *customization level* the behavior of the Spaceprobe system can be programmed. In particular, restructuring during digestion can be controlled by specifying *restructuring rules* and deductive inference can be controlled by specifying *inference rules.* Generally restructuring rules will, among other things, determine how spaces are set up.

The design philosophy dictates that rules creating spaces and contexts will apply in a data-directed manner, i.e., will apply when a statement is digested, and that context-climbing will apply in a goal-directed manner, i.e., when **infer_statement** is called. Parochial processes will apply in either direction as specified in the customization.

---

* For those readers who are not familiar with the Prolog language a few comments are in order. A variable in Prolog is a symbol that begins with a capital letter; that is why **bif** and **harry** are not capitalized here. The process of matching patterns to structures thereby binding variables is known as *unification.* Unification allows one procedure to communicate with another, since once a variable is bound to a structure it effectively behaves like that structure. For instance, the following calls **infer_statement** and *then* **digest_statement**.

```
?- infer_statement(sp_8 ! believes(bif, spy(X))),
     digest_statement(sp_8 ! believes(george, bulgarian(X))).
```

The call to **infer_statement** might bind **X**, say to **harry** as before. The subsequent call to **digest_statement** then serves to assert **sp_8 ! believes(george, bulgarian(harry))**. The two calls above in effect assert *George believes that the one who Bif believes to be a spy is Bulgarian.* If any call fails to do what it is supposed to in Prolog it is said to *fail.* If the call to **infer_statement** above fails, for instance because there is no information available about Bif's beliefs or about who Bif believes to be a spy, then execution will not proceed further, that is, the call to **digest_statement** would not be processed. Sterling and Shapiro (1986) provide a very thorough description of the Prolog language.

Most of this chapter deals with the options available for programming at the customization level.

Implementation Level

At the implementation level we discuss the parts of Spaceprobe that are fixed, that is, invisible to the programmer and not subject to programmer control. These include, for instance, optimizations on climbing inheritance contexts. We mention features at this level in passing because they play a role in realizing the full efficiency of the framework of partitioned representations.

CUSTOMIZING DIGESTION

In the simplest cases, the predicate **digest_statement** does nothing more than add something to the knowledge base (with some appropriate indexing, transparent to the programmer). In such a case, we say that a statement is *interned.* For example,

?- **digest_statement(sp_1 ! likes(george, mabel)).**

would probably add **likes(george, mabel)** to the space **sp_1** in exactly that form. Internment happens when Spaceprobe fails to find a restructuring rule that matches the statement to be digested.

More complex information, on the other hand, will generally match predeclared restructuring rule and will accordingly be restructured before internment. Data-directed *restructuring rules* can reform the statement in unlimited ways. They are intended to decompose statements into smaller parts that can be more easily processed. Among other things they can apply space initialization, space augmentation, and rules for creating certain kinds of secondary contexts.

For instance,

?- **digest_statement (sp_1 ! believes (hagar,**
has-eaten (siegfried, poison-apple-8) ==> dead (siegfried))

might actually cause the following statements to be interned.

sp_1 ! believes (hagar, {{sp_2}})
sp_2 ! has-eaten(siegfried, poison-apple-8) ==> {{sp_3}}
sp_3 ! {sp_2}

sp_3 ! has-eaten(siegfried, poison-apple-8)
sp_3 ! dead(siegfried)

Since the original statement can be reconstructed by context climbing, **digest_statement** does not store it explicitly.

Restructuring rules are declared by the customizer as Prolog facts of the form

restructure_rule(Pattern, Actions).

Pattern is a statement pattern, that is, it can potentially unify with a Spaceprobe statement. **Actions** is a sequence of Prolog procedure calls. Restructuring rules are like the production rules discussed in Chapter 3.

One of the simplest restructuring rules is:

restructure_rule(S ! P & Q,
[digest_statement(S ! P), digest_statement(S ! Q)]).

This implements the logical rule of *and-elimination* and ensures that it will be performed in a data-directed manner whenever its preconditions are satisfied. Given the rule for &, if we call

?- **digest_statement(sp_1 ! doctor(bif) & zodiac-sign(bif, orion)).**

The following will be interned in the absence of further relevant restructuring rules.

sp_1 ! doctor(bif)
sp_1 ! zodiac-sign(bif, orion)

RESTRUCTURING RULES FOR DISTRIBUTION

The design philosophy of Spaceprobe is to force all incoming information into forms that maximize *coherence* and *consolidation* in the use of spaces. Spaceprobe accordingly makes it easy to create restructuring rules that distribute information over spaces in accordance with the principles of partitioned representations. This maximizes the opportunities for parochial reasoning when answering queries in a goal-directed manner, and eliminates certain redundancies. Restructuring is accomplished with a constant order increase in time complexity.

This section gives an idea, through examples, of how knowledge is distributed over multiple spaces as part of the digestion process. We will see the use of the set of predicates defined in Spaceprobe that correspond to the partitioning rules defined in the last chapter. These are **sp_init** which applies *space initialization*, **sp_aug** which applies *space augmentation*, **sp_ident** which applies *space identity*, and **sp_distr** which applies *distributed space augmentation* if possible or space initialization otherwise. These rules of inference were discussed in Chapter 10.

In formulating the partitioning rules of PR we found the concept of *syntactic environment* to be critical. Because of the requirements of the underlying Prolog language, the notation for environments is somewhat different in Spaceprobe, and is borrowed roughly from the *lambda calculus*. An environment is always of the form,

lambda(V):S

where V is a variable, S is a sentence and V occurs in S. V is used to stand for the slot in S. For instance, instead of **possible(___)** we use **lambda(P):possible(P)**.

The following restructuring rule actually sets up a new space with its context as part of the restructuring.

```
restructure_rule( S0 ! possible(P),
    [ sp_init(S0!possible(P), lambda(X):possible(X), C, S1!P),
      digest_statement( S1 ! P),
      sp_ident(S0, S0 ! T),
      intern_statement( S1 ! T) ] ).
```

sp_init (*space initialization*) is one of only two procedures defined in Spaceprobe that can create a new space. (The other is **sp_distr** which conditionally *calls* **sp_init**.) It does this by splitting a statement **S0 ! P** into context **S0 ! C** and a simpler statement **S1 ! Q**, such that **S1** is a new space occurring as a space term in **C**. For instance, the call

```
sp_init(sp_3 ! possible(hot(coffee_6)), lambda(X) : possible(X),
New_Context, New_Statement ).
```

will in effect split **sp_3 ! possible(hot(coffee_6))** into two parts, **sp_3 ! possible({{sp_18}})**, where **sp_18** is a newly generated space name, and **sp_18 ! hot(coffee_6)**. These become the bindings of

New_Context and **New_Statement** respectively. **lambda(X) : possible(X)** is a pattern that specifies how to gut **possible(hot(coffee_6))** in order to produce a context and a statement. A lambda expression is always used as the second argument to **sp_init**. **sp_3 ! possible({{sp_18}})** will be interned automatically, but **sp_18 ! hot(coffee_6)** will not be immediately interned, since it is a candidate for further digestion. Notice that the restructuring rule goes on to digest **New_Statement**.

sp_ident (*space identity*) does something simple; in fact, it just saves a little typing and enhances readability. The call

?- **sp_ident(sp_3, Context).**

binds **Context** to the *identity context*, **sp_3 ! {sp_3}**. The usefulness of an identity context is that it can be retagged to create a inheritance context. The call to **intern_statement** adds such a inheritance context, **sp_18 ! {sp_3}**.

There are two reasons for automatically deriving inheritance contexts as opposed to other secondary contexts as part of the restructuring process. First, experience suggests that initializing these contexts creates an environment under which many useful inferences can be derived immediately by simple applications of context climbing over inheritance contexts in response to queries. For instance, in the example above, the context **sp_18 | [sp_3]** allows any knowledge tagged for **sp_3** to carry over directly to **sp_18**. Since **sp_18** has been initialized with a single standard sentence, most of the knowledge relevant to local inferences in **sp_18** will probably derive from **sp_3** in this manner. Second, context climbing over inheritance contexts is made especially efficient at the implementation level through special indexing mechanisms as discussed below.

Once the restructuring rule above is declared, if the call

?- **digest_statement(sp_1 ! possible(hot(coffee_6))).**

is made, something like the following would be interned.

sp_1 ! possible({{sp_19}})
sp_19 ! hot(coffee_6)
sp_19 ! {sp_1}

An important thing to note about the restructuring rule for **possible** is that it creates a new space every time another statement of possibility is digested. That is, it will not intern the embedded sentence in an already existing possibility space. This means that if we now call

```
?-    digest_statement(sp_1 ! possible(cold(coffee_6))).
```

something like the following will be interned.

```
sp_1  ! possible({{sp_19}})
sp_19 ! cold(coffee_6)
sp_19 ! {sp_1}
```

It is appropriate that we set up this second possibility space in the interests of *coherence*. If we were to intern **sp_19 ! cold(coffee_6)** this would mean that **coffee_6** could be both hot and cold at the same time.

On the other hand, conditional spaces should not be so duplicated.

```
restructure_rule( S0 ! P ==> Q,
   [ sp_distr(S0 ! P==>Q, lambda(X):P==>X, C, S1 ! Q),
     digest_statement(S1 ! P),
     digest_statement(S1 ! Q),
     sp_ident(S0, S0 ! T),
     intern_statement( S1 ! T) ]).
```

The restructuring rule for ==> looks a lot like that for **possible**. The main difference is that the procedure **sp_distr** (space distribution) is used instead of **sp_init** (space initialization). Both procedures are called the same way but do something slightly different. The call

```
?- sp_distr( sp_6 ! under_attack(enterprise) ==>
                doomed(enterprise),
     lambda(X):P ==> X, Context, New_Statement ).
```

begins by looking for an *existing* context of the form **sp_6 ! under_attack(enterprise) ==> X**. If it fails to find such a context, it has exactly the same result as **sp_init**, that is, it creates such a context, along with the new space. If it does find such a context, it will not create a new context or space but will apply **sp_aug** to add content to an existing space. In the latter case, **Context** will be bound to the already existing context and **New_statement** will be bound as in **sp_init**.

Notice that the statement **S1 ! P** is digested. **P** is satisfied in **S1**, since **P ==> P** is always satisfied in **S0** (or in any other space; it is a tautology). Notice also that this rule sets up a inheritance context, **S1 | T** much like the rule for **possible.**

Now let's look at the effect of the following two calls in sequence, assuming that no similar call has been made previously.

```
?- digest_statement(sp_6 ! under_attack(enterprise)
     ==> enemy_agent(spock) ).

?- digest_statement(sp_6 ! under_attack(enterprise)
     ==> doomed(enterprise) ).
```

The first call will intern something like

```
sp_6  ! under_attack(enterprise) ==> {{sp_22}}
sp_22 ! under_attack(enterprise)
sp_22 ! enemy_agent(spock)
sp_22 ! {sp_6}
```

The second call will intern only

```
sp_22 ! doomed(enterprise)
```

The second call to **digest_statement** will reuse the space and the context initiated by the first call. This makes sense, since if the enterprise is under attack then **enemy_agent(spock)** and **doomed(enterprise)** should be satisfied *together.*

One final point for the alert reader: the inheritance context **sp_22 ! {sp_6}** is *not* created twice. This is because **intern_statement** does a redundancy check at the implementation level so that it will never intern a statement or context that has already been interned. As a result, the customizer never has to worry about such redundancies.

Once an appropriate set of restructuring rules is declared, the content of each corresponding statement will be automatically and correctly distributed over multiple spaces by a simple call to **digest_statement.** The restructuring rules ensure that relevant parts of the meanings of certain predicates occurring in the intermediate representations are properly represented in terms of partitioned structures in a way that maximizes coherence and consolidation.

HANDLING QUERIES

The following call can be used to retrieve knowledge deductively in Spaceprobe.

?- **infer_statement(S ! P).**

infer_statement is like Prolog **call** in that it will try to derive **P**, possibly binding variables in **P** in the process. However, the derivation is made parochially for **S** and is accomplished in one of the following ways:

- By look-up, or
- By backward chaining to make an inference parochially in **S**, or
- By climbing a matching context.

Backward chaining can be customized. Look-up and climbing a matching context are options that are automatically invoked by Spaceprobe.

Look-Up

This is possible if a statement that unifies with **S ! P** has been interned. If **S** is an unbound variable, **infer_statement(S ! P)** will locate a space **S** in which **P** is satisfied. This can be used in contextualization in language understanding, for instance, to locate a space quickly in which a definite description has a referent. At the implementation level Spaceprobe uses several hash tables to index statements in a way that allows efficient access through alternative search heuristics.

Parochial Inference

Backward chaining is familiar from Prolog. The Spaceprobe analog of the Prolog rule is the *inference rule* declared by the programmer to perform an inference parochially within a space. An inference rule is declared by the programmer as a Prolog fact of the following form.

inference_rule(Sentence_Pattern, [Action, Action, ...]).

The actions specify procedurally how a query matching **Sentence_Pattern** can be answered. For instance,

inference_rule(P & Q, [infer_statement(P), infer_statement(Q)]).

In the recursive calls to **infer_statement** the space tag is normally omitted, as the current space in which the inference occurs parochially is understood by default. So, if

digest_statement (sp_18 ! enemy_agent (spock))
digest_statement (sp_18 ! doomed (enterprise))

are called, then

infer_statement (sp_18 ! enemy_agent (spock) & doomed (en

will succeed.

Modus ponens can be declared as a general rule that applies parochially within spaces as follows.

inference_rule(Q, [infer_statement(P ==> Q), infer_statement(P)]).

If the following have been called,

digest_statement(sp_2 ! car_salesman(X) ==>
politics (X, republican))
digest_statement(sp_2 ! car_salesman(bif))

then on the basis of the inference rule just given the call

infer_statement (sp_2 ! politics (bif, P))

will succeed and bind P to **republican.**

Context Climbing

The third way in which **infer_statement** can infer a statement is by *context climbing,* i.e., by locating a context that matches the query and making a recursive call to **infer_statement** for the appropriate query in the space referenced in the context. For instance, given

sp_1 ! believes(george, {{sp_8}}),
sp_8 ! phone(fred, 1234567)
sp_8 ! phone(fred, X) ==> phone(mary,X)

the query

infer_statement(sp_1 ! believes(george, phone(mary, N)))

will submit the query

infer_statement (sp_8 ! phone(mary, N))

Given an inference rule for modus ponens of the last section, this last query will find the binding **1234567** for **N**.

This last example demonstrates the relative ease with which certain inferences that are very difficult in traditional logic-based systems are handled in Spaceprobe. The knowledge used in this example would correspond to **believes(george, phone(fred, 1234567))**, and **believes(george, phone(fred, X) ==> phone(mary,X))** in a standard logic-based representation. (More typically there would be additional levels of embedding.) From these it is actually relatively difficult to infer **believes(george, phone(mary, 1234567))**.

The most common kind of context is the *inheritance context* of one of the forms

S1 ! {S2}
S1 ! default({S2})

The latter is like the secondary context **S1 | presumably: [S0]** discussed in earlier chapters. At the implementation level Spaceprobe does a special optimization to handle context climbing for these cases quickly as direct instances of look-up. For each space **S** mentioned in the data base the list of spaces in the transitive closure of the inheritance context relationship of **S** is maintained. This list is automatically updated whenever a inheritance context with **S** as a tag is added to the knowledge base. This is transparent to the customizer. With each space **S1** on the list is an indication of whether or not it is in the *default inheritance context of* **S**, i.e, whether or not a inheritance context of the form **S2 ! default({S3})** must be crossed to get from **S** to **S1**. When a query of the form **S ! P** is processed, **S** comes into *focus* and all sentences in the inheritance context of **S** are made directly *visible* without the need to explicitly apply context climbing on the inheritance contexts of **S**. The way in which visibility is implemented is similar to that of the inheritance mechanisms of CONNIVER (McDermott and Sussman 1972, McDermott 1983). As in CONNIVER, knowledge that would otherwise be visible from a default inheritance context of **S** can be canceled by explicitly removing it from **S**.

A Query about Siegfried

By way of example, let's briefly look at how Spaceprobe derives an inference, which we have seen to be complex in a standard logic-based system. This is an inference based on an internal representation that might be derived for the Siegfried story of Chapter 4, in particular the inference that the wizard believes that if Siegfried would work hard then he would be happy. We will trace the (recursive) calls to **infer_statement**, beginning with the query:

(1) **sp_2 ! believe (wizard_8, work_hard(siegfried) /==> happy (siegfried)).**

(1) is solved by *context-climbing* using the existing context **sp_2 ! believe(wizard_8, {{sp_3}})** and then solving:

(2) **sp_3 ! work_hard(siegfried) /==> happy(siegfried).**

(2) is solved by *context-climbing* using the context **sp_3 ! work_hard(siegfried) /==> {{sp_4}}** and then solving:

(3) **sp_4 ! happy(siegfried).**

(3) is solved by *backward chaining* using modus ponens and then solving each of the following:

(4) **sp_4 ! P ==> happy(siegfried).**

(5) **sp_4 ! P.**

(4) is solved by *look-up* using the inheritance context **sp_4 ! default({sp_3})** and the existing statement **sp_3 ! rich(X) ==> happy(X)**. This binds **P** in both (4) and (5) to **rich(siegfried)**. Thus (5) effectively becomes

sp_4 ! rich(siegfried).

Finally, (5) is solved immediately by *look-up*.

This completes the inference. This inference is fast not only because it is relatively short, but also because there is also generally no branching in the search space.

LANGUAGE UNDERSTANDING IN SPACEPROBE

I will exemplify the use of Spaceprobe in an application close to heart, language understanding. In the working language understanding systems that we have implemented, variations on the following algorithm are generally used.

loop

1. Read surface discourse sentence **D**.
2. Parse **D** to produce *intermediate representation* **P**, and identify *space cues* **C**.
3. Contextualize, using **C** and a list of *active spaces* to identify the focus space **S**.
4. Construct an internal representation by calling **digest_statement(S ! P)**.
5. Update the list of active spaces.

end loop

It is important to stress that this algorithm constitutes a very primitive model of discourse processing, one which divides understanding into discrete *serial* processing stages. Nevertheless, it captures certain aspects of the theory of language processing outlined in Chapter 4.

Parsing is fairly easily implemented in Prolog by supplying a *definite clause grammar* (Warren and Periera 1980). The intermediate structure has the syntactic form of an internal sentence, but is generally highly ambiguous. The construction stage combines space distribution with parochial processing, both under the control of restructuring rules. Let's look at some examples.

A contextualized intermediate structure produced by parsing *The wizard had a broom* might be

sp_2 ! the(wizard(X), broom(broom_3) & have(X,broom_3))

A restructuring rule implements the constructive rule described in Chapter 5 for definite descriptions:

```
restructure_rule( S ! the(D, P),
   [infer_statement( S ! D ),
    digest_statement(P)] ).
```

This rule issues a query **infer_statement(S ! D)** to find bindings for variables in **D**, normally binding variables in **P** at the same time. Then it digests **P**. For instance, if **sp_2 ! wizard(wizard_8)** is in the knowledge base, then digesting the statement above will first bind **X** to **wizard_8**, then will digest **broom (broom_3) & have (X, broom_3)**. This will cause the following to be interned (the restructuring rule for & will apply also).

```
sp_2 ! broom(broom_3)
sp_2 ! have(wizard_8, broom_3)
```

Notice that the rule for the is able to find a unique referent as long as there is only one statement unifying with **sp_2 ! wizard(X)**, regardless of how many wizards are represented in the knowledge base in various spaces. Partitioned representations are is doing much of the work of disambiguation by defining a restricted domain of reference. Discriminating a unique referent is generally difficult in standard logic-based systems (cf. Walker, et al. 1987, pp. 303-304).

Another interesting interaction between the rule for the and partitioned representations occurs when we digest the following statement, paraphrased *If Merlin has a broom, then the broom walks.*

```
sp_8 ! (broom(broom_9) & has(Merlin, broom_9)) ==>
       the(broom(X), walk(X))
```

These sentences are like the donkey sentences that Kamp (1980) talks about and that I described in Chapter 5. The problem is that *the broom* should refer to a broom, but the sentence makes no commitment to the existence of a broom for *the broom* to refer to. Kamp proposes that the rule of interpretation for *the* depends on a mental *discourse representation*, largely equivalent to what emerges here. In digesting this statement, the rule for ==>, and the rule for &, will first apply causing the following to be interned initially.

```
sp_8 ! (broom(broom_9) & has(Merlin, broom_9)
          ==> {{sp_12}}
sp_12 ! broom(broom_9)
sp_12 ! has(Merlin, broom_9)
```

At this point, the rule for ==> will try to digest the statement

sp_12 ! the(broom(X), walk(X))

The rule for **the** will call **infer_statement(sp_12 ! broom(X))**, which succeeds by *look-up*, binding **X** to **broom_9**. Therefore it will digest **sp_12 ! walk(broom_9)**.

The satisfaction of presuppositions in semantically complex discourses are also predicted when viewed in terms of processing parochially in spaces. We have seen that *Siegfried would stop drinking* should presuppose *Siegfried has drunk*. Disregarding the question of the actual function of presupposition in discourse, let's introduce a kind of presupposition *checker* for **stop** in the following way.

```
restructure_rule(S ! stop(X, P),
    [infer_statement(S ! beforehand(P)),
     digest_statement(S ! stop(X, P)) ] ).
```

The effect of this rule will be to prevent digestion of the statement S ! **stop(X, P)** unless the presupposition is satisfied, i.e., unless **infer_statement** succeeds. In the processing of the Siegfried story we have seen the following are interned before the sentence with *stop* is processed.

sp_3 ! alcoholic(siegfried)
sp_4 ! default({sp_3})

At some point the system will try to digest the statement

sp_4 ! stop(siegfried, drink(siegfried))

The rule for **stop** will then cause the following call.

?- **infer_statement(sp_4 ! beforehand(drink(siegfried)))**.

This will in fact succeed by *context-climbing* on the inheritance context **sp_4 ! default({sp_3})** to set up the query

sp_3 ! beforehand(drink(siegfried))

which should be inferable from **sp_3 ! alcoholic(Siegfried)** given appropriate inference rules relating **drink** to **alcoholic**. Ng (1989) demonstrates that this basic model of discourse processing leads to very accurate, correct and very general predictions about the satisfaction of presuppositions in semantically complex discourses in a manner consistent with the discussion of Chapter 6.

SUMMARY

In this chapter we have looked at a computational implementation of the theory of partitioned representations. We have seen how it achieves efficiency by appropriate application of the partitioning rules of inference in order to promote consolidation and coherence. We have seen that optimization of inheritance provides additional support for consolidation. Finally, we have seen how the implementation can be readily applied to the process of language understanding.

References

Aizawa, Kenneth, forthcoming, "Unreduced Mechanisms in Connectionist Theory," in Dinsmore, John, ed. *Closing the Gap: Symbolism vs. Connectionism*, Hillsdale, NJ: Erlbaum.

Allen, James and C.R. Perrault, 1980, "Analyzing Intention in Utterances," *Artificial Intelligence* **15**, 143-178.

Allen, James, 1983, "Maintaining Knowledge about Temporal Intervals," *Communication of the Association for Computing Machinery* **26:11**, 832-843.

Allen, R., 1966, *The Verb System of Present-day American English*, The Hague: Mouton.

Anderson, John R., 1983, *The Architecture of Cognition*, Cambridge, MA: Harvard University Press.

Anttila, R., 1973, "Linguistik und Philologie," in Renate Bartsch and Theo Vennemann, eds., *Linguistik und Nachbarwissenschaften*, Kronberg: Scriptor.

Asher, Nicholas, 1986, "Belief in Discourse Representation Theory," *Journal of Philosophical Logic* **15**, 127-189.

Bach, Emmon, 1967, "Have and Be in English Syntax," *Language* **43**, 462-485.

Ballim, Afzal and Yorick Wilks, forthcoming, *Artificial Believers*.

Barnden, John, 1989, "Belief, Metaphorically Speaking," *Proceedings of the Conference on Knowledge Representation*, Los Altos: Morgan Kaufman.

Barnden, John and Jordan Pollack, 1990, "Problems for High-Level Connectionism," in Barnden, John and Jordan Pollack, eds., *High-Level Connectionist Models*, Norwood, NJ: Ablex.

Blank, Douglas, Lisa Meeden and James Marshall, forthcoming, "Exploring the Symbolic/Subsymbolic Continuum: a Case Study of RAAM," in John Dinsmore, ed., *Closing the Gap: Symbolism vs. Connectionism*, Hillsdale, NJ: Erlbaum.

Bobrow, D.B. and B. Raphael, 1974, "New Programming Languages for Artificial Intelligence," *Computing Surveys* **6:3**, 155-174.

Bobrow, D. G. and T. Winograd, 1977, "An overview of KRL, A Knowledge Representation Language," *Cognitive Science* **1**, 3-46.

Brachman, Ronald, 1979, "On the Epistemological Status of Semantic Networks," in N. V. Findler, ed., *Associative Networks*, New York: Academic Press, 3-50.

Brachman, Ronald and James Schmolze, 1985, "An Overview of the KL-ONE Knowledge Representation System," *Cognitive Science* **9**, 171-216.

Bransford, J.D. and M.K. Johnson, 1972, "Contextual Prerequisites for

Understanding," *Journal of Verbal Learning and Verbal Behavior* **11**, 717-726.

Brownston, Lee; Robert Farrell; and Elaine Kant; Nancy Martin, 1985, *Programming Expert Systems in OPS5*, Reading, MA: Addison-Wesley.

Buchanan, Bruce and Edward Shortliffe, eds., 1984, *Rule-Based Expert Systems*, Reading, MA: Addison-Wesley.

Bull, William, 1960, *Time, Tense, and the Verb*, Berkeley: University of California Press.

Chafe, Wallace, 1970, *Meaning and the Structure of Language*, Chicago: University of Chicago Press.

Chomsky, Noam, 1965, *Aspects of the Theory of Syntax*, Cambridge, MA: MIT Press.

Chomsky, Noam, 1971, "Deep Structure, Surface Structure, and Semantic Interpretation," in Danny Steinber and Leon Jakobovits, eds., *Semantics*, London: Cambridge University Press, 185-216.

Clark, H.H. and S.E. Haviland, 1977, "Comprehension and the Given-New Contract," in R.O. Freedle, ed., *Discourse Production and Comprehension*, Norwood, NJ: Ablex.

Cicourel, Aaron, 1974, *Cognitive Sociology*, New York: Free Press.

Cohen, Paul and C. Raymond Perrault, 1979, "Elements of a Plan-Based Theory of Speech Acts," *Cognitive Science* **3**, 177-212.

Cole, Peter and Jerry Morgan, eds., 1975, *Speech Acts* (*Syntax and Semantics* 3), New York: Academic Press.

Comrie, Bernard, 1976, *Aspect*, London: Cambridge University Press.

Cottrell, G. W. and S. L. Small, 1983, "A Connectionist Scheme for Modeling Word Sense Disambiguation," *Cognition and Brain Theory* **6:1**, 89-120.

Creary, Louis, 1979, "Propositional Attitudes: Fregean Reasoning and Simulative Reasoning," *Proceedings of the 6th International Joint Conference on Artificial Intelligence*, 176-181.

Cresswell, M., 1972, *Logics and Languages*, London: Methuen.

Dennett, Daniel, 1978, *Brainstorms*, Bradford Press.

DeWeese, Gene, 1985, *Black Suits from Outer Space*, New York: Dell.

Dinsmore, John, 1979, *Pragmatics, Formal Theory and the Analysis of Presupposition*, Ph.D. dissertation, University of California at San Diego, Bloomington: Indiana University Linguistics Club.

Dinsmore, John, 1981a, *The Inheritance of Presupposition*, Amsterdam: Benjamins.

Dinsmore, John, 1981b, "Tense Choice and Time Specification in English," *Linguistics* **19**, 475-494.

Dinsmore, John, 1981c, "Towards a Unified Theory of Presupposition," *Journal of Pragmatics* **5**, 335-363.

Dinsmore, John, 1982, "On the Semantic Nature of Reichenbach's Tense System," *Glossa* **16**, 216-239.

Dinsmore, John, 1986, "Spaceprobe: A System for Representing Complex Knowledge," in *Proceedings of the First International Conference on Methodologies for Intelligent Systems*, New York: Association for Computing Machinery, 399-407.

Dinsmore, John and Christopher Moehle, 1990, "Artificial Intelligence Looks at Natural Language," *Poetics* **19:1-2**, 13-36, reprinted in Rolf Zwaan and Dietrich Meutsch, eds., *Computer Models and Technology in Media Research*, Amsterdam: Elsevier.

Dinsmore, John, 1991a, "The Use and Function of the English Past and Perfect," in Carol Georgopoulos and Roberta Ishihara, eds., *Essays in Honor of Yuki Kuroda*, Dordrecht: Kluwer, 101-117.

Dinsmore, John, 1991b, "Logic-Based Processing of Semantically Complex Natural Language Discourse," *New Generation Computing* 9:1.

Dinsmore, John, ed., forthcoming, *Closing the Gap: Symbolism vs. Connectionism*, Hillsdale, NJ: Erlbaum.

Dinsmore, John, forthcoming, Symbolism vs. Connectionism: a Difficult Marriage, in John Dinsmore, ed. *Closing the Gap: Symbolism vs. Connectionism*, Hillsdale, NJ: Erlbaum.

Donnellan, Keith, 1966, "Reference and Definite Descriptions," *Philosophical Review* **75**, 281-304.

Dowty, David, 1979, *Word Meaning and Montague Grammar*, Dordrecht: Reidel.

Dreyfus, Hubert and Stuart Dreyfus, 1986, *Mind over Machine*, New York: Free Press.

Erman, L.D. and U.R. Lesser, 1980, "The Hearsay Speech Understanding System: a Tutorial," in W.A. Lea, ed., *Trends in Speech Recognition*, Englewook Cliffs, NJ: Prentice-Hall.

Fahlman, Scott, 1979, *NETL: A System for Representing and Using Real-World Knowledge*, Cambridge, MA: MIT Press.

Fauconnier, Gilles, 1978, "Is There a Linguistic Level of Logical Representation?," *Theoretical Linguistics* **5**, 31-49.

Fauconnier, Gilles, 1985, *Mental Spaces: Aspects of Meaning Construction in Natural Language*, Cambridge, MA: Bradford/MIT Press.

Fauconnier, Gilles, 1986a, "Roles and Connecting Paths," in Charles Travis, ed., *Meaning and Interpretation*, Oxford: Blackwell, 19-44.

Fauconnier, Gilles, 1986b, "Quantification, Roles and Domains," in Umberto Eco, Marco Santambrogio and Patrizia Violi, eds., *Meaning and Mental Representations VS* **44/45**, 61-80.

Fikes, Richard and Nils Nilsson, 1971, "STRIPS: A New Approach to the Application of Theorem Proving to Problem Solving," *Artificial Intelligence* **2**, 189-208.

Fillmore, Charles, 1982, "Frame Semantics," in *Linguistics in the Morning Calm*, Linguistic Society of Korea, Seoul: Hanshin, 111-138.

Findler, N. V., ed., 1979, *Associative Networks*, New York: Academic Press. Fitch, Frederic, 1952, *Symbolic Logic: An Introduction*, New York: Roland Press.

Funt, B.V., 1980, "Problem-Solving with Diagrammatic Representations," *Artificial Intelligence* **13**, 201-230.

Gasser, Michael and Chan-Do Lee, forthcoming, "Where Do Underlying Representations Come From," in John Dinsmore, ed. *Closing the Gap: Symbolism vs. Connectionism*, Hillsdale, NJ: Erlbaum.

Gazdar, Gerald, 1979, *Pragmatics: Implicature, Presupposition and Logical Form*, New York: Academic Press.

Geach, Peter, 1952, *Reference and Generality*, Ithaca.

Genesereth, M. and Nils Nilsson, 1987, *Logical Foundations of Artificial Intelligence*, Los Altos, CA: Morgan Kaufman.

Givon, Talmy, 1980, *On Understanding Grammar*, New York: Academic Press.

Grice, Paul, 1975, "Logic and Conversation," in *Speech Acts (Syntax and Semantics 3)*, Peter Cole and Jerry Morgan, eds., New York: Academic Press, 41-58.

Grosz, Barbara, 1981, "Focusing and Description in Natural Language Dialogues" in Avrim Joshi, Bonnier Webber and Ivan Sag, eds., *Elements of Discourse*

Understanding, Cambridge: Cambridge University Press, 84-105.

Guenthner, Franz, 1987, "Linguistic Meaning in Discourse Representation Theory," *Synthese* 73, 569-598.

Hausser, R., 1976, "Presupposition in Montague Grammar," *Theoretical Linguistics* **3:3**, 245-280.

Hayes, Patrick, 1973, "The Frame Problem and Related Problems in Artificial Intelligence," in A. Elithorn and D. Jones, eds., *Artificial and Human Thinking*, Jossey-Bass, 45-59.

Hayes, Patrick, 1979a, "The Logic of Frames," in D. Metzing, ed., *Frame Conceptions and Text Understanding*, Berlin: Walter de Gruyter and Co., 46-61.

Hayes, Patrick, 1979b, "The Naive Physics Manifesto," in D. Mitchie, ed., *Expert Systems in the Microelectronic Age*, Edinburgh: Edinburgh University Press.

Hendrix, Gary, 1979, "Encoding Knowledge in Partitioned Semantic Networks," in Nicholas Findler, ed., *Associative Networks*, New York: Academic Press, 51-92.

Hillis, W. Daniel and Guy Steele, 1986, "Data Parallel Algorithms," *Communications of the ACM* **29:12**, 1170-1183.

Hintikka, Jaakko, 1962, *Knowledge and Belief*, Cornell University Press.

Hinton, Geoffry, 1981, "Implementing Semantic Networks in Parallel Hardware," in Geoffry Hinton and James A. Anderson, eds., 1981, *Parallel Models of Associative Memory*, Hillsdale, NJ: Erlbaum, 161-187.

Holland, John, Keith Holyoak, Richard Nisbett, and Paul Thagard, 1986, *Induction: Processes of Inference, Learning, and Discovery*, Cambridge, MA: MIT Press.

Horton, Diane and Graeme Hirst, 1988, "Presuppositions as Beliefs," *Proceedings of COLLING.*

Huddleston, R, 1969, "Some Observations on Tense and Deixis in English," *Language* **45**, 777-806.

Hughes, G.E. and M.J. Cresswell, 1968, *An Introduction to Modal Logic*, London: Methuen.

Inoue, K., 1979, "An Analysis of the English Present Perfect," *Linguistics* **19**, 561-589.

Itkonen, E., 1976, "Was für eine Wissenschaft ist die Linguistik eigentlich?" in Dieter Wunderlich, ed., *Wissenschaftstheorie der Linguistik*, Kronberg: Athenäum, 56-86.

Jackendoff, Ray, 1972, *Semantic Interpretation in Generative Grammar*, Cambridge, MA: MIT Press.

Jespersen, Otto, 1924, *The Philosophy of Grammar*, London: Allen and Unwin.

Johnson, Marion, 1981, "A Unified Theory of Tense and Aspect," in Philip Tedeschi and Annie Zaenen, eds., *Tense and Aspect (Syntax and Semantics 14)*, New York: Academic Press, 145-176.

Johnson, Mark, 1987, *The Body in the Mind*, Chicago: Chicago University Press.

Johnson-Laird, Philip, 1983, *Mental Models*, Cambridge, MA: Harvard University Press.

Joos, Martin, 1964, *The English Verb: Form and Meanings*, Madison: University of Wisconsin Press.

Kahneman, D. and A. Tversky, "The Simulation Heuristic," 1982, in D. Kahneman, P. Slovic and A. Tversky, eds., *Judgements under Uncertainty: Heuristics and Biases*, New York: Cambridge University Press, 201-208.

Kamp, Hans, 1979, "Events, Instants and Temporal Reference," in R. Baeuerle, U

Egli and A. von Stechow, eds., *Semantics from Different Points of View*, Berlin: Springer-Verlag, 376-417.

Kamp, Hans, 1980, "A Theory of Truth and Semantic Representation," in J.A.G. Groenendijk, T.M.V. Janssen and M.B.J. Stokhhof, eds., *Formal Methods in the Study of Language: Part I*, Amsterdam: Mathematisch Centrum, 277-322.

Kamp, Hans and Christian Rohrer, 1983, "Tense in Texts," in Roland Posner and Georg Meggle, eds., *Meaning, Use, and Interpretation*, Berlin: de Gruyter.

Karttunen, Lauri, 1973, "Presuppositions of Compound Sentences," *Linguistic Inquiry* **6**, 169-193.

Karttunen, Lauri and Stanley Peters, 1979, "Conventional Implicature," in Choon-Kyu Oh and David Dinneen , eds., *Presupposition (Syntax and Semantics 11)*, New York: Academic Press, 1-56.

Katz, Jerrold, 1972, *Semantic Theory*, New York: Harper and Row.

Katz, J.J., 1973, "On Defining Presupposition," *Linguistic Inquiry* **4**, 256-260.

Katz, Jerrold and D.T. Langendoen, 1976, "Pragmatics and Presupposition," *Language* **52**, 1-17.

Keenan, Edward and L. Schieffer, 1976, "Topic as a Discourse Notion," in Charles Li, ed., *Subject and Topic*, New York: Academic Press, 335-384.

Kosslyn, S.M., 1980, *Image and Mind*, Cambridge, MA: Harvard University Press.

Kripke, Saul, 1963, "Semantical Considerations on Modal Logic," *Acta Philosphica Fennica* **16**, 83-94.

Kwasny, Stan and Kanaan Faisal, forthcoming, "Symbolic Parsing via Sub-Symbolic Rules," in John Dinsmore, ed. *Closing the Gap: Symbolism vs. Connectionism*, Hillsdale, NJ: Erlbaum.

Lachter, Joel and Thomas G. Bever, 1988, "The Relation between Linguistic Structure and Associative Theories of Language Learning: A Constructive Critique of some Connectionist Learning Models," in Pinker, Steven and Jacque Mehler, eds., *Connections and Symbols*, Cambridge, MA: Bradford/MIT Press, 195-247.

Lakoff, George, 1987, *Women, Fire and Dangerous Things*, Chicago: University of Chicago Press.

Lakoff, George and Mark Johnson, 1980, *Metaphors We Live By*, Chicago: University of Chicago Press.

Langacker, Ronald, 1987, *Cognitive Grammar I*, Palo Alto, CA: Stanford University Press.

Lange, Trent, forthcoming, "Hybrid Connectionist Models: Temporary Bridges over the Gap Between the Symbolic and the Subsymbolic," in John Dinsmore, ed. *Closing the Gap: Symbolism vs. Connectionism*, Hillsdale, NJ: Erlbaum.

Langendoen, D.T. and H.B. Savin, 1971, "The Projection Problem for Presupposition," in Charles Fillmore and D.T. Langendoen, eds., *Studies in Linguistic Semantics*, New York: Holt, Rinehart and Winston.

Leech, Geoffrey, 1971, *Meaning and the English Verb*, London: Longman.

Lewis, David, 1969, *Convention: A Philosophical Study*, Cambridge, MA: Harvard University Press.

Lewis, David, 1973, *Counterfactuals*, Cambridge, MA: Harvard University Press.

Likhitaworn, Teerapong, 1986, *Partitioning Knowledge for Simulative Reasoning*, MS thesis, Department of Computer Science, Southern Illinois University.

Maida, Anthony, 1985, "Selecting a Humanly Understandable Knowledge Representation for Reasoning about Knowledge," *International Journal of*

Man-Machine Studies **22**, 151-161.

Marcus, Mitchell, 1978, "A Computational Account of Some Constraints on Language," in David Walz, ed., *Theoretical Issues in Natural Language Processing* **2**, Association for Computational Linguistics, 236-246.

Marcus, Mitchell, 1980, IA Theory of Syntactic Recognition for Natural Language, Cambridge, MA: MIT Press.

Marcus, Mitchell, 1981, *A Theory of Syntactic Recognition for Natural Language*, Cambridge, MA: MIT Press.

Marr, David, 1982, *Vision: A Computational Investigation into the Human Representation and Processing of Visual Information*, San Francisco: W.H. Freeman.

Martinet, A., 1962, *A Functional View of Language*, Oxford: Clarendon Press.

Martins, Joao, 1983, *Reasoning in Multiple Belief Spaces*, Tech. Report No. 203, Department of Computer Science, SUNY, Buffalo.

McCarthy, John, 1979, "First-Order Theories of Individual Concepts and Propositions," in J. Hayes and D. Michie, eds., *Machine Intelligence* **9**, New York: Halsted Press.

McCawley, James, 1971, "Tense and Time Reference in English," in Charles Fillmore and D. T. Langendoen, eds., *Studies in Linguistic Semantics*, New York: Holt, Rinehart, Winston, 97-114.

McClelland, J. L., D. E. Rumelhart and the PDP Research Group, eds., 1986, *Parallel Distributed Processing vol. 2*, Cambridge, MA: MIT Press.

McCoard, Robert, 1978, *The English Perfect*, Amsterdam: North Holland.

McDermott, Drew, 1983, "Contexts and Data Dependencies: A Synthesis," *IEEE Transactions on Pattern Analysis and Machine Intelligence* **5:3**, 237-246.

McDermott, Drew and John Doyle, 1980, "Non-Monotonic Logic I," *Artificial Intelligence* **13**, 41-72.

McDermott, Drew and G.J. Sussman, 1972, *The Conniver Reference Manual*, Technical Report Memo 259, MIT.

McKoon, G. and R. Ratcliff, 1980, "Priming in Item Recognition," *Journal of Verbal Learning and Verbal Behavior* **19**, 369-386.

Minsky, Marvin, 1975, "A framework for representing knowledge," in Patrick H Winston, ed., *The Psychology of Computer Vision*, New York: McGraw-Hill.

Minsky, Marvin and Seymour Papert, 1988, *Perceptrons, expanded edition*, Cambridge, MA: MIT Press.

Montague, Richard, 1974, *Formal Philosophy: Selected Papers of Richard Montague*, New Haven: Yale University Press.

Moore, Robert, 1976, "D-Script: A Computational Theory of Descriptions," *IEEE Transactions on Computers* **25:4**, 366-373.

Moore, Rober, 1985, "A Formal tehroy of Knowledge and Action," in J.r. Hobbs and Robert Moore, eds., *Formal Theories of the Commonsense World*, Norwood, NJ: Ablex.

Moore, Robert and Gary Hendrix, 1979, "Computational Models of Belief and the Semantics of Belief Sentences," SRI Technical Note **187**.

Morgan, Jerry, 1973, *Presupposition and the Representation of Meaning: Prolegomena*, Ph.D. Dissertation, University of Chicago.

Newell, Allen, 1982, "The Knowledge Level," *Artificial Intelligence* **18:1**.

Newell, Alan and Herbert Simon, 1972, *Human Problem Solving*, Englewood Cliffs, NJ: Prentice-Hall.

Newell, Alan and Herbert Simon, 1976, "Computer Science as an Empirical

Inquiry: Symbols and Search," ***Communications of the Association for Computing Machinery*** **19, 113-126** (Also in John Haugeland, ed., 1981, ***Mind Design***, Cambridge, MA, Bradford/MIT Press).

Ng Kee Hian, 1989, ***Presupposition and Partitioned Representations***, MS Thesis, Southern Illinois University at Carbondale.

Norman, Donald, 1976, ***Memory and Attention***, New York: Wiley.

Nunberg, Geoff, 1978, ***The Pragmatics of Reference***, Bloomington: Indiana University Linguistics Club.

Oh, Chu-Kyun and David Dineen, eds., 1979, ***Presupposition (Syntax and Semantics 11)***, New York: Academic Press.

Pereira, Fernando and David Warren, 1980, "Definite Clause Grammars for Language Analysis," ***Artificial Intelligence***, **13**, 231-278.

Pinker, Steven and Alan Prince, 1988, "On Language and Connectionism: Analysis of a Parallel Distributed Processing Model of Language Acquisition," in Pinker, Steven and Jacque Mehler, eds., ***Connections and Symbols***, Cambridge, MA: Bradford/MIT Press, 73-194.

Putnam, Hilary, 1973, "Reductionism and the Nature of Psychology," ***Cognition*** **2**, 131-146 (also in John Haugeland, ed., 1981, ***Mind Design***, Cambridge, MA: Bradford/MIT Press).

Putnam, Hilary, 1981, ***Reason, Truth and History***, Cambridge: Cambridge University Press.

Putnam, Hilary, 1988, ***Representation and Reality***, Cambridge, MA: Bradford/MIT Press.

Pylyshyn, Zenon, 1984, ***Computation and Cognition***, Cambridge, MA: Bradford/MIT Press.

Quillian, M. R., 1968, "Semantic Memory," in Marvin Minsky, ed., ***Semantic Information Processing***, Cambridge, MA: MIT Press.

Quine, W.V., 1953, ***From a Logical Point of View***, Cambridge, MA: Harvard University Press.

Reichenbach, Hans, 1947, ***Elements of Symbolic Logic***, New York: MacMillan.

Rips, Lance and Sandra Marcus, 1977, "Suppositions and the Analysis of Conditional Sentences," in Marces Just and Patricia Carpenter, eds., ***Cognitive Processes in Comprehension***, Hillsdale, NJ: Erlbaum, 185-220.

Roberts, Craig, 1986, ***Modal Subordination, Anaphora and Distributivity***, University of Massachussetts Ph.D. dissertation, Amherst, MA.

Roberts, Craig, 1989, "Modal Subordination and Pronominal Anaphora in Discourse," ***Linguistics and Philosophy*** **12**, 683-721.

Ross, John, 1967, ***Constraints on Variables in Syntax***, Ph.D. dissertation, MIT Dept. of Linguistics, Bloomington: Indiana University Linguistics Club.

Rumelhart, D. E, 1980, "Schemata: The Building Blocks of Cognition," in R. J. Spiro, B. C. Bruce and W. F. Brewer, eds., ***Theoretical Issues in Reading Comprehension***, Hillsdale, NJ: Lawrence Erlbaum.

Rumelhart, D. E., J. L. McClelland and the PDP Research Group, eds., 1986 ***Parallel Distributed Processing Volume 1***, Cambridge, MA: MIT Press.

Rumelhart, David, Paul Smolenskv, James McClelland and Geoffrey Hinton, 1986, "Schemata and Sequential Thought Processes in PDP Models," in McClelland, J. L. and D. E. Rumelhart, eds., ***Parallel Distributed Processing Volume 2***, Cambridge, MA: MIT Press.

Rumelhart, D. E., G. E. Hinton and R.J. Williams, "Learning Internal

Representations by Error Propagation," in Rumelhart, D. E., J. L. McClelland and the PDP Research Group, eds., *Parallel Distributed Processing Volume 1*, 318-362, Cambridge, MA: MIT Press.

de Saussure, Ferdinand, 1959, *Course in General Linguistics*, New York: McGraw-Hill.

Schank, Roger and Robert Abelson, 1977, *Scripts, Plans, Goals and Understanding*, Hillsdale, NJ: Lawrence Erlbaum.

Schank, Roger and Christopher Riesbeck, eds., 1981, *Inside Computer Understanding*, Hillsdale, NJ: Lawrence Erlbaum.

Schank, Roger, 1982, *Dynamic Memory*, Cambridge: Cambridge University Press.

Schiebe, Traugott, 1975, *Über Praesuppositionen zusammengesetzter Saetze im Deutschen*, Stockholm: Almquist and Wiksell.

Schwartz, Justin, forthcoming, "Who's Afraid of Multiple Realizability," in John Dinsmore, ed. *Closing the Gap: Symbolism vs. Connectionism*, Hillsdale, NJ: Erlbaum.

Searle, John, 1969, *Speech Acts: An Essay in the Philosophy of Language*, Cambridge: Cambridge University Press.

Searle, John, 1980, "Minds, Brains and Programs," *Behavioral and Brain Sciences* **3**, 417-424.

Sellars, Wilfred, 1954, "Presupposing," *Philosophical Review* **63**, 197-215.

Shapiro, Stuart, 1979, "The SNePS Semantic Network Processing System," in N. Findler, ed., *Associative Networks*, New York: Academic Press.

Sidner, Candice, 1983, "Focusing in the Comprehension of Definite Anaphora," in Michael Brady, ed., *Computational Models of Discourse*, Cambridge, MA: MIT Press, 267-330.

Smolensky, Paul, 1988, "On the Proper Treatment of Connectionism" (with commentaries by various people), *the Behavioral and Brain Sciences* **11**, 1-74.

Soames, Scott, 1979, "A Projection Problem for Speaker Presuppositions," *Linguistic Inquiry* **10:4**, 623-666.

Sowa, John, 1984, *Conceptual Structures: Information Processing in Mind and Machine*, Reading, MA: Addison-Wesley.

Sterling, Leon and Ehud Shapiro, 1986, *The Art of Prolog*, Cambridge, MA: MIT Press.

Strawson, P., 1954, "A Reply to Mr. Sellars," *Philosophical Review* **63**, 216-231.

Taylor, Barry, 1977, "Tense and Continuity," *Linguistics and Philosophy* **1**, 199-220.

Tversky A. and D. Kahnemann, 1973, Avalailibility: A Heuristic for Judging Frequency and Probability," *Cognitive Psychology* **5**, 207-232.

Van der Auwera, Johan, 1980, "On the Meaning of Basic Speech Acts," *Journal of Pragmatics* **4**, 253-264.

Walker, Adrian, Michael McCord, John Sowa, and Walter Wilson, 1987, *Knowledge Systems and Prolog*, Reading, MA: Addison-Wesley.

Walker, D. E. ed., 1978, *Understanding Spoken Language*, New York: North-Holland.

Warren, David and Fernando Periera, 1980, "Definite Clause Grammars for Language Analysis," *Artificial Intelligence* **13**, 231-278.

Waterman, Donald and Frederick Hayes-Roth, eds., 1978, *Pattern-Directed Inference Systems*, New York: Academic Press.

Webber, Bonnie Lynn, 1988, "Tense as Discourse Anaphor," *Computational Linguistics* **14:2**, 61-73.

Wells, Gary and Igor Gavanski, 1989, "Mental Simulation of Causality," *Journal of Personality and Social Psychology* **56:2**, 161-169.

Weyhrauch, Richard, 1980, "Prolegomena to a Theory of Formal Reasoning," *Artificial Intelligence* **13**, 133-170.

Wilks, Yorick and J. Bien, 1983, "Beliefs, Points of View and Multiple Environments," *Cognitive Science* **8**, 120-146.

Wilson, Deirdre, 1975, *Presupposition and Non-Truth Conditional Semantics*, New York: Academic Press.

Winograd, Terry and Fernando Flores, 1986, *Understanding Computers and Cognition*, Reading, MA: Addison-Wesley.

Author Index

Subject Index

STUDIES IN COGNITIVE SYSTEMS

Series Editor: James H. Fetzer, *University of Minnesota, Duluth*

1. J. H. Fetzer (ed.): *Aspects of Artificial Intelligence.* 1988
ISBN 1-55608-037-9; Pb 1-55608-038-7
2. J. Kulas, J.H. Fetzer and T.L. Rankin (eds.): *Philosophy, Language, and Artificial Intelligence.* Resources for Processing Natural Language. 1988
ISBN 1-55608-073-5
3. D.J. Cole, J.H. Fetzer and T.L. Rankin (eds.): *Philosophy, Mind and Cognitive Inquiry.* Resources for Understanding Mental Processes. 1990
ISBN 0-7923-0427-6
4. J.H. Fetzer: *Artificial Intelligence: Its Scope and Limits.* 1990
ISBN 0-7923-0505-1; Pb 0-7923-0548-5
5. H.E. Kyburg, Jr., R.P. Loui and G.N. Carlson (eds.): *Knowledge Representation and Defeasible Reasoning.* 1990 ISBN 0-7923-0677-5
6. J.H. Fetzer (ed.): *Epistemology and Cognition.* 1991 ISBN 0-7923-0892-1
7. E.C. Way: *Knowledge Representation and Metaphor.* 1991
ISBN 0-7923-1005-5
8. J. Dinsmore: *Partitioned Representations.* A Study in Mental Representation, Language Understanding and Linguistic Structure. 1991
ISBN 0-7923-1348-8

KLUWER ACADEMIC PUBLISHERS – DORDRECHT / BOSTON / LONDON

MIX
Papier aus verantwortungsvollen Quellen
Paper from responsible sources
FSC® C105338

If you have any concerns about our products,
you can contact us on
ProductSafety@springernature.com

In case Publisher is established outside the EU,
the EU authorized representative is:
Springer Nature Customer Service Center GmbH
Europaplatz 3, 69115 Heidelberg, Germany

Printed by Libri Plureos GmbH
in Hamburg, Germany